THE
ISRAELI
MIND

By the same author

Middle East Journey
Return to Glory
One Man's War
Digger (The Story of the Australian Soldier)
Scotland the Brave (The Story of the Scottish Soldier)
Jackboot (The Story of the German Soldier)
Tommy Atkins (The Story of the English Soldier)
Jack Tar (The Story of the English Seaman)
Fedayeen (The Arab-Israeli Dilemma)
The Arab Mind
The Face of War
British Campaign Medals
Codes and Ciphers
Anzacs at War
Boys in Battle
Women in Battle
The Walking Wounded
Links of Leadership
Swifter than Eagles
   (Biography of Marshal of the R.A.F. Sir John Salmond)
Surgeons in the Field
Americans in Battle
Letters from the Front 1914-18
The Hunger to Come (Food and Population Crises)
New Geography 1966-7
New Geography 1968-9
New Geography 1970-1
Anatomy of Captivity (Political Prisoners)
The French Foreign Legion
Devil's Goad
The Dagger of Islam
And other titles

THE
ISRAELI
MIND

JOHN LAFFIN

CASSELL
LONDON

CASSELL LTD.
35 Red Lion Square, London WC1R 4SG
and at Sydney, Auckland, Toronto, Johannesburg,
an affiliate of
Macmillan Publishing Co., Inc.,
New York.

First published 1979

ISBN 0 304 30399 2

Printed in Hong Kong

Contents

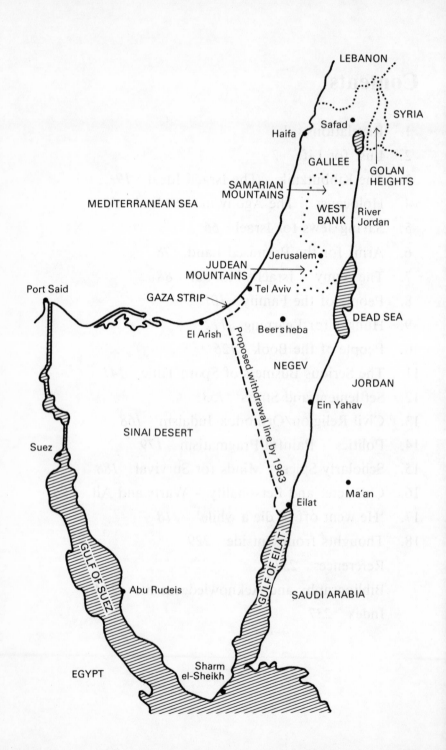

1 Revelations

'Living in Israel fills the whole of a person's body. All is demanded of men, of women and of children, daily and nightly.'

S.Y. Agnon, in his story *In the Heart of the Seas,* 1935 (thirteen years before the creation of the State of Israel).

'The object of State education is to base elementary education on the values of Jewish culture and the achievements of science, on love of the homeland and loyalty to the state and the Jewish people, on practice in agriculture, on pioneer training, and on striving for a society built on freedom, equality, tolerance, mutual assistance and love of mankind.'

Clause 2 of the Law formulating the aim of Israeli school education.

'Those faithful to Jewish independence refuse to be bound by foreign judgment.'

David Ben-Gurion, in a lecture to the High Command of the Israeli Army, 6 April, 1950. Quoted in *The Jerusalem Post.*

THE ISRAELI MIND

Two Israeli cabinet ministers were discussing the nation's dreadful economic problems. Said one, 'We must declare war on the United States. After we lose, the Americans will spend thousands of millions to rehabilitate us just as they did for Germany and Japan.' The second minister shook his head and asked, 'What if we win?'

A story current in the early 1960s.

'For most Jews in Israel...Zionism is not just an extra or a 614th commandment added on, but entails a complete revision of what constitutes "the Jewish way of life".'

Joseph S. Bentwich,
Education in Israel,
Routledge and Kegan Paul,
London, 1965.

'In a new and developing country versatility is not so much a virtue as a reaction to brute necessity.'

Ian McIntyre of the BBC in
his book, *The Proud Doers,*
B.B.C. Publications, 1968, p.110.

'That it [the Holocaust] is not happening again in reality is thanks to Israel as a living collective memory that it happened and determination that it shall not happen again.'

From an editorial in
The Jerusalem Post,
18 April, 1974.

2

'Israel has been living in its blood since it was created, and this reality leaves ineradicable scars on its inhabitants. You can't run away from the war; you live war, eat war, drink war with your morning coffee; you go to bed with the late telecast.'

Igael Tumarkin, Israeli
sculptor, painter and photo-
grapher, in *The Israel
Magazine,* July, 1974.

'If we go back to the vision and dreams we had when Israel was founded — of being a dynamic, morally creative society, based on the equality of man and true democratic principles, we can be a wonderful country. A sort of Denmark or a brave Holland with our own moral values.'

Member of the Knesset,
Shulamit Aloni, in a Press
interview, 31 August, 1974.

'We Israelis need honour as a tyre needs air...honour is the vindica-
tion of our identity, our existence, our way of life.'

Ruth Bondy, *The Israelis,*
Funk & Wagnall, 1969,
p.278.

'In Israel, we have three million citizens who think they are all prime ministers. The difference between them and me is that every one of them thinks he knows more than I do.'

Yitzhak Rabin, Prime
Minister, in a Press interview,
14 June, 1976.

3

THE ISRAELI MIND

'He stands as the perfect symbol of Israel's most precious asset — the hard, tough, gifted yet unspoiled and extrovert youth of her armed forces, in ceaseless service, on endless patrol, ever watchful, ever under pressure and touched by a rare nobility of spirit. Like their elders they want no more war, no more struggle, want only rest and a return to their homes.'

> Patrick Cosgrave, writing
> about a young Israeli officer
> in *The Sunday Telegraph,*
> 10 October, 1976.

'Israelis try to be good at everything, physical and spiritual.'

> Jill Tweedie, *The Guardian,*
> 22 November, 1976.

'The young Israeli has a robust peasant humour without the sour sadness of traditional Jewish wit. He is taller, more muscular, he stands and walks with the expansiveness of a cowboy. He is, surprisingly often, very handsome, either in a blunt Robert Redford way or in an evocation of the old prophets.'

> Jill Tweedie, *Ibid.*

'Spiritual contact with God has ceased for most Israeli writers, and indeed for the majority of Israel's citizens who no longer regard themselves as practising Jews; their religious conviction has been replaced by a national consciousness.'

> Benjamin Tammuz, in a
> foreword to *Meetings With
> the Angel,* André Deutsch,
> 1973.

4

'Attacks on Jews heighten the awareness of my Israelness. I then realise how good it is to be an Israeli.'

> Spoken by an Israeli student
> to the author, soon after the
> massacre of Israelis at the
> Munich Olympic Games,
> 1972.

'I love to wash my son's filthy army clothes when he comes home on leave. I never know when it will be the last thing I can do for him.'

> Spoken by an Israeli mother
> to the author, July, 1977.

'Poetry is taken much more seriously in Israel than it is in most places in the world...if a poet says something on a political issue, politicians and people who have nothing to do with poetry take it very seriously.'

> Yehuda Amichai, one of
> Israel's most prominent
> poets, in *The Jerusalem Post*,
> 21 February, 1978.

'It is important to be popular — but even more important to be alive.'

> Abba Eban, one-time Israeli
> Foreign Minister, in *Abba
> Eban: An Autobiography,*
> Weidenfeld and Nicolson,
> 1977.

THE ISRAELI MIND

'Israel is the only country in the world where miracles are a part of state planning.'

Chaim Weizmann,
first President of Israel,
speaking in 1950. Quoted in
*Chaim Weizmann: A
Biography by Several Hands*,
ed. M. Weisgal and
J. Carmichael, Weidenfeld
and Nicolson, 1962.

2 Lust for Life

On a journalistic visit to Israel in 1956 I spent a few days in Jerusalem, still torn apart after the first Israeli war of survival in
1947-49. I remember that visit mostly because of the people I
met, among them David and Anne Rubinger, who jointly ran a
photographic business. David, when serving in the British
Army, had met Anne while she was in a Displaced Persons
Camp in Germany and after he returned to Jerusalem he sent for
her. To Anne, pretty and black-haired — and recently a mother
when I met her — this was supreme fulfilment. 'It was like being
brought to heaven', she said. Her simple, spontaneous simile
impressed me because she obviously meant what she said.

On another occasion I was trying to find a vantage point to
look towards the Western (or Wailing) Wall. At that time the
armistice line of 1949 ran through the centre of Jerusalem,
leaving to Jordan the old walled city with almost all the holy
places of the three religions. The Jews were denied access to
theirs. A man of whom I asked directions offered to show me a
good viewpoint and as we walked I asked him if he was Polish,
as his accent seemed to indicate this. 'Oh no,' he said, 'I'm
Israeli'.

'So you're a Sabra?' I said, aware that the native-born Israeli
liked an opportunity to express his pride in 'original' citizenship.
A sabra is, literally, a prickly pear. Like the pear, the native-
born Israeli is supposed to be prickly on the outside, soft and
sweet in the centre.

'Oh no', my guide said again, 'I arrived in the country only
two days ago'.

7

It was true, he said, that he *had been* Polish. He did not explain further but it was clear that the moment he set foot in Israel he had totally invested himself with his new nationality. He felt different and *was* different from the man who had been on the immigrant ship when it docked at Haifa.

The third encounter which has stayed in my memory is the most eloquent, though it has no conversation. I visited a kibbutz, Mishmar Hasharon, north-east of Netanya — an old one, founded in 1925, on the fertile coastal plain. Walking through the fields I chanced upon a man of about 35, sleeves rolled up — he had a long gash of a scar right along the left forearm — and face to the sun as he knelt in the freshly ploughed earth. Apparently he had just got down from a battered old tractor which was towing his plough and he was sifting the soil through his fingers and letting it drop slowly back to the ground. There was something reverential rather than agricultural about the act. He dug his fingers into the earth several times and finally he tossed a handful of earth into the air and watched it fall against the sun's rays. Then he returned to his tractor without having noticed me. I have seen men in the throes of love for a woman, for money, for some prized possession, for their religion: this man was in love with the earth.

I learnt much about the Israeli mind during that visit.

The 'mind' of any race of people can be analysed by reference to a variety of complex influences — historical, religious, educational, literary, geographical — to name only a few. While individuals of the race might differ greatly, collectively they share the characteristics of a common culture, hence the mind — attitudes, opinions, outlook — which distinguishes them from any other race. Examples are illimitable. How much is the French mind the product of the French Revolution? To what extent are Australians' attitudes shaped by their geographical insularity? Can indecisiveness and procrastination in the English mind of the late-twentieth century be partly due to lack of confidence brought about by loss of international prestige?

This book is not primarily about Jews. That most Israelis are Jews is a simple fact; equally obvious is the fact that most Jews are not Israelis — only three million out of about fourteen million are. If I were to write a book about the mind of the American Jew — which I am not competent to write — I would produce a work very different from this one. This statement might provoke the question, 'But since many American Jews become Israelis by immigration where does the difference lie?'

One of my objectives is to explain the difference. In my observation, which seems to be supported by much scholarly research, any immigrant Jew — American, Russian, English, Dutch, Moroccan — changes profoundly on becoming an Israeli. He takes on the characteristics of the Sabra; and life in Israel, with its many dramatic and its many subtle aspects, brings about changes in his personality — of which he himself is often unaware.

David Ben-Gurion, Israel's first Prime Minister, saw the difference between Jews and Israelis. 'Put two Jews together and you have a political argument,' he said, 'Put two Israelis together and you have opposing political parties'.[1] Here he draws attention to the intensity which makes the Jew of Israel a different person from the Jew of the diaspora. Establishing the Jews as a nation state involved a total revolution in the attitudes of Jewry, no longer a minority within a host country, but a self-determining population as one state within the larger world.

As early in Israel's statehood as 1953 Dr Abraham Shumsky, a sociologist, found that 'the various Western groups which arrived in Israel before 1948 merged into a new nation and lost their previous ethnic belongingness and identification.'[2]

Nobody, it should be remembered, has lived in Israel — as a state — for longer than 30 years; the Jews of pre-1948 were Palestinians. Because of the nature of its establishment Israel is a country of ethnic medley. Apart from Sabras, one finds Egyptians, Algerians, Moroccans, Yemenis, Iraqis, Englishmen, Americans, Frenchmen, Poles, Greeks, Spaniards, Argentinians, Australians, Canadians, Irishmen, Russians, Belgians — and many others. They came to Israel as refugees, victims, escapees or volunteers with only two things in common — the penalty they paid for being Jews and their will to create a new Jewish nation from the diaspora of the old.

9

Even if no other factors had been involved in the development of an Israeli mind — and many other considerations did play a part — these two were enough to lay its foundation. And that mind has become as distinctive as the Arab mind or the Chinese or the Indian mind. It is a paradox that the Israeli state, an amalgam of many races, has been labelled racist. All nations are more or less racist in their varying degrees of national chauvinism — it would be strange if this were not so — but when applied to Israel the word is used pejoratively and abusively. With such a mixture of races and religions Israel is fiercely patriotic but patently not racist, even if it is demonstrable that Israelis sometimes betray signs of French-pride, American-arrogance and Swedish-chauvinism.

That there exists an Israeli mind to be analysed is an improbable fact of history. Theodor Hertzl, the father of modern Zionism, wrote of his idea, 'If you will it, it is no dream.' But the creation of Israel was really a preposterous dream. Dr Weizmann, Israel's first president, is reputed to have said, 'I don't say a Zionist must be insane, but it helps if he is.' I imagine that he meant that to be a Zionist — a Zionist is nothing more than a person wanting to return to Zion (Israel) — a man or woman has to be single-minded, and dedicated to the form of lunacy that inspired and carried through the *Mayflower* expedition, a venture that was as unlikely to succeed as the creation of a Jewish state.

The basic element of the Zionist dream was a craving for peace in a Jewish homeland. It is one of the great tragedies of history that the dream and the craving were shattered at the moment the dream came true. With a population of less than 650,000, many of them still recovering from the trauma of Nazi Europe, the new state, brought into being by the United Nations, was attacked by the Arab states. This experience fixed some of the characteristics of the Israeli mind, most notably a strong element of caution and a disinclination to believe in any more dreams.

The Israeli is a realist. He knows too well the terrible price of victory to want war; he fears too much the terrible price of defeat to be unready for war.

When I was gathering material for this book, an Israeli told me that his countrymen could not be adequately studied without reference to the national tensions. He meant, for instance, tension about national security, the tension between the orthodox Jew and the secular Israeli, the tension between political parties, the tension of poverty in a country which could be rich, and the tension of a whole people who long for peace but cannot have it.

There is another, more subtle tension, one which reverses the natural order known to most countries at peace. It is this: in Israel the young people are constantly closer to death than the old. Israeli servicemen have learned to live with death. The Arabs have seen to that. Since 1948 death has been one of the most obvious facts of life.

Less dramatic than Arab enmity and war and bombs, another enormous problem for Israel is the integration of Sabras, western-culture Jews, oriental Jews, eastern Jews, one with the other. Groups from the West were sophisticated and progressive, those from Islamic countries were under-developed and even primitive. As Jews, they all knew they were really one people — their enemies were constantly telling them this — but they had to *become* that one people. That this extraordinary fusion came about was the result of many factors, some the result of planning, others fortuitous — and not the least important was the enmity of the Arabs. It is high irony that the Arab states, in expelling their Jewish citizens not only made Israel stronger numerically but provided a bonding agent second only in importance to Judaism.

Israel is a place you see but don't believe. No matter what you imagine before going there for the first time, it turns out to be different. Physically, it is smaller and with fewer people than you imagine. It is a tiny country, just one per cent of the size of the Arab land mass or a little more than the area of Wales or New Jersey. In its number of inhabitants, the entire State of Israel is no larger than Berlin, Sydney or the Manchester conurbation. The city of Cairo has almost three times the population of the whole of Israel.

11

In other ways, Israel is improbable. Any student of geography who studies maps and charts of Israel's rainfall, temperatures, soil types, terrain and so on would conclude that it could not possibly support three million people. By studying the country's raw materials — this would not take long to do — he must also conclude that the nation could not develop a viable industrial economy. And any economics student, with a glance at the staggering bill for defence, could tell that the nation's balance sheet must show an adverse balance. Yet, somehow, the Israelis have made the country a going concern. It would be all too simple to attribute this solely to American money. By sheer hard work and inventiveness, the people of Israel have made this unpromising scrap of land into what it is and in the process have evolved from a heterogeneous mass into a homogenous purposeful nationality that is, distinct from the Jewish nationality.

Surely in the course of centuries no race of people has excited such a combination of admiration, dislike, envy, fear, respect, incredulity and wonder as the modern Israelis. All these reactions were evident at the time of the Entebbe raid of July 1976, applauded by practically the entire world. When an Israeli commando force rescued a planeload of Jewish hostages held by terrorists at the Ugandan airport most people were intrigued by the finesse of the military operation. Perceptive commentators read more into the exploit than mere military skill. On the day of the raid BBC TV asked me to stand by for the programme *Panorama,* to comment on the terrorist organization responsible for the hijacking. During a break before the programme went on the air the presenter, David Dimbleby, said to me, 'It's the Israelis' political will that is so outstanding; how many other countries would have such will in similar circumstances?'

No other one, I believe. It is the nature of modern nations to play safe. Voting at the United Nations proves the point; many a nation will abstain rather than vote against an embarrassing or inconvenient motion. The political will to embark on the Entebbe operation shows a particular aspect of the Israeli mind and is the result of certain processes of thought, one of which was revealed at a press conference after the raid when Shimon

Peres then the Defence Minister, was asked by a journalist, 'What made you do it?'

Peres replied at once, 'The alternative.'

Bialik, the poet laureate of the Hebrew revival, had expressed much the same sentiment a long time before Peres. He wrote: 'Only where there is a feeling that there is no way out is there utter devotion; and devotion is the touchstone of every truth in the world.'[3]

Peres had no way out at the time of Entebbe, no alternative other than to allow the terrorists' captives to perish. The utter devotion Bialik refers to was evident not only in the Entebbe operation but in the task of survival the Israelis have set themselves; they have no way out.

There is nothing very mysterious about the Israeli mind, and nothing at all sinister, but for a variety of reasons the mind and its goals have often been misunderstood or misrepresented. This can be shown by reference to David Ben-Gurion, who is so often labelled 'a socialist' in a way that presumes that this explains everything about him. Ben-Gurion, like others in his group, was a non-Marxist socialist for whom socialism was a means, not an end. The dream of this group was not only to create a more just and free society for all but to regenerate the Jewish people within their own state. Jewish society of the future was to be a hard, pure society of workers not ruled by any leisure class, a society of natural human dignity based on pristine principles of social democracy.

Ben-Gurion lived to see Israel become, basically, a welfare state competing in a capitalist world.

No study of modern Israel and its people can ignore the way in which the Jewish people maintained and preserved their spiritual connection with the land of Palestine or Canaan or Judea (or whatever we want to call it) for 19 centuries. For 18 of those centuries the Palestine passion — the longing, the dream and the spiritual preparation for the homeland — was strong in the Jewish people. This steadfastness in looking on Palestine as the focus of national culture is one of mankind's most remarkable stories. Never in the periods of greatest persecution did the Jews as a people renounce their faith in liberation and in Ha'aretz, the land, as it was called through all those years.

With this in mind it becomes easy to understand Israeli tenacity and huge endeavour, to see why nothing could stop these people from building their new state. The ideology of Zionism gave the Jews passion and purpose, the Holocaust gave them impetus. A great deal of the anguish connected with the Middle East conflict might have been prevented if the world at large had only realized that nothing could weaken this three-strand strength of passion, purpose and impetus, but that on the contrary every attack, verbal or physical, would only strengthen it. Norman Bentwich, in one of his books about Israel,[4] refers to the 'triple cord of faith, will and memory' that links Jerusalem to the nation. Still more anguish will be averted if the strength of this cord is appreciated.

Two of the most significant Zionist slogans over the years have been: 'A light unto the nations' and 'A teaching shall go forth from Jerusalem'. As a nation, Israel is insistent on its sense of mission. Israel has saved itself by its own exertions and many Israelis think the country could save the world by its example. I believe that Israel does have a role to play in teaching and illuminating, not in the religious sense, but in philosophical and political issues. This new-old state could be an intellectual centre, when more of its energies can be diverted from the all-consuming need to survive. The educated Israeli believes that his state has something valuable to offer — a place of conference and consensus, of study, debate and publication.

Many modern students of Israel have referred to frustration as a principal facet of national mood. I prefer to use the word exasperation. In particular, Israelis are exasperated by demands to abandon their Zionism; this means being asked to dismantle an institutional apparatus of statehood and advanced economy, society and culture, achieved painfully and at great cost by its pioneers and maintained with dedication by millions of Jews imbued with a national consciousness. The Israelis cannot understand why others cannot see that this demand is preposterous, and their exasperation becomes chronic.

14

Yet, a particularly intriguing feature of the Israeli mind is its ability to find humour in adversity and under pressure. This can be illustrated here by a few quotations from the satirist Ephraim Kishon, possibly the world's most published humorist.

'Some people,' Kishon says, 'regard Dr Kissinger as the grave-digger of the Jewish State; others think it only looks that way.'[5]

- Even the few friends we have in the world — and you can count those on the thumb of one hand — don't want to hear us tell them [about the Palestinian problem].

- No doubt the Sabena hijackers [Tel Aviv Airport, May 1972] made the mistake of their lives by landing at Lydda airport of all places, thus giving our boys the advantage of the home-team. Indirectly their failure also led to strained relations between ourselves and the Red Cross in Geneva, seeing that we saved the passengers from being burnt alive in the booby-trapped plane *without* calling on the services of that human-itarian and strictly neutral body. Adding insult to injury, we freed the hostages and caught the killers by a shabby, spiteful, a well-nigh *illegal* trick.

- If there's one thing that bothers us more than this intolerable defence burden every Israeli carries on his back, it's that other people think we enjoy it.

Kishon is often naive and Maxime Rodinson, the French orientalist and non-communist Marxist, has said that 'The good conscience of the Israelis is a sign of their naivety.'[6] He means that what they do, they do in good conscience and with good intentions, and that they believe that this is all that can be expected of them. In short, they are sure that what they do is right. But, Rodinson believes, they are sometimes naive in this belief. For instance (he does not propose the example, but I do) the Israelis believed that in bulldozing Arab slums and rebuild-ing — for the same occupants — good homes with running water and electric light they were performing a humanitarian act and that it would be recognized as such. This was politically naive. The Arabs resented the helping hand.

Throughout history the Jew has not fitted into categories. He is the world's perpetual protestant and no ignoring of the

15

past can ignore his extraordinary position. In the modern world the Israeli also refuses to be put into categories and to conform to what other people think he should be. This enrages the international community, which sees conformity as a virtue. The frustration engendered by Israel's failure to conform has led to many patronising comments by foreign politicians and journalists — particularly Americans — such as 'Israel must be disciplined for its own good'. Or, 'The Israelis must be saved from themselves'.

The inference which may be drawn is that the Israelis are irrational, ignorant of cause and effect and that they are somehow detached from the world, as individuals and as a people. But neither this country nor its individual citizens can afford to be detached from daily events and live for themselves alone. To the Israeli, it seems that his country is at the centre of the world's attention. He doesn't want it that way, but this is how it is. His country's fate is always in the balance and somebody always seems to be attacking its politics or its citizens. To paraphrase Churchill; never in the field of international relations has such a small nation with so few people been so much traduced and vilified so persistently by so many other nations.

Much can be learned about any people from their national anthem. The Israelis' anthem, 'Hatikvah', is short and direct.

> So long as still within our breasts
> The Jewish heart beats true,
> So long as still towards the Easts,
> To Zion looks the Jew,
> So long our hopes are not yet lost —
> Two thousand years we cherished them —
> To live in freedom in the land
> of Zion and Jerusalem.

There are values here which ought to reveal much to the more perceptive of the Israelis' friends and enemies.

While songs and literature can reveal much about a people, just watching them is even more instructive, especially when they do not know they are being watched, or don't care. One evening I saw a wedding near the Tomb of David, in a maze of medieval buildings on the south side of Jerusalem. Guests had gathered for the marriage of an orthodox Jewish girl and a convert, a student at a certain 'yeshiva' or seminary. It is a liberal seminary because it accepts convert-students and even permits girls to study there. As we were not official guests we could watch without being involved. The wedding took place in a sunken courtyard — and, in the orthodox tradition, in the open air. The bride and groom were almost hidden by the wedding canopy so everybody had to get into contorted positions to see them. As night fell torches flared to give the scene a mystic quality. Grace was pronounced and the feasting and singing began. The men danced in a large circle — and what a spectacle it was. Bearded rabbis, respectable older men in dark suits, students in shirt sleeves, little boys — round they whirled, feet thumping the ground, bodies twisting. The women danced, too, as they gently and gracefully encircled the bride. A young man did a balancing trick with bottles, reminiscent of the performance in *Fiddler on the Roof*, and another youth turned cartwheels through a hoop held by a couple of little boys. It was all unashamed showing-off.

After all this jollity a few older men restored order — apparently by sheer force of personality, as they did not shout. Then rabbis evoked the Seven Blessings upon the young couple, who looked moved by the proceedings.

This book does not analyse the Israeli Arabs — those Arabs, both Moslem and Christian who, since 1948, have lived within the borders of the State of Israel, who are entitled to Israeli passports and who vote in Israeli elections. Numbering more than 500,000, these Israeli Arabs mostly reside in the north of the country. They have much in common with the oriental Jews who lived for generations in Arab lands before they were driven out and found refuge in Israel. The Arabs living within Israel's borders are Israeli citizens and they have benefited from Israel's development. For instance, the first Arab women in the world to vote were those of Israel. In 1977 the elementary school attendance for Arab boys was 98 per cent, compared with 65 per cent in British Mandate days, and for girls 90 per cent, compared with 15 during the Mandate.[7] I have not included the Israeli Arabs in this book because I would need several more chapters and it would become uneconomically long. In any case, I am more concerned to study the Jewish Israelis — the race most people mean when they refer to 'the Israelis'.

3 The Kibbutznik –
The Israeli Ideal

The kibbutz* is the oldest of Israeli institutions, the most important, and the most basic in any analysis of the Israeli mind. Of all things Israeli it is also the best known outside Israel; it has had a moral and political impact around the world.

A study in depth of the kibbutz and its cousin, the moshav,** and of the people who live in them is essential to an understanding of Israeli attitudes and values for kibbutzim are repositories of national values, such as patriotism. Their people are proud of their intellectual-physical dualism. Human and humane, kibbutzniks are conscious of being True Israelis and it is on the kibbutz that one finds the ideal by which others are assessed. Truly the kibbutz is the tool of 'Israelification'.

For many foreigners the kibbutz has romantic connotations of young pioneering farmers working in primitive conditions, of groups of sunburnt, like-minded people who, after a backbreaking day in the fields, dance and sing around their camp fire at night. To me personally, when I saw the kibbutz in my and its early years, it was an exciting emblem of courage and enterprise in the face of adversity and an escape from the tensions of Western 'civilization'. The Israelis do not see it as an escape. The Hebrew word which best describes the motivation of those who choose life on a kibbutz is hagshama, meaning 'dedication',

*Kibbutz or kevuzah (plural kibbutzim, kevuzat) literally translated the word means group; the residents of a kibbutz are kibbutzniks.
**A moshav (plural, moshavim) does *not* hold all property in common. It is described in detail later in the chapter.

though a kibbutznik I know says a better translation is 'putting ideals into action'.

To the sociologist, the psychologist, the political scientist and the educationist, from their various viewpoints, the kibbutz is an intriguing experiment and the subject of endless analysis.

As a phenomenon, the kibbutz is a unique product of the Zionist labour movement and the Jewish national revival. No theoretical utopian project, it was developed by Jewish workers inspired by ideas of social justice as an integral part of the Zionist effort to resettle the homeland. Ever since its inception the kibbutz movement has fostered the economic, political, cultural and security activities required to carry out that purpose. From the internal and Zionist point of view, 'the most profound contribution of the kibbutz has been the creation and perpetuation of the image of the New Jew and the True Israeli'.[1]

There is an awareness about kibbutz members, a vitality, as if they are aware of a dimension in life that escapes the rest of us. The kibbutzniks show this awareness in the vitality of their talk, the vivacity of their actions and their tranquillity in repose.

Despite those common traits there is no 'pure breed', no exact model of the kibbutz. There are four distinct kibbutz movements, each giving expression to a political-philosophical approach — from orthodox religious to atheist, from 'left' to 'right', from a belief in life in small communities (400-500 people) to a belief in life in larger communities (perhaps 1,500). Even within each movement there are variations. The initial residents came from different backgrounds in 80 countries — from peaceful middle-class homes and from concentration camps. Although all kibbutzim may look alike to visitors, in the eyes of kibbutz members themselves each one has its own personality which they sense the moment they drive through the gates. Each has tended to alter over time, to adapt to new scientific knowledge and to changes in the realities of life in Israel. Yet, there is a commonality in the kibbutz experience.

There was a time when the kibbutz was the heart and essence of the whole country — because there was no state. In its absence the kibbutz was the miniature or prototype of the state to come. State activities are derived from what was learnt on the kibbutz. Historically, therefore, the kibbutz is the foundation of modern Israel, while to the Israeli himself it represents an emotional, intellectual and ideological ideal — that of genuine community and co-operation. For many years before the establishment of the state of Israel it was the compass which gave direction to the individual Jewish settler and to those inspired people who struggled to bring about a return to the homeland. Seven decades after the first communal settlement bonded itself to the land, the kibbutz might not remain the compass, but it does give stability to a volatile society.

Kibbutzim and kibbutzniks have an importance out of all proportion to their numbers — 90,000 people in 259 kibbutzim. They comprise only four per cent of the total population but their proportion among army officers is nearly four times as high, and a quarter of the casualties in the Six-Day War were soldiers from kibbutzim. Overall, kibbutzim account for about 15 per cent of the gross national product.

To understand the kibbutznik mind and the effect of the kibbutz on the mind of the Israeli generally it is necessary to trace the growth of the communal settlement from an intriguing dream to an instrument of policy and, further, to what it is today — a major influence on the activities of the state of Israel.

Its influence has always been a mixture of the moral and the practical — ranging from settlement and security functions to the absorption of immigrants and the provision of leading personnel for Zionist and government service.

The first kibbutz was founded in 1909 at Degania on the southern shore of the Sea of Galilee by a group of pioneers who, after working at first as employees on a farm of the Palestine Land Development Company, undertook collective responsibility for the working of the farm. The Degania youngsters came from Eastern Europe from middle-class families and they believed in the Tolstoyan philosophy of self-labour. The 750 acres they were given belonged to the Jewish National Fund; it was swamp, unproductive, malaria-infested, and open to Arab raids.

Another group, which started work at Kinneret in the same year, became an independent kibbutz in 1913. By 1914, 11 kibbutzim were established on Jewish National Fund land under the responsibility of the Zionist organization; the number grew to 29 by 1918.

These early kibbutzim had small memberships based upon the idea that the community should be small enough to constitute a kind of enlarged family in which every person is aware of his responsibility for all the others. The kibbutzniks saw manual labour as self-fulfilment; to take a wild, desolate and lonely piece of ground and turn it into a ploughed, productive field — that was profound satisfaction. It was not only a matter of livelihood, but one of value, akin to composing poetry. During the Third Aliyah (the third wave of emigration) after the First World War, when larger numbers of pioneering settlers arrived, Schlomo Lavie and others proposed the establishment of large, self-sufficient villages combining agriculture with industry, for which the name kibbutz was used. The first of this type in 1921 was En Harod. Some communities were inspired by the ideas of the social philosopher Aaron David Gordon who lived in Degania, dying there in 1922.

Gordon's work *Philosophy of Labour* gave the kibbutz its ideological background and his theories had a profound influence on his colleagues and contemporaries. He believed in the change of the individual before the transformation or rebirth of the state, in the development of man as a social being and the evolvement of personal responsibility, before a materialist social revolution. He realized that the rootless Jew could achieve harmonious creativity through physical labour on the land, which would become a new identification with nature and represent revival of social and national awareness. Gordon's belief in the dignity of labour and the individual personality deeply affected the Jewish labour movement. Other kibbutz founders cherished the tradition of the Gedud ha-Avodah 'the Labour Legion' of the early 1920s, which regarded itself as a militant constructive task force, and whose policy was to establish large communes.

THE KIBBUTZNIK – THE ISRAELI IDEAL

In their early days the kibbutzim received their manpower mainly from the pioneering youth movements abroad. These strongly motivated young people — the kibbutzniks of popular legend — provided the movements with a practical ideal of pioneering settlement on the land in order to make a major contribution to the building of the Jewish National Home and create a model and a basis for the socialist society of the future. The new settlements played an important part in expanding Jewish settlement and safeguarding the growing community from Arab raids.

In the late 1930s when the British administration was systematically trying to prevent the establishment of Jewish settlements the settlers evolved their 'tower and stockade' tactics; they could set up a kibbutz in a single night, complete with stockade and watchtower. British troops sent to the area would find an entire protected settlement which could hardly be dismantled without a pitched battle. The tower and stockade system forestalled official British destruction and foiled many an Arab attack. The kibbutzim served as bases for the Hagana defence force and later for the Palmach, its commando section. Arms were hidden in the kibbutzim, ammunition was made there and Jewish leaders on the run were spirited from one kibbutz to another.

Political life was rudimentary and informal in the early days of the kibbutz. The small group of a dozen or so young people decided everything directly, and the participation of each individual was taken for granted. Ideologically and practically there was no difficulty about including women; as part of the group they were always present and they shared the discussion and decision-making. Women with strong personalities quickly emerged in political activity. One was Golda Meir, a member of Kibbutz Merchavia. She was not at first well received because she was married and a 'spoilt American', considered incapable of hard work. The kibbutzniks had misjudged Golda and she came unscathed through the backbreaking work of harvesting almonds. Then they sent her to dig pits, which was really hard work. Golda mastered that, too. Later she became an expert on poultry and in bread-making. Valuing hygiene, she asked that the dining room tables be covered with linoleum and that the waiters not smoke while waiting on tables. This gained her the label of 'witch' — meaning that she was nagging and domineering. Her perseverance and obvious good intentions eventually brought about her unqualified acceptance by the kibbutz.

The powers of the kibbutz over its members used to be total. For instance, the committee of a kibbutz in the Jordan Valley six decades ago decided that it could afford no more children and one young woman, already pregnant, was told to have an abortion. She refused, and in due course gave birth to a son she named Moshe — Moshe Dayan.

Fully to appreciate the vitality and drive of the kibbutz and moshav it is essential to understand that most of the Jews coming as refugees from Europe after 1945 were hungry for security. Cruelly maltreated by the Nazis and later profoundly embittered by official British indifference to their plight in post-war Europe, many saw that salvation lay only in self-help. Abandoned by Christianity — as they thought — they could trust only another Jew. The kibbutz or moshav provided mutuality and security and a place for wounds to heal. Here, after centuries of oppression, the survivors of European Jewry could labour in peace, or so they thought.

Most of the new villages established under emergency conditions during and immediately after the Second World War, especially in the Negev, were kibbutzim. By the time of Independence in May 1948, they numbered 149 out of the 291 Jewish villages in the country. In 1948 and 1949 the momentum of kibbutzim expansion continued; out of 175 new villages founded during those two years, 79 were kibbutzim.

They were difficult and dangerous years; during Israel's various wars of survival — 1947-49, 1956, 1967, 1973 — the kibbutzim have been command posts or strong-points or places of last-ditch defence. This has given them a special place in the Israeli consciousness and invested some with the kind of aura which Dunkirk has in the British consciousness or Lexington and Concord in the American. Probably the most evocative kibbutz name in Israel is Yad Mordechai — named in honour of

Mordechai Anielewicz, commander of the Warsaw ghetto fighters. On the edge of the Negev, just north of Gaza, it was founded in 1943 by Polish and Galician Jews, many of whom had fought with anti-Nazi partisans. They believed that in Palestine they would be able to lay aside their weapons for ploughs and hammers, but they were mistaken. On 18 May, 1948 Yad Mordechai was attacked by Egyptian soldiers marching up the coast towards Tel Aviv. The state, only a few days old and struggling to organize a defence against enemies now attacking it on three fronts, needed Yad Mardechai to hold out until Hagana could get reinforcements to the area.

The handful of kibbutzniks, armed only with small arms, held Yad Mordechai against repeated attacks by aircraft, tanks, artillery and at least 3,000 Egyptian troops. After an epic five-day struggle and 50 per cent casualties the kibbutzniks had to abandon the ruins of Yad Mordechai. The Egyptians burned it to ash. After the enemy had been driven south, the survivors returned, re-established their kibbutz, and later made part of it into a museum of the battle. Within the grounds they also built an imaginative memorial to victims of the Holocaust.

The courage and sacrifice of the kibbutz settlers at this time profoundly influenced Israelis and made them all the more determined to strengthen their country ready for the inevitable further assaults upon it.

Youngsters born or brought up in Israel, including the second or third generation from older kibbutzim and graduates of Youth Aliyah and Israel youth movements, became more prominent among the founders of new kibbutzim, especially in the Negev and, after the Six-Day War, in the Golan Heights and the Jordan Valley. Political attitudes were now more diverse. Some of the later kibbutzim did not regard themselves as a part of the socialist movement while a number of kibbutzim were established by religious Jews and combined communal life with fulfillment of the Torah, the Jewish book of holy law.

Gradually, mainly for ideological, ethnic or economic reasons, the various kibbutzim banded into unions or movements. The differences in principle and practice between one federation and another can be tremendous. A summary of each of the four main groups makes some of these differences clear.

Union of Collective Settlements: Ihud ha-Kevuzot ve-ha-kibbutzim

Founded in 1951, by 1976 this group comprised 76 communities with a total population of about 27,000. The Ihud is considered the most liberal of the major kibbutz federations, since it imposes less social or political discipline. In some of its villages children sleep in their parents' home, and in many settlements people may possess personal funds and spend their money more or less as they wish. Some of the settlements are not socialist.

The National Kibbutz Movement: Ha-kibbutz ha-Arzi ha-Shomer ha-Za'ir

Founded in 1927, this federation had 76 kibbutzim by 1971. Its ideological basis is a belief in the kibbutz as an instrument for fulfilling the Zionist ideal, furthering the class struggle and building a Socialist society. Its founding members came from Poland and Galicia in 1919 and in 1920 established their first kibbutz, Bet Alfa, in 1922. In 1927 four of the six ha-Shomer ha-Za'ir kibbutzim founded the Young Guard (Ha-kibbutzim ha-Arzi).

The outlook of Ha-kibbutz ha-Arzi is that the kibbutz is an autonomous unit of social life, comprising all spheres of economic, social, cultural, political and educational activity. Through continual democratic process, the movement aims at developing a common outlook on life that unites all its members — 'Ideological collectivism'. While insistent on Jewish political independence, Ha-kibbutz ha-Arzi members seek Jewish-Arab co-operation — or, as it has been put in the movement's manifesto, 'the defence of Israel's security coupled with unremitting efforts to achieve peace'.

The United Kibbutz Movement: Ha-kibbutz ha-Me'uhad

Founded in 1927, ha-Me'uhad is based on these principles: The kibbutz should be a large settlement with no predetermined limit to the number of members; it should be open to all comers; it should engage in all forms of production; it should play a role in the integration of newcomers to Israel by aiming at a membership representing a wide range of geographic origin. Members of Ha-kibbutz ha-Me'uhad have been prominent among the leaders of the Israel labour movement and the Hagana, as officers in the Israel forces in the War of Independence, cabinet ministers, authors and artists. It has 62 settlements with a population of more than 26,000.

The Religious Kibbutz: Ha-kibbutz Ha-Dati

Established in 1935 by four religious pioneer groups, the movement was well developed before 1948 — when Arab invaders destroyed six of its villages and killed many of the adult population. Most of the religious kibbutzim had a second period of growth during the 1960s and all 11, with a total population of 4,000, are prosperous. The fundamental principle of Ha-kibbutz Ha-Dati is to combine religious practice with labour. As its more articulate kibbutzniks will tell a visitor, 'Our religious socialism is founded on prophetic concepts of social justice and talmudic principles of human relations and good government... We regard democracy as a basic value of the kibbutz and not merely as a corollary of equality... Communal ownership is important not only for economic reasons but as an expression of religious and human attitudes'.* A religious kibbutz has problems which the non-orthodox do not face. For instance, the kitchen of the communal dining-room must be twice as big as the others because it is divided; one half for the preparation of meat and the other half for the preparation of dairy meals and dishes. The kibbutzniks must stock two sets of cutlery and two sets of china — and yet a third set for use only at Passover.

Over the years each of the kibbutz organizations has associated itself to some degree with one of the Israel political

*This is my synthesis of many descriptions I have heard.

parties. With the passage of time many of the initial differences between one type of kibbutz and another have disappeared. Most of the small ones which were purely agricultural have established industries, and there is no difference between the small kevuzah of 40 or 50 members and the large kibbutz of 1,500. Givat Brenner is the largest with 1,660. Some kibbutzim used to be strongly pro-Soviet, but with the intensified Soviet hostility towards Israel, the attitude of the U.S.S.R. has ceased to be a dividing factor, especially since the Six-Day War.

Since its inception the movement has been supported by Zionist and Israel governmental agencies with leases of national land, technical advice, development projects and long-term financing. Through a special corps, Nahal, composed of youth movement graduates, the defence forces train the foundation members of future kibbutzim and help in their establishment. Sites for new kibbutzim have been chosen to fit into the pattern of national settlement and defence policy, often in defiance of economic viability. Many of them are in border areas and form an important part of the regional defence system.

The administration of any kibbutz is based on a weekly general meeting of membership, which formulates policy, elects officers and supervises the working of the kibbutz. The governing body of each community is the secretariat, consisting of the secretary, the treasurer, the chairmen of some of the key committees, the production manager, and a few others. Other committees manage education, cultural activities, personal problems and matters of principle, economic planning, and co-ordination of work. All elective positions are rotated every year or two.

According to general kibbutz values, members also rotated their duties and were expected to carry out a specific task for a limited period only, then no identification between a member and any special type of work could result. This arrangement broke down when the need for specialization arose. Also it does not pay a kibbutz to turn one of its members into a highly qualified engineer and then expect him to take his turn in the kitchen.

A kibbutz has no judicial institutions; it has considerable autonomy in judging its members and does so through the general assembly and certain committees. Behaviour considered deviant is dealt with internally; only the rare incidents of such misconduct as fraud, larceny and murder are handed over to the state police. (Only one murder is known to have been committed within a kibbutz and only one act of embezzlement.)

A kibbutz is democracy in action, even to the point of errors in judgment. A secretary or divisional manager can be over-ruled by the committee and the committee can be over-ruled by the kibbutz general meeting. For example, at Kibbutz Nachshon the secretary and committee proposed to buy an air conditioning unit for the dining hall but they were over-ruled by the general membership which decided on a sophisticated washing-up machine.

Candidates for membership are usually accepted after a year's probation. Since kibbutzim are incorporated co-operative enterprises, members generally transfer all their assets, other than strictly personal effects, to the kibbutz. If a member decides to leave he is entitled to his personal effects, and — since a government decision of 1972 — to a cash grant proportional to the time he has been with the kibbutz.

The kibbutz has always stood in interesting opposition to the Israeli system of private property. Capitalistic individualism and competition did not influence the kibbutz system. In the late 1950s, thousands of kibbutz members received millions of German marks in reparation payments. This seductive external influence could have resulted in the desertion of the kibbutz by thousands of members who preferred to keep the funds rather than turn them over to the kibbutz treasury, but the number of people who did leave was surprisingly small — about one family in a hundred.

The first occasion in a kibbutz when the family became the unit of consumption occurred in the now legendary case of the man who brought home an electric kettle from the Jewish Brigade of the British Army after the Second World War. He was considered a dangerous renegade and was ordered to hand

29

the kettle over to the kibbutz as common property. When he refused some people followed his example and acquired electric kettles from illegitimate sources. This insubordination spread and the idealists prophesied the end of the kibbutz. I was told, in 1950, that possession of an electric kettle was 'bourgeois softness'. But members went on sipping tea in their apartments; the practice became a ceremony — and cakes and biscuits were served with the tea. Tea soon became legitimate, and to the foreign visitor it is one of the most attractive aspects of kibbutz life.

At one time the very existence of a bedroom was considered effete, bourgeois and indecent. Only a pampered person indulging his sexual appetite needed a bedroom. The oldtime kibbutznik — and for that matter, the city-dweller of the Yishuv* — slept in the living room on an iron bedstead which during the day became a settee; later the iron bed gave away to corner sofas which opened up and folded back in a variety of patterns.

In 1956 the favourite kibbutz hate was the private shower; it would surely undermine the principle of kibbutz life. When everybody had a private shower the great fear of self-indulgence was the personal or family refrigerator. More recently it has been air-conditioning, which is 'damnably bourgeois' according to one kibbutz secretary. Sooner or later all kibbutz homes and public rooms will have air conditioning — and the kibbutz principles will be just as strong as ever. The old-timers are much more flexible than they used to be — or perhaps they have learned that things which they used to regard as threats to the true path of socialism are mere matters of personal taste and habit.

Every kibbutz I have visited is lacking in some of the more obvious refinements one expects in western society. For instance, the kibbutz dining-room has no table cloths; the emphasis is on the purely functional. The bedroom is for sleeping (and, of course, love-making); there is no space for a

*Yishuv — the term for pre-State Israel.

single thing other than a bed — although an entire wall is given over to built-in cupboards. Kibbutzniks say that a person can have as much privacy as he wants, but it is the privacy of the mind. There are few physical bolt holes. The lack of privacy has one obvious result: there is little adultery and less divorce. Family togetherness is so important that spouses are supposed to eat with their partners in the dining room, always sit with them in the general assembly, when films are shown, or at other cultural events. It is preferred that they do their night-guard duty together; if they don't they will become the subject of gossip, an absorbing kibbutz pastime, though usually without malice or spite.*

Kibbutz society strives for the simultaneous solution of social, economic and cultural problems on the basis of co-operation, equality and mutual aid. Such a society, even though it takes the existence of the family for granted, cannot leave education within the family as a single, isolated entity. The responsibility for the education of the child is largely taken away from the family, and becomes the responsibility of the kibbutz society. The idea that children are the responsibility of the whole community is as old as Plato, who outlined a similar programme in *The Republic.*

Kibbutz education aims mainly at the interweaving of the individual and the community — the development of an adult in whom personal initiative and maturity will combine with devotion to the community and with the acceptance of the communal way of life. Music is an essential part of education from the earliest age and nearly every child sings and dances and plays the recorder or accordion. I can recall some beautiful evenings spent listening to youthful singing and watching the dancing, for which the young performers made their own music.

The most controversial aspect of collective education is that from birth the children live in separate children's houses, where

*For a literary description of kibbutz life, see Amos Oz's novel, *Elsewhere, Perhaps,* Helen and Kurt Wolff, London, 1973. Translated by Node Lange.

they are under the care of professionally-trained kibbutz members. Every day, when the parents have finished work the children come home to stay with them until bedtime. Experience has strengthened the conviction that the parents are the most important factor in the education and healthy development of their children. Collective education does not question the unique ties between parent and child; the problem has not been how to weaken them but on the contrary how to make them into a more stable and permanent source of security and how to integrate them into education for communal life.

The children's houses include bedrooms, a kitchenette and dining hall, playroom and workshop, toilet and showers, sheltered courtyard equipped with sand-box, gymnastic equipment and a pool and classrooms. Both the building and the facilities are adapted to the needs of different ages, but all are inclusive units for living and learning. A kibbutz playground is often an intriguing place with its exercises in ingenuity.

The formal educational pattern is based on five separate but progressive frameworks. After the birth of a child and the subsequent period of rest, the mother returns to her ordinary duties and functions in work and society, and the infant is cared for by trained nurses. From the infants' house the children are moved to the toddlers' section where they remain until their fourth year. They are placed in play-groups of about six, each with a permanent nurse, and meet their parents during the afternoons. Between the ages of four and seven the children live in kindergartens and then move to the primary division (seven to 12 years) where groups of about 20 live in special quarters with a matron and teacher-leader. In the final secondary division, academic and social activities become particularly important. Each group has its special instructor and teaching stresses agriculture. Children in the final grade take full part in the working and social life of the kibbutz and are admitted formally to the community at the age of 18.

The teacher-pupil relationship is necessarily close and informal, since the teacher is not just that but a neighbour and family friend as well. Essentially, the children's house is a mini-kibbutz conducting its own affairs with the advice of teachers and group leaders.

Despite the children's separate existence, kibbutz members spend almost an hour a day more wholly in child care than do parents in the cities or development towns. In recent years some kibbutzim have changed the system to provide for children sleeping in the homes of their parents. Advocates of this change say that it enhances the psychological security of the child and strengthens the family. The kibbutz educational system and its effect on children has been extensively studied, like most things in Israel. Research has not revealed much damage caused by maternal deprivation but any deleterious effects are overcome at a later age by the strong group-supportive environment. The importance of children in the kibbutz system is paramount; they are the real wealth of the kibbutz and their welfare and development is by far the most important kibbutz 'industry'.

Kibbutz boys and girls who have been reared together in the same children's house very rarely marry each other, in violation of the sociological law of propinquity, which holds that people marry people who are geographically near and with whom they share a set of life experiences. In effect, the child's colleagues have become family. Sharing mixed-sex rooms with members of their own kibbutz is not embarrassing or complicated; sexual attraction does not occur between co-socialized children. In contrast, youngsters of the Kibbutz Arzi Movement, which has a different policy, at adolescence are suddenly forced to adjust to sharing mixed-sex bedrooms with students from other kibbutzim. Perhaps because of this the highest proportion of inter-kibbutz marriages within a federation exist in the Arzi movement.

Girls usually engage in courtship much earlier than boys and go through its preliminary phases within their own kibbutzim. At 15 or 16 they are going out with boys four or five years older and by the time they are 16 or 17 they may visit their boyfriends in their rooms. From the time kibbutz women become fecund they are routinely provided with contraceptives; if they have children, it is because they have chosen to.

33

In the early kibbutzim the ideal marriage relationship was not based on sexuality, even though the ultimate need for it was acknowledged. The emphasis was on intimate friendship and ideological and personal sympathy. It took a long time for people to decide who would be their partners for life, for permanence was expected. Once the decision had been made, all the couple had to do was to ask for a separate room or tent; there was no ceremony.

When a boy on leave from the army brings his girlfriend home it is taken for granted that she will spend the night in his room; his room-mate, if also on leave, must find other lodgings — this is a peer's duty. In the modern kibbutz it is generally assumed that a deep emotional relationship is a precondition of sexual intercourse. When a boy and girl live together their association is considered 'serious'. Young people are never formally interfered with but those who change partners become the subject of gossip — and therefore of the pressures of public opinion. Parents play no part in mate selection and the few who try are severely admonished.

Should an affair seem to be serious people begin to ask, sometimes slyly, 'When are we going to drink?' (at the wedding). When a generally recognized couple shows affection in public the only acceptable outcome is marriage — or at least the decision to marry. Many couples live together for a long time before the wedding. No formal engagement takes place and the wedding date is set after consultation with the housing committee, which will say when the couple can expect to be allocated an apartment, and with the couple's parents. It seems that trial marriages rarely founder, though I know of a young woman so disappointed in love that she decided never to marry. (But she was unwilling to forego the experience of motherhood so she asked a man outside the kibbutz to make her pregnant; she reared the child in the kibbutz and neither mother nor child suffered socially or economically.) It should be said that on the kibbutz no woman, whether pregnant, old, a new mother, a mother of five, unmarried, or divorced, need depend on her husband, father or any other man. Economic support and legal status are hers by virtue of her membership in the collective. Illegitimate children — though they are rare — do not suffer economic disadvantage or moral handicap. The kibbutz system, unlike the nuclear-family system of Europe and North America, does not penalize one-parent families.

A kibbutz wedding ceremony is a gala occasion; never again will boy or girl be at the centre of so much attention. Convention, usually so casually regarded on the kibbutz, comes into play and the bride acquires a wedding dress, veil, special shoes and the day before the wedding visits a hairdresser and beautician. As in other societies, the boy has less to do — simply to buy the wedding rings and visit a rabbi to arrange the ceremony. The bride's parents are not saddled with crippling debts, as so often happens elsewhere; the kibbutz organizes the wedding feast for the kibbutz members and perhaps 300 or so guests from outside. The culture committee prepares the entertainment programme.

Generally kibbutzniks are irreverent — in founding the kibbutz their grandparents hoped to get away from old-time religion — so the religious wedding ceremony is not taken very seriously; it is a mere duty to the state. The wedding feast — the messiba — is much more important, especially in its more ritualistic aspect. A text from the *Song of Songs* is both recited and sung and the kibbutz secretary hands the couple a parchment document, essentially an agreement to pay the wife a certain sum in the event of divorce; on the kibbutz this is merely symbolic.

The jolly part of the evening consists of light entertainment and the recital of humorous events from the couple's life and love story, together with songs and dances.

A mood of apprehension settles over the kibbutz when a young woman goes to the hospital to have a baby and there is much rejoicing when news comes through of a safe delivery. When the mother returns with the baby there is a reception at the clubhouse.

In some kibbutzim the third, and in a few even the fourth, generation has reached maturity and in a number the kibbutz-born — the Sabras — are the dominant group. Significantly, over 75 per cent of kibbutz-born Sabras have remained in the kibbutz; the cities have either not attracted them or they need the support of the group in which they have grown up. Some who have moved to the towns and cities have had difficulty in adjusting to the different way of life, for example, handling money.

Some women have at times been disappointed in their relationship with the kibbutz community — a fact readily conceded by kibbutzim leadership. They were freed from household chores so that they could work at other tasks but this practice has become increasingly difficult as a kibbutz grows older and pressure is generated for increased work in child care and household services. Some kibbutzim are doing remarkable work in accepting and re-educating troubled urban boys and girls, a social service which requires trained female staff. Since the 1960s kibbutzim have been improving the status of women by bettering physical conditions of work in the services, by raising the status of a job through training and study, and by reducing working hours for women with families.

Kibbutz life is necessarily disciplined — not by rules but by constant respect and regard for other people and by always being on guard against displays of destructive emotion such as fear and anger. Joy and pleasure are freely expressed. When people live in such close and constant proximity as they do on a kibbutz there is little natural privacy, so they contrive an artificial privacy by keeping their thoughts to themselves, except on very special occasions. Perhaps this self-sufficiency is damaging. 'When everything is so controlled you stop being sensitive to other people and then you stop saying, "Hallo, how are you?" People never say "How are you?" here. There's no such thing except when there's been some tragedy. People are afraid to expose themselves, to reveal themselves.'*

This disinclination to exposure or revelation extended, until recently, to politics. The kibbutz has always taken politics seriously but kibbutzniks usually arrived at their political views

* Noa Daniel, of Kibbutz Ma'abarot, quoted by Yigal Pe'eri in *Hashavua,* the weekly journal of the Hashomer Hatza'ir movement. Miss Daniel, a dancing teacher, told Pe'eri that she 'had never seen her pupils let go unless there was some special reason'. (April 1977).

by no more complex process than by reading them in the news-paper of their particular movement. Allan Shapiro, a kibbutznik who lectures on political science at Haifa University, says that in extreme cases the kibbutznik is, politically speaking, 'something of an enthused robot'.

Traditionally, each kibbutz was one-party. This was under-standable enough, for if rows in the family are unsettling, the strains and tensions of a political division could tear a kibbutz apart. For instance, conflicting opinions about the Korean War — though of no local significance to Israel — had profound and polarizing effects in some kibbutzim. At times like this most people are intent on reducing the political temperature — achieved by reverting to the safety of the movement's official policy. At one time the Ihud movement secretariat advised its affiliated kibbutzim to ban pre-election rallies on kibbutz premises.

The few political 'deviants' were tolerated but expected not to engage in organized activities on behalf of their party. Some-times these deviants were people who had married out of their political faith; for many years unions between members of dif-ferent kibbutz movements were jokingly referred to as mixed marriages.

All this is changing rapidly. The movement press is no longer so powerful or so uncritically read by its readers. Political infor-mation and opinion is coming into the kibbutz by radio and tele-vision, with the wide range of commercial newspapers, and through the many meetings of kibbutzniks. It is now legitimate to deviate from the kibbutz party line, if indeed one exists. On ceremonial occasions some kibbutzim still display the red flag together with the Israeli national flag. A child explained this odd juxtaposition to me in this way: 'The red flag is the flag of the working class. The blue and white one is ours'.

In the mid-1970s kibbutz rank and file members were demanding open debates on political issues. This inevitably made kibbutz politics more volatile, a healthy sign since debate produces more flexible minds. Towards the end of 1976 Israeli political scientists were aware that the great mass of kibbutzniks

37

were developing a more acute political consciousness, and they interpreted this as a quest for the revival of the kibbutz spirit.

Inevitably, the kibbutznik tends to become institutionalized if only because administrative machinery exists to handle his every problem. Yet, surprisingly, every kibbutz has its individualists and a young foreign Christian volunteer has told me that the kibbutz on which she worked was 'a breeding ground for eccentrics'. Certainly kibbutzniks are far from complacent. The most restive are often the older people, who fret because they have not achieved all their aspirations and because, as they see it, their sons and daughters do not have the bright ideological spark which they themselves had. Some sons and daughters readily admit this.

In recent years Western youth culture has penetrated the kibbutz. Pop music, clothing fads, sexual experimentation and other activities have had their effect on kibbutz youngsters. This has created a hidden but real conflict between the new influences and the ascribed ideologies for kibbutz children of action, performance and creativity.

But the high regard for labour has not changed. The kibbutz movement places equal value on all kinds of work and while there is a good deal of mobility many people take up more or less permanent jobs. It has even become necessary to hire outside labour, in contradiction to the movement's socialist principles. A growing problem is how to absorb the increasing proportion of members who wish to pursue academic or professional careers, often outside the kibbutz, while retaining their membership.

In a kibbutz the individual is under subtle pressures to succeed. For instance, since funds are limited not all the kibbutzniks who want to undertake a special course of education can do so. The committee, perhaps with outside assessments of the potential of the competing kibbutzniks, must make a selection, so it chooses Uri and turns down Moshe and Dan. Uri is aware that he must justify the committee's selection and he is forever aware that Moshe and Dan and their families will be watching his progress. He must not fail.

Every kibbutz provides total welfare, from housing to hair shampoo and honeymoons. With the rise in the standard of living personal tastes are not merely tolerated but encouraged, especially in clothing, furnishings, hobbies, vacations — all paid for by the kibbutz. Many a kibbutz has a large wardrobe of expensive suits and good quality sports jackets, party dresses and special occasion dresses; they are at the disposal of the kibbutznik who needs a dark suit for a funeral or a chic gown for a wedding. A couple can choose clothes suitable for a European vacation, the holiday over, the clothes are returned to the wardrobe. The image of the poor, pioneering kibbutznik no longer has relevance, though some kibbutznik administrators would like to retain it if only to justify the special income tax rates, free education, and other benefits accorded to kibbutzniks.

In a society where money is never used it is hardly surprising that most kibbutzniks detest materialism. 'We are glad to be liberated from the communications media and the cash-and-carry hang-up', one of them told me. They are hungry for culture but not television culture, even though it is much easier at the end of a hard day to watch television than to read a book of serious poetry or to study Arabic.

Kibbutzim exceed large cities in theatre attendance, and museum visiting. The kibbutzniks people spend much more time in studies and book-reading than do urban dwellers, perhaps because of the large libraries possessed by most kibbutzim.

Despite their rejection of materialism, kibbutzniks, as several have admitted to me, are always worrying about their image as the 'real Israelis', always having to prove themselves. There is not much wrong with such intensity of purpose, though it can lead to people becoming too deliberate and losing their natural spontaneity. Second and third generation kibbutzniks are not as inspired as their elders. As a 33-year-old second-generation kibbutznik observed, 'Most people stay in the kibbutz because they've got it good here. No ideology about it. The quality of life of the kibbutzim is good. The people are first class. And you know that your life isn't going to run into any hitches at all.'[2]

Kibbutz life also does not run into class antagonisms since a kibbutz has no 'important people' or 'personalities'. David Ben-Gurion, newly-resigned as Prime Minister in 1953 (he later made a comeback) went to live on the Negev kibbutz of Sde-Boker. Checking the duty roster, he found that while everyone else was listed by first name, he was Mr Ben-Gurion. It was 'Mr Ben-Gurion's' duty to tend the sheep. He had to tell the others that he was entitled to no special label; he was just David.

According to sociological studies any class stratification that does exist is based on the social prestige of kinds of work. In addition, there are some differences in personal possessions, due to outside sources of income such as gifts or inheritances.

In their range of industrial activity the kibbutzim of the 1970s are vastly different from those of the early 1950s. The principal fields are electronic, electrical and control products; food and food preparation; textiles and leather products; chemicals and pharmaceuticals; building materials; decorative and art products. Kibbutz Ein Hamifratz make corrugated cardboard, Ruppin turns out auxiliary equipment for physics teaching, Sarid produces grindstones, Sham produces optical lenses, and Nachshon has developed a sophisticated process for making sapphires. Almost every kibbutz has its specialty, depending on the skills of its members.

Kibbutz Tsor'a, near Beit Shemesh between Jerusalem and Tel Aviv, has a fashion project, producing attractive dresses, skirts and blouses in Israel-made fabrics. Under the trade-name Canaan, and under the direction of Jerusalem designer Tova Shidlovsky, the project is financially successful. The project manager, Avraham Ben Zvi, has interested foreign buyers in Canaan products. The manager and the foremen of the kibbutz work team get exactly the same non-salary as the workers, and have exactly the same standard of living. The foreign buyers who go to Kibbutz Tsor'a cannot understand this, for they do not comprehend that work is still an end in itself.

At least 30 kibbutzim earn good money from their guest houses or 'kibbutz inns'. Providing comfortable accommodation, good quality — and large — meals, swimming pools and other sporting facilities, the best of the guest houses compare favourably with four- or five-star hotels, but are generally cheaper. Many city Israelis spend their annual holidays on a kibbutz and several have told me that here they review their 'pledge to Israel'.

The more liberal kibbutzim are constantly experimenting with new economic, cultural and educational ideas. In 1969 Kibbutz Kfar Blum in Upper Galilee — one of the early kibbutzim established by former Americans — began a 10th grade high school programme for American students — 38 hours a week of classroom work and nine hours work on the kibbutz. The class is limited to 25 and by the summer of 1976, 147 had completed the year's course; 34 of these either stayed in Israel or returned there later to become temporary residents or permanent immigrants; 43 stayed to continue their high school education in Israel.

Enterprise shows itself in many ways. For a good many years it was a Sabbath custom to visit a kibbutz — if only because kibbutz kitchens serve the best food in Israel and the kibbutzniks are generous. The kibbutzniks put up with these 'raids' for years and then decided they had to stop. Not wishing to put up barricades or be rude they solved the problem by getting brief announcements into the newspapers — 'XYZ Kibbutz is suffering from foot and mouth disease and is in quarantine' or 'ABC Kibbutz reports an outbreak of gastro-enteritis'. These devices were enough to break the city people of the kibbutz-sabbath-visit habit, for a while at least. Generally, there is a good deal of social contact between kibbutzniks and town people.

Many kibbutzim are physically very agreeable, with generous grounds and rich flora through which wind stone paths. I particularly remember Ofer in northern Israel, where the comfortable apartments have good-sized porches where the kibbutzniks lounge after a day's hard work. In fact, work never stops in Ofer, day or night, it's just that different people are working. The casual visitor might well get the impression that a kibbutz is an endless holiday camp. The whole atmosphere is one of a pleasant camp — the hanging lights along the paths through shrubs and gardens, the sunlounging furniture on the lawns outside almost every little home, the landscaped swimming pool, the casual dress of the kibbutzniks, the relaxed air of the kibbutz club and its outdoor television where the members sit in comfortable cane chairs to watch the outsize television screen.

The impression of an everlasting picnic can be misleading. Some kibbutzim have tragic histories. One such place is Kibbutz Gezer, off the Tel Aviv-Jerusalem Highway. Established in 1945, it was severely battered during the War of Independence; the Arab Legion held the kibbutz for a few hours and before Jewish reinforcements could retake it, the Arabs slew 19 kibbutzniks and captured 15 women (they were released a few days later).

After that setback, no attempts to make the place thrive ever succeeded. From 1971 it had a bad reputation and in the next two years an astonishing 600 people passed through the kibbutz, many of them drifters, drug-addicts and dropouts. Gezer did not even possess a paved road and by 1974 it was quietly dying.

Thirty Americans held on and worked hard to revive the place. This attempt attracted candidates for membership, as well as foreign volunteers who wanted the experience of building a kibbutz apart from just working on one. By the end of 1977 the farm was flourishing, with 200 dairy cows, 12,000 chickens, melon gardens, and cotton fields. In response to an appeal for books to start a library, the Schocken publishing house sent Gezer everything on its list. The library, like the club room and the free store, never closes. Much of the credit for Gezer's success belongs to the English-speaking members of neighbouring Kibbutz Tsor'a who trained the American newcomers in agriculture and management. Other help comes from the 'Friends of Gezer' — mostly members' parents — which operates in the U.S.

The real secret of Gezer is sweat. Field crops demand daily attention — before the day begins. Irrigation crews and the midnight milking shift pass each other in the dark. Growing cotton means endless weeding by hand. The harvesting and sorting of melons is back-breaking. Every kibbutznik — men and women — is at work on agriculture. The women are set a good example by the chief administrator — a woman.

Somehow the men find time and energy for a regular Saturday afternoon game of baseball — which helps to stamp Gezer as American. Most of the kibbutzniks know Hebrew or are learning it but the official kibbutz language is English. These American Jews are already Israelis because they have rejected many of the values of American Jewishness; this is why they find themselves at Gezer. For most of them, Gezer is their first permanent commitment. As one told me, 'We came from a highly materialistic, mobile and selfish culture; here we have found the alternative we wanted'. And another said, 'Gezer is a state of mind'.

The site of Gezer has a history of 4,500 years; here Joshua defeated a Canaan king, the ancient Egyptians wrested the place from the Hebrews and later a Pharaoh presented it to Solomon as part of a dowry. The Maccabees built a major fortress there. Now that it is a flourishing kibbutz it is unlikely to fall again.

Kibbutzim operate their own psychology clinics for children and in co-operation with institutions of higher learning offer courses in specific branches of technology, agriculture, and kibbutz management. Cultural activities are wide-ranging, from choirs and orchestras to regional schools for adult education up to university level.

The practical success of the kibbutz system became strikingly evident in 1963 when the different kibbutz movements combined in a national federation — Berit Na-Tenu'ah ha-Kibbutzit (Kibbutz Movement Alliance). Such an all-embracing organization, though inevitably bureaucratic, was essential to handle combined interests and activities, such as land, water, financing, housing, planning, costs, new settlements, taxes and marketing budgets and to be the representative of kibbutz-movement affairs in negotiations with the government, the Jewish Agency and other institutions. With the movement increasing in size by 2-3 per cent a year bureaucracy inevitably becomes more complex. Kibbutz industrial plants are federated in the Association of Kibbutz Industry, which represents them externally. The Alliance's Education and Research Authority is responsible for the whole widespread network of post high-school and university education in the Kibbutz Movement. It operates Israel's largest teacher training college.

Interest in the kibbutz as a social phenomenon is universal and the federation serves as a centre for information, communication and reference. It maintains offices in several cities abroad to handle the stream of young foreigners who volunteer to work on a kibbutz. Aged from 18 to 26, these young people undertake to spend from three months to a year on a kibbutz, working six hours a day (the kibbutznik works eight) and sharing wholly in the life of the kibbutz. Unpaid, except for a small amount of pocket money after the first month, the volunteers are an indispensable part of the kibbutz system, if only because they replace young men serving in the armed forces. The presence of volunteers also permits kibbutzniks to take vacations. Not originally conceived as a public relations operation, the volunteer system has nevertheless proved to be just that. Few people who have worked on a kibbutz can have left without a profound respect for the Israelis with whom they lived and worked. The experience is healthy for the Israelis too, since the volunteers — it is not unusual to find a dozen nationalities on a single kibbutz — bring into this restricted environment many stimulating ideas, attitudes and experiences. The young foreign volunteers do not do all the worst jobs. Most work in kibbutzim is repetitive and does not require great intellectual powers, and for every volunteer who does a boring job at least two out of three kibbutzniks are doing exactly the same work. The main problem for the volunteer is learning that work in a kibbutz is not supposed to be something you get through in order to earn your leisure. Work is supposed to be a large part of the purpose of life, a large part of its satisfaction.

While the kibbutz system has been well publicised the moshav movement is relatively unknown or wrongly considered merely as part of the kibbutz movement. In fact it is quite separate and so different as to show another facet of personality among Israelis.

The moshav is a co-operative smallholders' village combining some features of both co-operative and private farming. The idea came about during the First World War when many newcomers wanted a type of settlement which would express not only national and social aspirations, as in a kibbutz, but give opportunities for individual initiative and independent farm management as well. Not the group but the family, living together, would be the fundamental unit, and mixed farming was the economic basis.

The first two moshavim, both in the Jezreel Valley, were founded in 1921 by ex-kibbutzniks who wanted rather more independence than their kibbutz could offer. By 1948, when the state was established, the nation had 58 moshavim. The reality of the new Jewish homeland brought to Israel a great many desperate families with many children and elderly dependants. Many were Jewish refugees from Arab lands, others were survivors of the Holocaust. These people were totally unsuited to life on kibbutzim; the moshav was the only way of settling this influx of immigrants. With the help of veterans from established moshavim, 250 new ones were established between 1949 and 1956 and 100,000 new Israelis were settled in this way. Gradually each moshav aligned itself with a particular group, usually on a regional basis, for co-operative buying, storage, canning, packing and marketing. By 1976 Israel had 347 moshavim with a combined population of about 125,000.

Each moshav elects its management, which helps members to obtain credit, purchase seed, distribute fertilizer and fodder, and to market the produce. It also allocates the co-operatively owned farming equipment. The moshav provides education in local or regional schools, fosters cultural activities and provides medical care. The economic and functional similarities between kibbutz and moshav are obvious; it is in life-style that the greatest differences exist. The members do not live communally — for instance, they do not dine together — and they do not pool their money. As a consequence, moshav members have more privacy and family life than kibbutzniks and they can be more idiosyncratic.

45

The kibbutz and moshav are second only to the United States in farm technology and in some ways are ahead of the U.S. During the later 1960s and early 1970s thousands of officials, sociologists, town planners and economists from Asia, Africa and Latin America visited Israel to study the moshav system as a solution to the problems of agricultural settlement in their own countries. The moshav movement organized study courses for these visitors and provided and paid for many instructors to establish and advise settlements set up in many parts of the Third World. Unfortunately, Arab anti-Israel propaganda and political pressure induced many poor nations to cut their ties with Israel, to their own detriment. An outstanding farming-practice innovation of the century, the moshav movement, could transform agriculture in a large number of nations desperately in need of it.

The flexible Israeli mind produced another variation, the moshav shittufi, a form of settlement combining features of the kibbutz and the moshav. Its originators were men who thought that the kibbutz was too wedded to collectivism and the moshav too inclined to individualism. They decided that the answer was to adopt the productive system of the kibbutz while preserving the family unit of the moshav. The village's lands and installations are collectively owned and operated but each family has its own domestic economy and care of children. Mothers work outside the home for two or three hours a day five days a week.

From the moshav shittufi's farming and other enterprises — which unlike a moshav proper, may include manufacturing or assembly — each family is allotted a sum to meet its own needs while the village as a whole provides education for the children, medical services and cultural activities. The first two moshavim shittufiyyim, one in Lower Galilee and the other near Mount Gilboa, were established in 1936 and by the 1970s the movement had 27 settlements with a total population of 5,700.

On the east side of Tel Aviv-Haifa motorway, just north of the Netanya turn-off, is a shop with a large vividly painted sign urging motorists to DRIVE IN. Surprisingly, the shop is part of a moshav, Beit Herut, and its specialities are art posters, sausages and salamis. Beit Herut is a good example of the enterprise now beginning to transform the moshav; this particular one relies for its prosperity on high-class silk screen printing, turkey farming and meat processing.

All the art works come from the Shohar printing press, which employs 80 people about 20 of them being members of the community. Most of the others are Yemenite settlers from nearby moshavim. The moshav was founded by Americans and now about 60 of the 90 families in Beit Herut are American. Male members of Beit Herut are all expected to work in some enterprise or other of the moshav, for which they all get a standard salary. Women are not obliged to work; if they do, they earn extra money. Most of them are fully occupied running their homes, which are comfortable villas. Since the moshav has no community laundry or dining room, a housewife's day is much the same as in the Western world.

Two moshav shittufiyyim are Christian. The more recently established is Yad Ha-Shemona, in the Judean Hills, overlooking the settlement of Neve Ilan to the south; to the west, on a clear day, you can see the Mediterranean. Yad Ha-Shemona was founded in 1974 when 20 men, women and children from Finland arrived on a 'sacred mission'. The Finns wanted to make amends for an incident when eight Jews were handed over by a Finnish government minister to the Nazis in 1942. Only one survived the concentration camps. Yad Ha-Shemona was to be a memorial to the eight.

By the end of 1976 Yad Ha-Shemona had 40 inhabitants, 35 of them from Finland, and will eventually have 150. The settlement exists economically through aid and contributions, Scandinavian tourism — 6,000 visitors in 1976 — and from a small furniture factory. Some members work outside the moshav and their income helps the moshav budget.

A visitor to Yad Ha-Shemona might well get the impression that he is back in the pioneering pre-state days, for the moshav's own buildings and its guest houses have been put up — and are being extended — through pick-and-shovel sweat. The members do everything by hand, even to the making of building blocks.

This is partly because of a taste for honest labour, and partly because they cannot afford machinery. The 2,000 trees planted by the residents and their visitors will eventually make the settlement an oasis of green on the brown hillsides of Judea.

Collectively, the kibbutzim, moshavim and moshavim shittufiyyim, and the diversity within all three, illustrate the Israeli mind's own diversity. Each kibbutz might be collective — but it is a collection of like-minded individuals, uniform in purpose, different in person. A man or woman happy and fulfilled in one kibbutz could be profoundly dissatisfied in another. Each has its own character and ethos. Each makes demands from its members — from total commitment at one end of the scale to courteous interest at the other. The paradox of the kibbutz is that while it must lead to conformity and uniformity and sometimes to introversion and rigidity, it yet produces individual minds and it remains the vital heart of a complex society. It has replaced the rat-race by social relations which, if they have not yet abolished conflict, can face it openly and boldly.

After a visit to kibbutz Lehavot Habashan on the Syrian border, in March 1967, Simone de Beauvoir wrote to the kibbutzniks: 'I saw the effort you have put into the kibbutz and the miracle which you have succeeded in achieving. I also saw a community of people that is different from all others which I have met until now. There is no explanation or alienation within it and it lives with a sense of full equality and freedom. What you have accomplished can serve as an example to the world ... I hope that the world will follow your example.'*

Kibbutzim are not utopias — utopias are other-worldly while kibbutzim are of this world, providing an alternative way of life which deserves consideration by the growing number of people disenchanted with the deepening social alienation generated by modern life. But these people need to realize that on the kibbutz there is no 'they' to blame, there is only 'we'. In difficult periods there is nobody to complain to, no system to vent hatred upon; the work has to be done and is done.

*My translation of the de Beauvoir letter.

THE KIBBUTZNIK – THE ISRAELI IDEAL

In its fourth generation, the kibbutz might well have an even greater impact on the world outside Israel than it has had inside. Certainly it was a specifically Israeli invention to deal with local conditions but given much wider application and adaptation what has been called 'the only true socialist experience of our time' could prove to be Israel's greatest contribution to the welfare of mankind in the twentieth century.

4 Holocaust –
The Agony in the Mind

The Holocaust* — the genocidal tragedy which struck the Jews of Europe under the Nazi regime — was the most profound influence in the shaping of the Israeli mind. The agonies of that time, the reaction to it and the painful attempt to understand it have affected Israelis as individuals, as a society, and as a nation. The barbarous treatment of European Jewry and the murder of six million men, women and children was so monstrous that it defies the imagination. Normal human speech is powerless to describe it.

The two major events in Jewish life — as distinct from Israeli attitudes — in the twentieth century are the Holocaust and the establishment of the state of Israel. It is impossible from both the factual and spiritual viewpoint to separate the two. They are interdependent.

The very fact that the Jews and Israelis label the period 1933-45 'The Holocaust' indicates the extent to which it has affected their outlook. Details of the Holocaust are too well known and are to be found in too many places to need repeating here. Sufficient to say that never before in history has a people been subjected to such inhumanity. The Holocaust was a time-divide, in the way that the coming of Christ is regarded. The philosopher T.W. Adorno claims that to write poetry after Auschwitz is 'barbaric'.

*The Holocaust was also known as the Catastrophe, the Sho'ah or the Hurban.

The extremely long Holocaust entry in *Encyclopaedia Judaica* begins with the assertion that the Holocaust 'is undoubtedly the most tragic period of Jewish Diaspora history and indeed of mankind as a whole'. A catalogue of the degradations, humiliations and cruelties perpetrated by the Germans against the Jews, even if given only a few lines of description for each, would fill volumes.

For the non-Jew the main question about the Holocaust has always been, 'How could one people commit such a heinous crime against another people?' For the Jew and Israeli there have been *two* main questions. The other one is, 'How could our people so readily have acquiesced in their own destruction?'

Encyclopaedia Judaica adopts a rather defensive attitude. 'Any attempt to apply to the victims of the Holocaust or of comparable situations standards of behaviour of a civilised society must fail'.

From time to time various writers have pointed out that some Jews fought against the Nazi tyranny, even inside the concentration camps. The dangerous flights of Jewish inmates from extermination camps was a form of resistance that brought the story of the slaughter of a people before the world; there were 76 successful flights out of a total of 667 known attempts.

A particular form of defiant behaviour *vis-à-vis* the Nazis and pro-Nazi authorities was that of the He-Halutz and other Zionist youth groups, who had to traverse dangerous routes to reach Palestine. However much physical courage was shown by a relative few the stark fact remains: millions of European Jews went passively to their deaths. Their abandonment and betrayal by the free world is hardly relevant to the fact of their passivity. In the formation of the Israeli mind frustration and exasperation caused by the inability to understand the apparent docility of the Jews under the German jackboot is second only in importance to the occurrence of the Holocaust.

Realistically viewed, the behaviour of the Jewish masses in the various stages of the Holocaust is in a general way only what could have been expected from any group having to face all-pervading terror and overwhelming power of a ruthless enemy, such as the Nazis. In some respects, perhaps, it was more than could be reasonably expected; in spite of continuous terror and the bestiality of the persecutors, few inmates of camps descended to the level of animals. But an *Encyclopaedia Judaica* writer makes the point that standards of normal society did not apply in the ghettos and concentration camps. Theft, egotism, lack of consideration for others, disregard for laws, were all abhorred in pre-concentration camp days. Inside the concentration camp, however, it was normal behaviour.

I *suspect* that all Jews changed after Hitler. I *know* that those who were to become Israelis changed. The Jews sent to Europe as the war was ending to rescue the survivors were immediately aware that these people had undergone profound changes. A certain type of change was evident among the children, the 'Children of the Camps' as they are called. They had survived the Nazi concentration prisons, only to find themselves in camps for displaced persons, and later still in British detention camps in Cyprus or in Palestine itself. Having spent their vital years of childhood in the Nazi death camps these children had learnt that the only way to avoid the fate that had overtaken their parents and families was to fight for life, with teeth and nails if necessary. The danger from the Nazis had ceased but the children could not adjust; to them every unknown person was an enemy and each new situation a threat to their lives. Self-preservation was their only motivation. The adult agents, despite their many pressing tasks, tried to help the young people to regain a sense of normal values.

One of the great agents, Yisrael Gal, illustrates some of the difficulties in handling the insecure and maladjusted youngsters.[1]

> At Czestochowa [Poland] we found a group [of teenagers] mainly of girls, but with a few boys. They were there in that camp and they did not want to budge ... They did not believe that the Germans would not return. The war was not over yet. 'Where should we go? Here we have a place to live and some food to eat.'

[One of us] tried to persuade them. The thing that in the end broke the ice was that he lied to them and told them we were emissaries from Palestine. [The agents had not come direct from Palestine.] My language is too poor to describe what happened after that. We sat and cried, all of us. That was the discussion — crying, that was all. The moment they heard we were from Palestine we could not disillusion them ... They overwhelmed us, kissed us, these children — they thought they were already on the way to Palestine.

Once they were in Palestine these young people reached adulthood with the fixed intensity of purpose that what had happened to them must never happen to their children. In a sense they and their parents, after 1948, used the Holocaust to give an extra stamp of authority to the new state which still needed to justify its authenticity.

But a great many Jews, abroad and in Israel, were unable to face and unravel the implications of the genocide in Europe. They were unwilling, perhaps pathologically so, to examine the failure of Jewish agencies to rescue their brethren; nor could they bring themselves to investigate the failure of the gentile world to prevent the catastrophe. Perhaps they were afraid of the answers.* Not that the Israelis wished to forget — all over the nation public monuments and ceremonies keep the memory alive almost to the point of torment. The most prominent institution is Yad Vashem (the name is derived from Isaiah 56:5) the Martyrs' and Heroes Remembrance Authority. The aim of Yad Vashem is to preserve the memory of the murdered and to gather all material about the Jewish life that was destroyed. The vast library contains, among much else, 2½ million pages of documents. The buildings include a museum — which contains a complete model of Treblinka death camp — a memorial hall and a synagogue. A visit to Yad Vashem with its pathetic reminders

*When the Sinai war of 1956 extended the privilege of military pride and confidence from the generation of 1948 to the population at large it redeemed the apparent passivity of European Jewry in the hands of its butchers and the people felt better able to cope with the memories.

of vanished European Jewry moves one to tears. A particularly disturbing exhibit is a large irregular lump of gold, perhaps four of five pounds in weight; it was formed from many gold fillings taken from the teeth of Jews murdered by the Nazis. Seized after the war, it is one of Yad Vashem's more macabre illustrations of the Nazis' inhumanity.

Official history, as taught in Israel's schools, used to give an almost morbid prominence to the Holocaust and its appalling details. As psychologists would have expected, this tended to evoke a response of rejection rather than identification on the part of the children born in Israel. While their parents felt profound sorrow and compassion for the Nazis' victims, Israeli youth reacted with shame and disgust. The thoughtful young saw, or thought they saw, why Zionism repudiated Jewish nationhood as practised in Europe.

Gradually, a greater emphasis was placed on the heroism of Jewish resistance during the Nazi era, sometimes extending and magnifying its significance. As I have indicated, it is undeniable that there was much heroism but I am sometimes intellectually embarrassed by friends who tell me about Jewish resistance as if it were commensurate with, say, French or Yugoslav resistance. It is a defence mechanism, a way of trying to conceal the ugly truth that resistance was slight compared to the real resistance movements. Perhaps too it is a way of assuaging the gnawing sense of guilt about whether the Jewish Agency and other organizations did all that was possible to save the Jews of Europe from annihilation. Did Zionist statecraft and the concentration on attaining statehood impede rescue, even contribute to the toll of Jewish life?

From time to time Israeli society has flagellated itself with Holocaust whips. The Kastner case was one such whip. Dr Israel Kastner was a senior official of Mapai (a political party) who had been a Zionist leader of Hungarian Jewry during the war. On behalf of the Jewish rescue committee of Budapest he had in 1944 conducted negotiations with Adolf Eichmann and other Nazis for the release of a number of Hungary's million Jews from their impending slaughter. In 1953 Malkiel Gruenwald, right-wing editor of a private newsletter, circulated an accusation that Kastner had collaborated with the Nazis in the murder of hundreds of thousands of Hungarian Jews in return for the escape of a few hundred of his own relatives and Zionist friends. The Attorney-General instituted a suit for criminal libel against Gruenwald but to the government's dismay the district court found that Gruenwald's charges were valid. The ramifications of the case brought down the Sharett government and public emotions were agitated. The Hungarian survivors and other European groups were bitter, and Kastner was murdered — proof of the national tensions. The supreme court, on appeal, posthumously restored Kastner's honour but by a majority of only one.

The Israelis naturally place primary blame for the Holocaust on the Germans but with a few exceptions they attach secondary blame to other nations. Well-read Israelis — and that includes most of the policy-makers and opinion-formers — know that at Evian-les-Bains, France, in July 1938 the Holocaust could probably have been halted. Here, 15 weeks after Hitler annexed Austria, delegates from 32 nations met to determine how they could rescue the Jews of the 'Greater German Reich' and help them to establish new lives elsewhere. The conference[2] had been organized by President Roosevelt and all the delegates were important men — three ambassadors, three ministers, 13 special envoys and 13 other diplomats of senior status. It was an impressive list of nations too — Argentina, Australia, Brazil, Colombia, Denmark, the U.S.A., Great Britain, France, Belgium, Sweden, Norway, countries of Latin America and Africa. Grandiosely, they saw themselves as 'Nations of Asylum'.

Also attending were leading officials of 39 refugee bodies, including 20 Jewish organizations, who had come to present the delegates with eyewitness accounts, reports, statistics, photographs — all of which culminated in the irrefutable conclusion that the Jews of Hitler's Reich were doomed unless they could be got out of Germany and Austria. And they could get out — then. It was easy. The official German policy in 1938 was to get the Jews out. Only one problem remained: who would let the Jews *in*?

A bit of black humour was circulating in the Reich at the time. A Jew goes into a travel agent: he wants to take a trip. The agent sets a globe on the counter before him. 'There,' he says, 'the world. Choose.' Slowly the Jew turns the globe, studying it carefully. Finally he looks up and says, 'Have you got anything else?'

The conference spent the first two days in heated argument about which country would chair the proceedings — the U.S.A., France or Britain. The honour eventually went to the United States. Then the 39 representatives of the refugee organizations were told that their submissions must all be completed within an afternoon. The first speakers got 10 minutes each, the later ones five minutes, including the World Jewish Congress, representing seven million Jews. The delegation of Jews of the Reich were refused permission to speak and could only submit a written memorandum. The Jews of Palestine had sent a direct and forceful orator, Golda Meyerson (Meir); she too was not allowed to speak.

At that time Germany had only 350,000 Jews, Austria 222,000. It would not have been difficult for the 'Nations of Asylum' to have saved the lot and some observers were guessing that the U.S. alone would take them all. (A generation later it took 585,000 Cuban and Vietnamese refugees.) The nations' delegates then explained what they would do. U.S. Special Ambassador Myron Taylor said that the severe American restrictions imposed on Jewish refugees would be lifted and that 27,730 would be admitted each year. Canada explained that it could accept only experienced agricultural workers; the Jews of Germany and Austria were all mercantile or professional people. Brazil, vast and underpopulated, had enacted a new law — every visa application must be accompanied by a certificate of baptism; Brazil therefore could accept no Jews. Australia, one of whose official slogans was 'populate or perish' (it had about 7,400,000 people in 3,000,000 square miles) could accept only 15,000 refugees over a three year period. The French delegate said that his country had already taken in 200,000 Jews and had reached 'saturation point'. (He was mistaken: the 200,000 included French Jews.) The United Kingdom, champion of the oppressed, said that a rush of Jewish refugees 'might arouse anti-Semitic feeling in Great Britain'. Switzerland, the nation of the Red Cross, said, 'Switzerland has as little use for these Jews as Germany and will take measures to protect herself from being swamped by Jews'. Nicaragua, Costa Rica, Honduras officially classified intellectuals and merchants as undesirables — knowing that half the Jews in Austria and Germany fell into the intellectual category and most of the other half were businessmen. The Dominican Republic announced that it would accept 100,000 refugees — a decision hailed as 'noble'. But the Dominicans played one of the dirtiest tricks of all; by creating various obstructions they found that they could in fact admit only 500 Jews. Only Holland and Denmark opened their borders.

On top of all this, came an unanimous resolution that only those Jews who could pay their own way would be accepted. And in formulating a final resolution the conference decided to omit any 'contentious' reference to Hitler's Third Reich.

After the 'Crystal Night' of 9 and 10 November 1938 — so-called after the glass from the windows of Jewish homes and businesses that littered the streets — thousands of ordinary people of the 'Countries of Asylum' petitioned their governments to open their gates to the Jews of the Reich. George Rublee, director of the Intergovernmental Committee on Refugees, suggested a simple plan: Each of the 32 nations should accept 25,000 Jews. If only half had agreed, every Jew in the Reich could have been saved.

Not one agreed — though Britain took 9,000 Jewish children.

Golda Meir later wrote, 'After the conference at Evian-les-Bains it became chillingly clear that the Jewish people were entirely on their own'.[3]

In Hitler's view the Evian Conference gave him approval for his 'Jewish programme'. The French Government proved that his assessment was correct, for its Foreign Ministry wrote to the German Foreign Minister '... None of the States [present at the

Jewish refugee conference] would dispute the absolute right of the German government to take, with regard to certain of its citizens, such measures as are within its sovereign powers'.[4]

Many Israelis contend that had the nations attending the Evian Conference shown their sympathy and support for the European Jews and had they protested about Nazi maltreatment of the German and Austrian Jews, Hitler would not have embarked on his programme of genocide. I consider this to be a valid contention and so, among other writers, does the American Peggy Mann '... After a staunch expression of world opinion [at Evian] backed by world action it seems almost inconceivable that Hitler would have proceeded with his "final solution".'[5]

After Evian it is small wonder that the Israelis do not trust other nations and other people to protect them in an emergency. Once war had engulfed Europe many people could still have been rescued. Small numbers *were* rescued from the extermination machine by the Danes, who organized mass rescue flights, by the Swedes, and by the Swiss, who issued protective papers for Hungarian Jews.

The intelligence services of the Allies were well informed about the 'events of the East', the euphemism of the time for mass murder. Jewish sources were active in disseminating information on the massacres, particularly in the Polish-Soviet area. Jews in free countries tried to prod their governments into action but the general attitude of the Allies was influenced by certain Allied interests, such as the British White Paper on Palestine. They were also afraid that by openly helping Jews they would play into the hands of Hitler's propaganda about a 'Jewish war'. Consequently, the Allies upheld the view that a general victory alone could save the Jews. This led to situations which the Jews (and later the Israelis) found inexplicable. For instance, the synthetic rubber works seven kilometers from Birkenau concentration camp was bombed in April 1944, the town of Auschwitz three miles from Birkenau was bombed in July 1944, and the hospital and SS barracks, 15 yards from the extermination sites, were bombed in December 1944 — but no action was ever taken against the camp installations easily recognized by the smoking fire of the crematoria and unguarded by anti-aircraft batteries. With precision bombing there would have been little risk of killing the prisoners.

Actual rescue operations by the Allies were taken very late and were often clumsy and useless.

The Christian churches did little to help; most even failed to register their objection to Nazi cruelties, let alone condemn them. Pope Pius XI seems to have limited his concern to Catholic non-Aryans. None of his encyclicals mentioned or criticized anti-semitism as such. The Roman Congregation of Seminaries and Universities issued a statement (13 April, 1938) and attacked eight theses taken from the Nazi doctrine as erroneous but did not refer to anti-semitism. Pius XII, enthroned in 1939, was a Germanophile. The Vatican received detailed information about the murder of Jews in the concentration camps from 1942 on, but Pius XII restricted all his public utterances to carefully phrased expressions of sympathy for the victims of injustice. His policy was one of neutrality. He remained silent during the arrest of Roman Jews — though the Germans had expected him to protest. On 18 October, 1943 more than 1,000 — two-thirds women and children — were sent to Auschwitz death camp without a protest from the Vatican.*

It has been argued that the Pope could have saved numerous lives. Some scholars say that he might well have stopped the machinery of destruction altogether by threatening excommunication of Hitler, Goebbels and other leading Nazis of the Catholic faith. At the very least, it has been suggested, a public denunciation of the mass murders, broadcast widely over Vati-

---

*The Vatican's knowledge of the Nazi atrocities and its failure to act is described in G. Reitlinger's definitive *The Final Solution* (Valentine Mitchell 1953, now in Sphere paperback.) Reitlinger quotes the German ambassador to the Holy See: "Although pressed on all sides the Pope did not allow himself to be drawn into any demonstration of reproof at the deportation of the Jews of Rome ...." In Reitlinger's opinion Pope Pius was affected by "plain physical fear, not that this makes the silence of the Holy See any more defensible."

can radio by Pius XII, would have revealed to Jews and Christians alike what deportation to eastern Europe actually meant.

There is no way of proving or disproving these arguments and this is not the point. The fact of history is that the Vatican appears to have given little help. Protestant leaders in Britain, the U.S.A., France, Switzerland and Sweden made certain protests, but the historical fact here is that they appeared to have had little *political* effect. During the war the Protestants of Germany maintained their silence, with the notable exception of Bishop Wurm of Württemberg. Only in the occupied countries did the Church show any real fight, especially the Catholic and Protestant churches in Holland.

The effect on the Israeli mind of all this has been the conviction — cynical or bitter or resigned — that in the face of any new threat Israelis can no more expect the support from Christian church leaders than from political ones. 'If they did not support us in the time of our greatest need we would be naive to expect them to support us in lesser crises', an Israeli scholar told me.

The individual Israeli tries not to show how relieved he is that fate spared him from the Holocaust. More collectively, the European trauma has been a pervasive motif in the political consciousness of Israel, accounting in large part for the characteristically apocalyptic response of the Israelis to the issues of security posed by Arab enmity.

The threat of another holocaust is still keenly felt; according to one survey, made in 1977 by the Sociology Department of Tel Aviv University, 70 per cent of Israeli Jews said that such a danger exists — though surprisingly to the western mind about half think it is more likely to happen abroad. Neither age, education or country of origin makes much difference in these feelings. Even in the late 1970s the Israeli mind was not ready to see the Holocaust in retrospect, and will never see it in 'perspective' as some European gentiles — pro-Israeli as well as anti-Israeli — keep urging. How can such a monstrous and sustained evil *have* perspective? It remains a chronic nightmare and it is responsible for much of what a thoughtless world considers 'Israeli intransigence'.

The Holocaust has led to incidents in Israel which could not happen elsewhere. That which involved Joseph Foxenbrauner and Bruno Fink will illustrate the point. One summer's day Foxenbrauner sat down to his lunch in a crowded Tel Aviv cafeteria and glimpsed a tattoo on the arm of a man who had to squeeze past his seat. It was a concentration camp number — in this case 108062. Foxenbrauner went to the other man's table and bared his own arm and number — 108061. They had both been arrested in Krakow, Poland on 15 May, 1943, and sent to Auschwitz, where they had been tattooed.

Nazi whim separated the two men almost at once. Foxenbrauner was sent to Ibishowitz to work in coal mines and later was force-marched towards Buchenwald to escape the Russian drive into Germany; he was the only one of a group of 200 to survive this journey. In Buchenwald a Christian helped Foxenbrauner to pass as a gentile. Stealing the parts to make a radio transmitter, Foxenbrauner made contact with the headquarters of General Patton's Third U.S. Army and maintained it for a week while the Germans desperately tried to locate the illicit radio.

Fink was sent from Auschwitz to Birkenau as a sick bay attendant, then for some 'infringement' he was sent to a 'correction camp' where the prisoners carried bags of cement all day. Fink escaped back to the main camp and then volunteered to work in a factory in Silesia, before being later transported in a cattle truck to Gonez-Kirchen from where the Americans liberated him on 6 May, 1945. At that time he weighed 88 lb.

The story of Foxenbrauner and Fink made a good story for a *Ma'ariv* reporter. Other such reunions have taken place from time to time, though the chances of another two survivors with consecutive numbers must be remote.

The Holocaust affected more than individuals' outlook. Together with mass immigration from a hundred sources, largely non-Zionist in composition, it challenged the relevance of the nineteenth century ideological foundations of the state. Zionism had elaborated the myth of a Jewish nation in order to create a Jewish state. Immediately upon its establishment the state then became the foremost instrument for the creation of a new nation, the Israelis. Realizing this, Israel's first Prime Minister, David Ben-Gurion, worked hard to place the ancient Jewish heritage at the centre of consciousness, as a source of inspiration and as a vital instrument of national unification. He made a great backward leap of two thousand years, and more remarkably he induced millions of others to make the same leap.

The early Israelis arrived in their new land with little in the way of tangible belongings but with a tremendous variety of cultural, social and educational freight. There was only one way to produce a viable mix — by giving all these immigrants the same reference point and a common language. The reference point was the remote past, the language Hebrew. In this way an ideology was produced to transcend the geographical and historical backgrounds of the settlers. The Holocaust was the cement which strengthened the mix.

The land itself helped the nationalizing process; among its vivid ancient relics, the biblical prophets and the heroic Maccabees came alive. The nationalizing process had two important effects. It helped the non-orthodox majority to establish common roots and it differentiated the Israelis from the non-orthodox majority of Jews *abroad*.

The power of political independence, accentuated by the Holocaust, was the most inspiring and unifying source of national life, at least for the older generation. It was stronger than either politicism of Zionism or the religiosity of Judaism in its inspiration and unification.

There were significant differences between oriental immigrants and the refugees from the West. For many oriental Jews their new life in Israel represented a fulfilment of their Jewish heritage but for most of the refugees from the West it was a repudiation of their Jewish past. This was why national political independence was such a heady wine. The symbols of sovereignty and statehood — the flag, the presidency, the government, parliament, and especially the army — became the foci of strong national identification both in Israel and the diaspora. They created the strengths which had been so sorely missed during the period of the Holocaust.

For the younger generation it was necessary to develop a positive Jewish dimension to national life. The school system was the key institution for regulating the effervescent nature of national consciousness, to give uniformity, direction and continuity to the collective fellowship. A plan was evolved which was to become the whole basis of political stability. The way in which this scheme worked is interesting as an illustration of the quality of pragmatism and compromise in the Israeli mind. Bible studies — not to be confused with religious studies — were made a prominent part of the curriculum in secular schools to reinforce the tendency to identify with the ancient past on Israel soil. The Bible was taught as geography, literature and national history. This weakened links with the Jews abroad, where the Bible belonged to religious education for orthodox and non-orthodox alike. In the mid-1950s an inspector of schools raised the issue of specific Jewish consciousness as a problem for the secular schools and after much discussion 'Jewish consciousness' was included in the curriculum as an explicit requirement. However, it produced an 'Israeli consciousness' rather than a Jewish one, partly because religious practices were presented as exotic rituals that people used to perform but which were now irrelevant, post-Holocaust.

This modern consciousness is largely the result of the Holocaust, which keeps rising like a spectre in the minds of most Israelis. With the making by NBC of the 9½-hour television 'docu-drama' *Holocaust* in 1978 the spectre might have temporarily loomed larger. As documentary fiction, *Holocaust* ranked second only to the series *Roots* as popular viewing in the United States. Some Israelis say the four-episode programme was immoral. Many were understandably ambivalent: they wanted the world to know what happened but they themselves find even the make-believe almost unbearable. Unfortunately, *Holocaust* did not supply enough political and economic context for its drama; a young viewer, trying to comprehend what happened, would not understand why the German people allowed it to happen, nor why the Jews themselves did not appreciate what was going on earlier. No television production can plumb horror so vast and yet so individual.

Israeli public archives have copies of all the black and white photographs of the Holocaust known to have been taken. Black and white is appropriate for the Holocaust and for the attitude it has produced: if you didn't try to save us from Hitler you were against us; if you don't stand with us when our enemies again try to wipe us out you are against us. With you or without you, there will never be another holocaust.

The capture and trial of the arch war criminal Adolf Eichmann, one of the master minds of the Holocaust, deeply affected the Israeli mind. We in the West tend to see Eichmann's capture and trial as a triumph for retribution and as evidence of the powers of Israeli secret agents. In Ben-Gurion's hands it was more than that; it was the first great emotional re-affirmation of Israel's national being after the War of Independence of 1948-49, and it immeasurably strengthened Israeli confidence.

For a full two years, from his seizure in Argentina to the disposal of his ashes in the Mediterranean, Eichmann dominated the mind of the Israeli public. The older generation was able to subdue its nightmare by catharsis while the youth of Israel was shown the validity of the Zionist movement which had brought the nation into being. Young people accepted that validity.

The thorough process of the law in the Eichmann case strengthened the country both as a state and as a nation. The procedure was exhaustive — the trial taking four months, and the deliberations of the court another four. Eichmann was permitted to appeal to the supreme court and when this appeal was denied he petitioned the head of state for clemency. In view of the man's heinous, total and self-confessed guilt, it is unlikely that the courts of any civilized nation would have imposed less than the death penalty,* but the penalty was of less consequence than the truth and scope of the Nazi crime which came to light. For the first time young Israelis were tested to the limit of their

---

*Israel introduced the death penalty for terrorist murder in May 1979, by a majority cabinet decision. Eichmann's execution is the only one carried out by Israel.

imagination and comprehension to understand the fate of European Jewry. The inhibiting and embittering grief of the survivors found an outlet. All Israelis became aware, as the story unfolded, of how alone Europe's Jews had been. And they realized their own aloneness among a sea of Arabs, who had declared undying hatred for Jews.

The tremendous effect on Israelis was probably not fully understood outside Israel. The Jews of Europe had been hated by the Nazis and had been savaged by them — but they, the Israelis, knew how to fight any Arab attempt to annihilate them. Apart from this, the Israelis felt different from the Jews abroad — and this heightened their national consciousness, the Israeli mind. The Israelis felt that they held their destiny in their hands while the Jews abroad had chosen to share somebody else's destiny.

The new notion among Jews of being masters of their own destiny was well illustrated on Martyrs' and Heroes Remembrance Day, 29 April, 1973, when Yigal Allon, who was then Deputy Prime Minister and Minister of Education and Culture, was the principal speaker. This was the key passage of his speech, delivered at Yad Vashem:

The spirit of Fascism continues to rove the world ... behind a variety of guises. No one calling himself human — least of all a Jew — can be absolved of the duty to fight this many-faced evil. For every Jew should be considered as having eluded destruction ... whether born in Israel or the diaspora. Every Jew is a survivor, for Fascism declared total war of annihilation against the Jewish people as a whole. We believed in Life, Freedom, the strength of the spirit. We paid a heavy price. But we also learned a lesson. It is: Woe to the nation of the spirit that lacks physical strength to defend its life, its belief and freedom. In those ghastly days we swore to become strong ... By virtue of that oath, we are here now, in the free country of the Jewish people that has risen from its ashes and remembers.

5 Saving Jews for Israel

The Israeli mind was in the process of development long before the state of Israel existed. In embryonic form it was present in the Jews of the Yishuv, and the founders of Zionism, notably Theodor Herzl. He recognized that life in Palestine (which was to become Israel) would produce a more self-reliant, worldly person than Jewry of the diaspora had created. I do not intend to go into Zionism in this book — because it is irrelevant, not because it is complex. Indeed, Zionism is simple and straightforward; it is only a passionate policy for the return of the Jews to their homeland.

The Jewish farmers of the Yishuv, whether Sabra or European immigrants, were the stock onto which later immigrants were grafted during the times of the 'ingathering of the exiles'. The Israelis-to-be came from many places and they were ingathered in many ways by hundreds of dedicated, intelligent people. A useful — and significant — starting point is 5 March, 1933, the day of Hitler's accession to power. On that day the Youth Aliyah was founded to bring Jewish children out from Germany and settle them on the land.

Aliyah is one of the emotive words in Israeli political development. It can be understood only by its translation — immigration. Formed from the Hebrew verb 'to climb' it symbolizes the rebirth of the nation, the return of the people scattered in alien societies to their own homeland.

The idea of a youth intake had been initiated the year before when six German Jewish boys arrived at the Ben-Shemen Agricultural School, itself founded by Dr Siegfried Lehmann as a 'youth village' for Jewish youngsters left homeless after the First World War. His ideas influenced several other nation-builders, principally Henrietta Szold, 'Mother of the Yishuv'. As Youth Aliya got under way, she would meet the ships and take an almost personal interest in each child. The first group, sixty strong, arrived at En Harod in 1934 and was successfully settled. At the German end, those adults who could see Hitler's writing on the wall, despatched one group after another to be either absorbed into a foster-kibbutz or sent to form a new kibbutz.

In a way, early Zionist ideology was at work here in an attempt to mould a new type of person, free from the secular and religious conventions of the parents' world.

The novel Youth Aliya method of re-education was successful for two main reasons:

- The kibbutz itself was an educative environment. The youngsters lived and worked in daily contact with men and women devoted to an ideal and living that ideal. For youth coming from Nazi Germany, the kibbutz was a ray of hope in a world of night.

- The youth-group was allowed a large measure of autonomy and soon developed into a close-knit unit. The boys and girls, separated from their families, felt the need to belong to this new family, and to follow it through all adversity. The following extract from a girl's diary describes how the resolution was taken to form a 'nucleus', that is, of a new kibbutz.

  'We are crowded, more than thirty of us in a small tent, and, in an atmosphere of genuine sincerity, concluded our discussion. Twilight changed to night, but we hardly noticed the lapse of time. We just sensed that something big was happening. We felt that now the links between us had been drawn tight, that a community for life was being formed'.

By the outbreak of the Second World War more than 5,000 boys and girls had been rescued from Nazidom, and a system existed for continuing the rescue, though with greater difficultly, while the war was in progress. The need for rescue was desperate, partly because the two great western European Powers, Britain and France, did not acknowledge that European

Jewry was threatened with extinction and when the evidence became too strong to ignore it was too late for help. Later, when the British and Americans could have rescued some of the threatened Jews they failed to seize the opportunity.[1]

The Jews of the Yishuv had long known that they could rely on nobody but themselves, especially as the British were determined to limit the number of Jewish immigrants to Palestine. Exasperated by British refusal to understand the seriousness of the situation in Europe, and Palestinian Jews began to organize illicit immigration. In 1934 the first known attempt to organize sailings of 'illegals' to Palestine in defiance of the British restrictions was made by Levi Schwartz, a member of the Jewish underground army, Hagana. Under the auspices of the Polish Zionist youth movement, Schwartz set up a base in Athens and acquired a tiny Adriatic freighter, the *Velos*. The ship safely landed 340 illegals on its first trip but the British caught it on the second voyage.

After the *Velos* an unknown number of small boats landed immigrants at night — 10 to 20 passengers on each trip. Those boats which landed successfully were little heard about; the illegals were spirited away to a kibbutz where they quietly became new citizens. Many people never reached their destination, they died en route of starvation or drowned when heavy seas overturned their boats. The boats were usually provided by Egyptian, Greek or Italian racketeers and were often ill-equipped and unseaworthy.

In the Polish town of Kazimierz in the summer of 1937 two Palestinian kibbutzniks, Yulik Braginski and Dani Shind, founded the organization of Aliya Bet. It meant 'Class 2 Immigration' — the illegal kind, in contrast to Aliya A, standing for 'Class 1' or British-sponsored immigration. The activities of Aliya Bet's operators and others who came after them are important indicators of certain qualities of the Israeli mind at its best — resourcefulness, intelligence, stubborn determination, imagination.

In Kazimierz to attend a convention, Braginski and Shind found thousands of Polish Jews living on training farms in arduous conditions. Sleeping on wooden shelves, they often went hungry because they lived on what they could make doing intermittent day work at the nearby farms. Only one or two legal certificates for entry to Palestine were available to each farm each year. These young men and women were desperately needed in Palestine to work in the fields by day and to help hold off the attacks by Arab terrorists at night, so Braginski and Shind offered to organize an illegal ship. Levi Schwartz and David Nameri, who would organize the landing operations, joined the group. The proposal was approved by Yishuv leaders Berl Ketznelson and Eliahu Golomb and, reluctantly, by David Ben-Gurion, although he was opposed to freelance activity of this kind.

No relaxation of restrictions could be expected from the British. A working idea of the scarcity of entry permits can be gained by noting the number available for the Jews of Vienna, one of the largest centres of Jewish population, in 1938 — just 32 certificates. In 1939, under the terms of the White Paper, the British decreed that over the next five years a total of 75,000 Jewish immigrants would be permitted, after which immigration would cease.

The outbreak of war clipped the wings of the fledgling Aliya Bet. Shipments resumed when the Nazis were driven from the Mediterranean shores in 1944 but most Jewish leaders believed that illegal entry would be unnecessary if the Labour Party were to win the first British post-war election. When the Labour Party was swept into office and Ernest Bevin became the new Foreign Minister the Jews of Palestine were delighted. They were confident that he would wish to help his fellow socialists, who formed the majority of the Zionist movement, that it would be easier for Jewish refugees to get into Palestine, and the atrocious conditions under which they were living in Europe would be ended.

The shock when Bevin set his face against the Jews' hopes was profound. Ten thousand Jews took part in a rally near the concentration camp of Bergen-Belsen where an effigy of Bevin, adorned with a swastika-daubed Union Jack, was hanged and later burned.

For men and women who had struggled and schemed to rescue the tormented Jews of Europe, Bevin's anti-homeland stance was just one more problem to be challenged. Aliya Bet was already in existence; its operations only had to be intensified. The outrageously successful agent Yehudah Arazi had begun a boat-building venture in Italy and his little boats took refugees to Palestine and returned with Aliya agents to be smuggled into Europe. Arazi's boats were so small that the British Navy, patrolling the coast on the lookout for illegal arrivals, did not bother to stop and check them. But in each of these tiny boats, built for a crew of three, were packed up to 80 refugees.

The first attempts to get bigger ships through the blockade were unsuccessful. Arazi, with characteristic dash, decided in the summer of 1945 that he could succeed where others might fail and he acquired the freighter the *Fede* — as well as the whole-hearted co-operation of the port authorities of La Spezia on the Italian Riviera. But his plans went wildly wrong. A British gunboat blocked the small harbour while troops arrived and surrounded the ship. The British order was abrupt: 'Disembark your passengers or we will take them off by force.'

The British did not yet know that aboard the *Fede* was Arazi, the most wanted Zionist agent in Italy. Acting as the refugees' 'representative', Arazi retorted that he had given orders to blow up the ship with everybody on board the moment a British soldier laid hands on a Jewish emigrant. Unless the British troops were withdrawn at once he could not answer for their safety. Since secrecy no longer counted, he sent telegrams to Truman, Stalin and Attlee: 1,000 SURVIVORS OF HITLER'S DEATH CAMPS ARE CROWDED IN SMALL SHIP IN AN ALLIED PORT AND BESIEGED BY HUGE FORCE OF BRITISH TANKS INFANTRY AND WARSHIPS.

Publicity was instantaneous. Italians who crowded to the gates where Arazi daily made inflammatory speeches, demonstrated in favour of the Jews; the British Army commander's house was attacked and reporters converged on the scene from all over Europe. Arazi hung a sign over the port gates — THE GATE OF ZION — held press conferences and stirred the pot of protest. Backed by Aliya Bet's European chief, Shaul Avigur, Arazi proclaimed a hunger strike. Near the 'Gate of Zion' he hung a board bearing two numbers — one denoting the number of hours of the hunger strike, the other the number of refugees who had lost consciousness through lack of food. By the 63rd hour the deck of the *Fede* was covered by unconscious bodies and an unearthly quiet settled over the ship. Arazi held a last press conference and said that no more communiques would be issued until the ship was released. He refused to see representatives from the British Embassy in Rome but sent a cable to Attlee warning that he would be held personally responsible for any loss of life on the ship. Messages of sympathy arrived in La Spezia and in Palestine Golda Meir and other leaders went on hunger strike in sympathy with the *Fede* refugees.

A group of senior British Army officers and civilians arrived, among them Harold Laski, Chairman of the British Labour Party. Arazi played his trump card, telling Laski that from the following day 10 refugees would commit suicide on the deck in public every day. Laski, appalled, telephoned the British Prime Minister (who used to enjoy recounting this story) to say that a lunatic was leading a group of 1,000 desperate people and that the British must make some gesture.

Laski secured a truce and the refugees called off their hunger strike. The British offered various compromises but Arazi held to his demands. On 8 May, 1946, 33 days after they had captured the ship, the British gave way. The *Fede's* passengers could go to Palestine without conditions. The only one who did not make the trip was Yehudah Arazi. He slipped through the cordon of British agents and went back to work.*

In the United States Dani Shind was now buying much better ships for Aliya Bet and their capture by the British could not be risked. Somebody suggested a simple but effective scheme. The refugees would leave a European port aboard one of the newer, faster ships which would rendezvous with a hulk just outside

*For a lengthy account of Arazi's exploit, and other stories about 'illegal' immigration, see Ehud Avriel's *Open the Gates!* Weidenfeld and Nicolson, 1975.

Palestinian waters, where the Royal Navy would hardly dare interfere — that would have been piracy. The passengers would tranship to the hulk where they would endure an uncomfortable 24 hours while the British escorted them into a Palestine port. The hulk was expendable, the British administration would be embarrassed by the arrival of more 'illegals' — and the expensive ship would return for another load.

The British responded by taking seized ships not to Palestine but to Cyprus where the refugees were interned. Conditions aboard the Aliya Bet ships were horrible. Some were rigged as fishing vessels and when British planes or ships were spotted the refugees huddled together under heavy tarpaulins. In Mediterranean heat this was a terrible ordeal. Some ships built as freighters without passenger accommodation carried as many as 4,000 men, women and children in their holds. They could come up on deck only by night.

Shlomo Zimmerman produced what was known as 'Scheme D' based on 'genuine forged' immigration permits while other agents brought parties of illegals through Egypt, where the British would least expect them. Despite all the British efforts to block the traffic the flow continued.

British action was sometimes brutal. The *Exodus* incident of 1947 is too well known, if only through Leon Uris' book of the same name, to need detailed recounting here. This refugee ship, grossly overloaded with 4,767 people, was attacked by the British 22 miles from the Palestine coast. Exhausted and bitter, the Jews were tugged into Haifa harbour, from where they were deported to Germany, the very country which had destroyed them. In retrospect, it can be seen that the *Exodus* incident — if atrocity is not a more accurate word — ensured that the Jews would fight to the last.

All over Europe Aliya Bet agents were arranging shipping, false documents, bribes and gathering information. Since they were in constant danger from British Intelligence, the agents needed to be highly professional.

Getting the refugees safely out of Europe was difficult enough; receiving them in Palestine was hazardous. David Nameri, who had become chief of landing operations, organized teams to receive the illegals. His security unit used recorded folk songs which were played loudly as signals to the ships. One song meant 'Attention: British ambush on beach'. Another: 'Sea too rough for landing'. A third: 'All safe, approach shore'. Songs and codes were changed with each ship.

Nameri's guides led the illegals to an orange grove or packing house, where a Receiving Group interviewed and registered them and gave them false identity papers. A Dispersion Group decided where to send the new settlers and the Transport Group got them to their destination, somehow. The British were not the only danger. Arabs organized beach patrols to track down Jewish illegals and rob and beat them before selling them at so much a head to the British.

The price in captures was high. From 1946 to February 1948, according to a report submitted to the War Office by Sir Gordon MacMillan, the last commander-in-chief of British forces in Palestine, the British intercepted 47 shiploads of 'illegal' immigrants, interning 65,307 of them in detention camps on Cyprus.

Throughout the war years and until 1948 Aliya Bet brought Jews from Arab countries into Palestine through northern border settlements such as Kfar Gil'adi, Dan, Daphna, Ayelet HaShaher and Hanita. Almost every night groups of illegals escorted by the handpicked members of a group known as 'The Unit' slipped across the border. The Jews paid Arabs to bring the refugees, sometimes from deep in Arab lands. With their escort services so greatly in demand the Arabs, who were competing with one another for the refugee trade, raised their prices and frequently also informed the British police and collected bounty money. Jewish women were raped by their Arab guides and Jews from Syria were robbed and murdered within sight of Palestine.

When the Jews dispensed with Arab help, the Arab guides started a campaign of threats and blackmail against The Unit. They would hold up transports near the border and threaten at gunpoint to inform the police unless they were paid for their silence. The Aliya Bet agents paid, but for protection they created 'The Black Unit', so-called because most of its men were

73

dark-skinned Jews from Arab countries. Passing for Arabs without difficulty, they set up ambushes near the border and waited for the Arabs to turn up for negotiations with Jewish representatives. The Arabs appeared with guns and knives and a higher demand for every Jew they brought to Palestine. The Black Unit's one sub-machine-gun wiped out the Arab gang. After several such episodes prices dropped to a reasonable level and betrayals were greatly reduced.

While Aliya Bet was moving Israelis-to-be from European ports to the Palestinian coast, agents of another human salvage organization, Brichah, were rescuing Jews from inside Europe. Most of these agents were Palestinian-born Jews but more than 1,000 men and women of 12 countries worked full time for Brichah and during the two years of its operations in Poland and Soviet-dominated eastern Europe at least 20 of these agents were killed. Many others were arrested by the Communists.

Brichah officials received no salaries, only food, some clothing and a little pocket money. One name which crops up frequently in official and unofficial records of Brichah is that of Ruth Klieger. She had begun work in Rumania in 1938 and was later to be active in Sofia, Belgrade, Istanbul, Cairo, Paris, Germany and South America. Intelligent, resourceful, professional, she used her femininity — though never her sex — to get what she wanted, and she worked through her many friends and acquaintances. Through influential American friends she was given the rank of colonel in the U.S. Army. This gave her the entrée to almost anywhere she wanted to go.

Ruth Klieger's policy was to take advantage of chaos in Europe while it lasted and her most urgent task was to recover Jewish children who had been placed by their parents in monasteries or in the homes of Christians. Later David Ben-Gurion officially changed Ruth's name from Klieger to Aliav, a corruption of 'Aliya' — the cause for which she had done so much.

Only a few key personnel were professional agents; most were volunteers. As Brichah grew many helpers came from among the refugees bound for Palestine. The real heroes were the tough, determined and dependable boys and girls aged 16 to 21. One Hungarian-Jewish boy of 19, whose family had been killed by the Nazis, lived by his wits after liberation until he met the Brichah commander in Hungary and asked for a job. With intelligence, physical endurance and courage, he became a competent escort and trouble-shooter. When three key Brichah workers were arrested by Soviet police the Jewish boy got them out of prison by glib talk and cleverly offered bribes. People with all kinds of special skills were needed; those with a string of languages; others who could handle money, or who were experts with radio. Other important people in the Brichah system were the scouts who were constantly on the search for easier and safer border crossing points. The dangers were very real. On the night of 3 May, 1946 a picked group of 26 members of a Zionist youth movement were stopped near Nowy Sacz by Polish fascists — embittered by the defeat of the Nazis — taken off the track and 13 of them brutally murdered.

A vital link in the Brichah chain was the Jewish Brigade, the military unit of Palestinian Jews who had served in the British Army. Most of these soldiers were also members of Hagana. When the war ended in May 1945 the Brigade had reached the area where the frontier of northern Italy meets that of both Yugoslavia and Austria. Here the Palestinian Jews linked with the European Jews, many of them in dreadful condition from their years in concentration camps. For its own relief work, the Hagana men in the Jewish Brigade appropriated vast stores of clothing and other supplies such as soap, medicines and medical equipment. Often the brigade was the only relief organization on the spot and many newly-freed Jews, weak, ill, helpless and without money would have died without this help. Unofficially, men of the Jewish Brigade — more popularly the 'Pimpernel Brigade' — set up shelters and bases for the refugees and taught them Hebrew as well as the manual skills they would need in the farming communities in Palestine.

Most Jewish refugees were in the Allied Displaced Persons camps in the British and American zones. Brichah agents manoeuvred themselves into administrative posts in all these camps, the better to arrange movements out of the camps towards Palestine and of other refugees into the camp from areas further east in Europe. The great need was for documents.

The Jewish 'Operation Documents', set up during the war, continued to be immensely helpful. 'Operation Documents' had brought off some outstanding anti-Nazi coups. Now these master forgers turned to the manufacture of birth, baptism, marriage and death certificates, working papers, certificates of unfitness for military services, soldiers' pay books, travel orders, identity cards, certificates of citizenship for such 'safe' states as San Salvador or the Vatican. They even produced passports and, on occasions, certificates 'signed' by the Allied commander-in-chief — General Eisenhower or his successors — by General de Gaulle and even by the Pope. Every piece of paper was complete with official stamps and seals.

Of course the survivors of the Nazis' extermination programme possessed no papers but they had soon found it was pointless trying to explain this to their liberators or to the government officials of the countries in which the refugees found themselves when the war ended. No papers, no progress. The Russians and the British were particularly obstructive in the matter of documents, the British partly because they believed that by withholding or delaying documents they could keep the Jews from moving towards Palestine. Operation Documents proved them wrong. Sometimes documents were genuine, made out by Red Cross officials, diplomats who sympathised with the Jews, friendly priests — or consular officials who could be bought.

The occupying powers — the U.S., Britain, France and the Soviet Union — and various European governments challenged Brichah's indiscriminate movement of refugees on the grounds that Nazi war criminals or collaborators could pose as refugees and escape punishment. This was absurd, since the Jews were the most insistent of all people that no war criminals should escape. Many war criminals tried to pose as refugees but it is doubtful if more than a handful succeeded in posing as Jewish refugees. The Brichah men, often trained in intelligence work, could spot a phony refugee.

Transport was a major problem. Most of Brichah's refugees had to make at least part of their journey on foot and travelling could be arduous. In its early days Brichah used the trucks of the Jewish Brigade; any Jewish Tommy returning to Italy from army business in Austria could be depended upon to fill his truck with refugees. British High Command moved the Brigade from the border area but this did not stop its members from helping Brichah. They toured monasteries and convents in Holland, Belgium and France to collect Jewish children who had survived the war but now had no relations to claim them.

Refugees' baggage travelled on army trucks. The drivers, Brichah men in illegal army uniforms, carried forged papers identifying their cargo as the personal property of American officers who had been transferred. The great difficulty was not in transporting this 'hot' baggage but in persuading refugees to part with it temporarily; they had been through all this before, with the Nazis.

The need for Aliya Bet and Brichah ended when Israel became a state in May 1948. Several leading agents confessed later that they were sorry that the excitement had gone out of their lives, though some continued to find it in the Israeli secret services. The greatest Aliya Bet agent of them all, Yehudah Arazi, became a hotel manger in Israel and died prematurely in his fifties. Ehud Avriel rose to be one of Israel's most distinguished diplomats. Shaul Avigur, the chief, held key positions in the Prime Minister's Office and the Ministry of Foreign Affairs. Levi Schwartz worked for many years as an official of Zim, Israel's merchant shipping line. Ephraim Dekel, former Hagana intelligence commander and Brichah chief in Europe in 1947, became director of the Ministry of Defence Naval Section. Ruth Klieger, after several government jobs, retired to domestic obscurity.

They had been secret service agents of a very special kind and members of a remarkable organization which had rescued 400,000 Jews. Brichah-Aliya Bet is a testament to the power of human ingenuity, dogged determination against staggering odds and the perseverance of the human spirit in the face of monstrous cruelty and indifference. Ingenuity and determination were built-in characteristics of the Israeli mind.

6 Arms for the Promised Land

The rescue and rehabilitation of European Jews shows Israeli determination, inventiveness, shrewdness and sheer will to triumph over daunting obstacles. The acquisition of arms to defend the farmers of the Yishuv and later the settlers of the new state was carried through with no less dedication and intelligence.

During the period when the Turks held Palestine and much of Arabia the Jewish settlers were usually able to acquire sufficient arms and ammunition to protect themselves from marauding Arabs. After the British defeat of the Turks in 1917 and the subsequent British occupation weapons became gradually more difficult to get but British and Turkish rifles and revolvers, bought, stolen, or found during the war kept the Yishuv reasonably well armed. Increased supply became vital when larger numbers of unarmed Jews began to reach Palestine.

For a time the Jewish leaders, who hated the idea of constant friction and fighting with the Arabs, trusted in British protection; they believed that this victorious and powerful army could guarantee peace and security for all. The Arab assault on the Jewish settlements in Upper Galilee in March 1920, the imminent danger to those in Lower Galilee in the summer of that year and the failure of the self-defence activities openly organized by Vladimir Jabotinsky during the Passover riots in Jerusalem the same year destroyed all illusions about peace.

In March 1921 a defence committee was set up consisting of Israel Shohat, Eliahu Golomb, Joseph Baratz, Hayyim Sturmann and Levi Shkolnik (later, as Levi Eshkol, Prime

Minister of Israel). Agents went to Vienna to buy arms and ship them to Palestine in beehives, refrigerators, steamrollers and anything else that would conceal revolvers and hand grenades.

When the British Mandate for the administration of Palestine became effective in September 1923 the British discouraged the possession of arms and later made it illegal. On paper, the British were as much opposed to the Arabs having weapons as the Jews but at times the Jews were driven to believe that British policy was designed to strengthen the Arabs and weaken the Jews to the point where the Arabs could eliminate the Jews. Part of the truth is that the British could more easily prevent the Jews from acquiring arms than they could the Arabs, who had a much greater freedom of movement in desert transactions which were safe from British interference. Despite this, for most of the period between 1923 and 1948, the British were uneven in their policy on arms, giving more latitude to the Arabs than to the Jews. A British police officer who served in Palestine in the 1930s told me, 'The police could more happily allow the Arabs to have arms because they were lousy shots and as they never looked after their weapons they were unreliable. The Jews learned how to care for their rifles and revolvers and how to fire them. The Arabs were terrorists but the Jews were the greater potential threat.'

With the establishment of a definite military structure in Hagana a greater supply of arms became essential, especially after 1929 when the need to maintain, expand and strengthen Hagana was recognized by all parts of the Yishuv. Some of these arms arrived in unexpected ways. For instance, in October 1935 a mysterious munitions consignment reached Jaffa. The weapons were hidden in cement sacks, addressed to an unknown Isaac Katan in Tel Aviv. When the cement sacks were opened customs officers found 300 rifles, 500 bayonets and 400,000 rounds of ammunition. The discovery led to Arab demonstrations, caused a widespread attack in the Arab press and on 26 October resulted in an Arab protest strike in Jaffa. The munitions were not intended for the Jews but belonged to an international syndicate trying to get weapons into Abyssinia in a roundabout way. But Hagana got its hands on the weapons and they travelled no further than Palestine.

Opportunism in acquiring arms was too uncertain; system was needed. The Yishuv needed capable men in Europe to organize the purchase and despatch of weapons. One of the first Rechech (arms procurement) men sent abroad on a definite mission was the enterprising Yehuda Arazi. In 1937 Arazi made a deal with the Polish Government for the supply of rifles, machine-guns and ammunition — to be transported to Palestine in steam-rollers. Poland allowed into the country, on Arazi's request, Hagana instructors to teach the use of weapons to young Jews about to emigrate. Even so, at the end of 1937 Hagana had no more than 6,000 rifles and 220 machine-guns for its 20 branches and 20,000 members.

During the Second World War normal purchases were out of the question but as the Arabs were stealing British weapons Hagana kept pace by the same means. In 1939-40 the British arrested many Hagana members and made searches for arms caches. The British troops met with opposition which reached the stage of bloodshed at Ramat ha-Kovesh in 1943. Show trials of Hagana members accused of stealing arms from British depots were held.

As the world war was ending, Hagana and various other Jewish bodies went back to systematic arms procurement and Rechech became only slightly less important than the rescue of refugees and their passage to Palestine. It was now all too clear to the Yishuv leaders that they would be forced to fight the British if they were to establish Palestine as a Jewish state. But to do battle with Britain, which in 1945 had the third most powerful army in the world, would need much greater military strength than the Yishuv possessed. The Jewish leaders also knew that trouble with the Arabs could only become worse.

Immediately after the war Ben-Gurion and Reuven Shiloach, a senior Jewish Agency official, went to the United States where they persuaded a small group of Jewish millionaires to form a dummy company for buying the latest machines for arms manu-facturing. The Rechech man on the spot in the U.S. was Haim

Slavine, then aged 41, who was instructed by Ben-Gurion to buy an armaments industry for the non-existent Israeli state. Slavine visited factories, auction rooms, scrap merchants, buying up machine tools which were being sold off as war-surplus material. Smuggled past British customs in Palestine, his machines were hidden in underground factories beneath the fields of kibbutz-im. By 1948 they were producing hundreds of sub machine-guns each day.

The Jewish leaders believed that the minimum army needed to protect the Yishuv was 16,000 men. Early in 1947 they chose Xiel Federmann, a Frenchman who had arrived in Palestine in 1940, to find in Europe the material to equip this army secretly and cheaply. Nosing around likely sources of army equipment, Federmann located in the Antwerp docks district an astonishing hoard of Allied war surplus — acres of warehouses piled to the ceiling. The delighted Federmann gazed on hundreds of ambulances, staff cars, jeeps, tanks, bulldozers and half-tracks; mountains of tents of every size; thousands of radios and field telephones; thousands of miles of wire and cable; huge piles of clothing and a variety of miscellaneous service equipment so vast that Federmann soon gave up trying to catalogue it.

While making out his shopping list Federmann came across one doubtful item — a U.S. army pack-rack, a timber frame designed to help a man carry a heavier load than normal. Since the packs were only 20 cents each, Federmann marked down 300. He thought they just might be useful for something. They were; when the Jews of Jerusalem were starving under the effects of the Arab siege other Jews loaded those pack-racks to capacity and humped food over the tortuous hills into the hungry city.

In the U.S.A. a campaign called 'Materials for Palestine' got under way — a massive collection taken up all over the nation for the Jews of Palestine. Run by the 'Sonneborn Institute', a group of dedicated Zionists, the campaign gathered in such offerings as 350,000 sandbags (from Wisconsin), 25,000 helmets (New Jersey), 100 tons of barbed wire (Chicago), 600 mine detectors (Minneapolis), 92,000 flares (Ohio), two corvettes

(Virginia), and supplies of medicines, bandages and surgical equipment (Louisiana).[1]

Under the overall command of Shaul Avigur, the Hagana chief in Europe, so many talented, determined Jews were involved in the secret acquisition of arms that it is difficult to select the most outstanding. The most versatile and spectacular was probably Arazi, who paid a bribe of $200,000 to Nicaraguan government ministers to be appointed 'Special Ambassador of Nicaragua for Europe'. His cover job, as 'Don José Arazi', was to procure arms for the Nicaraguan army and his first purchase consisted of five 20-millimetre Hispano Suiza anti-aircraft guns and 15,000 shells. He also negotiated the purchase of Hagana's first field artillery pieces — five old French mountain guns nicknamed 'Napoleonchika'.

Imaginative in his approach, Arazi gave his group of agents in Italy special cover documents — United Nations diplomatic passports of his own design. These forgeries were so successful that when the first real U.N. diplomats arrived at Rome airport they were arrested by the Italian police for travelling on false documents.

Hagana also got many of its weapons through Ehud Avriel, the agent for Brichach and Aliya Bet. Ultimately he held the greatest responsibility of the all Rechech operators. Born in Vienna in 1917, Avriel was a Hagana member by 1938 and in the next 10 years was involved in exploits which called for courage, diplomatic and commercial skill and immense perseverance.

In 1947, when Ben-Gurion knew that the United Nations' decision on partition was imminent — and therefore war with the Arabs inevitable — he sent for Avriel, then working peaceably on his farm. He was to assume command of Rechech activities in Europe but, Ben-Gurion said, the old piecemeal efforts were no longer enough. Rechech had to move fast and take great risks — Avriel would have carte blanche authority and access to a million dollars in a Zurich bank.

Raising the vast sums of money needed for the dealings of Avriel, Arazi, Slavine and others was a basic part of Rechech activities. While the many Israelis and Jews worked for nothing more than their living costs and the foreign volunteers for little more than this, the arms suppliers wanted total cash payment when the goods were handed over. That the money was available was mostly due to the work of Golda Meir, in 1948 political secretary of the Jewish Agency. Ben-Gurion sent her to the U.S.A. to raise the money and she arrived in New York with $10 in her handbag. She left a month later with $50,000,000. Ben Gurion was to say, 'It will be recorded that it was thanks to a Jewish woman that the Jewish state was born'.[2]

The million dollars in hand gave Avriel confidence, and in Paris he made contact with Robert Adam, a businessman who had connections with the famous Czech arms factory at Brno. Avriel would be able to buy 10,000 rifles and a million rounds of ammunition, Adam said, but he would need official credentials from some nation. Avriel could produce such credentials, as he had in stock the official stationery of what he still calls 'Country X', which is probably Mexico. With Adam as escort and introduction, Avriel completed the deal in Brno next day.

The problem of getting arms and equipment to Palestine/Israel was enormous. The Rechech agents were engaged in a constant battle of wits with British and American spies, the Royal Navy, and the authorities of many countries. The difficulties did not end when Israel was declared a state. Shippers, insurers and captains were apprehensive about war dangers in eastern Mediterranean waters and many nations, anxious to appear neutral, prevented the Israelis from openly despatching war material from their soil.

With much difficulty and many delays Avriel got his purchases out of Czechoslovakia and onto the *S.S. Nora* at a Yugoslav port. The cargo of 10,000 rifles, two-and-a-half million rounds of ammunition and 500 machine-guns were concealed by a great consignment of onions. During a storm, *Nora* was driven into a bay in which the skipper saw, too late, two British destroyers. He calmly anchored between them, saluted them in the maritime fashion and had the satisfaction of seeing his greeting returned.

In several parts of the world Jewish agents had aircraft waiting to fly to the new state — in Panama a nearly new Constellation and 10 war-surplus C-46s; in California, Constellations, Mustang fighters and three Flying Fortresses; in France and Germany 25 Norseman transports; in Corsica four British Beaufighters which had been eased out of Britain by a fake movie company on the pretext that they were to be used in a film. Two former Second World War pilots, one Jew the other Christian, made clandestine purchases of planes in Paris involving over $2,000,000. Among the planes they acquired were a Mosquito bomber fighter, and some Spitfires bought from R.A.F. surplus stocks. They bought a few Russian-style Yak fighters in from eastern Europe.

When war broke out — conflicts were in progress even before 15 May, the day of Israel's statehood — Israel was far from ready. The strength of the five Arab nations opposing them was overwhelming. Jordan's Arab Legion was British-trained and led and quantities of British arms and ammunition mysteriously found their way from the British depots, which were closing down in Palestine, into Arab hands.

To counter all this Avriel was buying big. In Prague, in June alone, he bought eight million rounds of ammunition, 22 light tanks and 400 machine-guns. From Tel Aviv came an order to buy from the Czechs 10 Messerschmitt 109s, at $400,000 the batch, and to take an option on 15 more. But how was Avriel to get these aircraft to Israel, since they could not fly such a distance without a refuelling stop? Ben-Gurion put on the pressure. The Egyptian Air Force had control of Israel's skies and civilian casualties were increasing. Avriel persuaded his Czech friends to lend him a complete air base near the town of Zatec. Here Avriel and his helpers took the fighters apart and fitted them inside the DC4 owned by Ocean Trade Airways. Ocean Trade Airways' entire staff comprised three Americans and the DC4 was their only aircraft. They had been hired for the Czech arms job by a Jewish former R.A.F. pilot, Freddy Fredkens, operating on orders from Avriel. For a fee of $10,000 the Americans were risking their lives and their DC4. With the first Messerschmitt load they took the Israeli Air Force's first fighter pilots — Mordechai Hod and Ezer Weizmann.*

In less than six months the Israeli Air Force would comprise 15 C-46s, three B-17 Flying Fortresses, three Constellations, five Mustangs, four Boston bombers, two DC-4s, 10 DC-3s, 20 Messerschmitts, seven Ansons and four Beaufighters. Volunteers and mercenaries, Zionists, Jews and non-Jews arrived to fly them.

After desperate shortages, supplies of heartening quantity, quality and variety were arriving in Israel by 15 June. Yehuda Arazi turned up triumphantly with 20 surplus Sherman tanks from Italy — only to find that Israel did not possess a marine crane capable of swinging a weighty Sherman ashore. Arazi was unworried. He returned to Italy and bought a 50-ton crane.

Not all schemes involving arms ships succeeded and one, involving the *S.S. Altalena,* was a disaster. The Irgun organization which, like the Stern Gang, operated independently of Hagana, planned to bring in a shipload of arms at one minute past midnight on 15 May, 1948 — the first day of independence. The British could not then attempt to stop the ship. The *Altalena* had become available late in 1947 but money for the arms trickled in so slowly that the ship did not reach Israeli waters until 20 June. On board were 5,000 rifles and 100 Irgun men.

Ben-Gurion regarded Irgun as a dangerous source of dissidence and was determined to destroy it as a military organization. His assessment was accurate for Irgun's leader, Menachem Begin, was beginning to mobilize his men to 'take over the government'.† Eluding Israeli naval ships, *Altalena* headed for Tel Aviv where the captain tried to beach her — only to ground the ship 100 yards offshore on the wreck of an old immigrant ship sunk by the British. Shooting developed between Irgun and Hagana and when two battalions of Irgun men deserted their

---

*Each turn was to command the Israeli Air Force in its greatest days. Weizmann became Defence Minister in 1977.
†For details of the struggle for authority between the provisional government and Irgun — Ben-Gurion versus Begin — see Arthur Koestler's *Promise and Fulfilment*, Macmillan, 1949, in which he gives and account of the *Altalena* affair.

frontline posts to help the *Altalena,* a civil war seemed imminent. Ben-Gurion told Yigal Allon, chief of the Palmach, 'The very existence of the State is threatened, especially if Tel Aviv falls to the rebels. You will have to kill Jews today'.[3]

Allon was outnumbered but a Hagana field gun firing from the shore decided the battle by setting fire to *Altalena;* ship and cargo were lost. Official figures show 14 Irgun men and two Palmach soldiers killed and another 100 wounded. The military wing of Irgun was dissolved and Israel saved from disastrous factional warfare. Ben-Gurion's critics see the incident as a failure of intelligence, saying that he could have had Irgun's leaders arrested, the *Altalena* unloaded and its cargo confiscated, that it was not necessary to fire on a ship which was flying the white flag, nor on small boats which were carrying wounded to the shore. But Ben-Gurion's intelligence was sound; he knew that Begin could only be beaten by a decisive show of strength and force — and this the tough little leader displayed. Begin temporarily gave up his struggle to become the Israelis' leader but, a much changed man, he succeeded in 1977.

No account of Israeli inventiveness would be complete without some mention of the Palestinian Jews' secret manufacture of arms, which had begun late in the 1920s in sheds and cellars on the kibbutzim where Hagana's leaders lived. By 1935 the industry was producing hand grenades, and by 1941 it was sophisticated enough to make mortars, sub machine-guns and shells. Two decades later Israel's arms industry was producing weapons equal in quality to anything made by the world's great arms companies but, in a sense, the clandestine inventiveness of the Palestinian Jew reached its peak soon after the Arabs began their siege of Jerusalem in 1948. The Israelis had only one experienced gunner, an English-language teacher in a Jewish school who was not particularly keen on gunnery. On the morning of 15 May he was drafted into the army and put in charge of the local mortar battery but this duty bored him. After a few weeks he went to his C.O. and is reported to have said, 'Your mortars are lousy, I think this one will work better'.

He placed on the officer's desk a missile resembling in weight and shape an aerial bomb which he had made in his spare time. 'This is fired from a mortar I call Fritzel', he said. 'I think you might like to try it out; it has a longer range than any mortar I know of'. Experiments proved that he was right. He had built a new weapon which was to play a vital part in the defence of Jerusalem and the Negev settlements. General Yaacov Dori, Hagana's Chief-of-Staff said, 'God knows whether we would have won the war without Fritzel'.[4]

7 The Army – Israel's Honour

On 1 July, 1975, a middle-aged Israeli, Eliezer Whartman, wrote an article in *The Jerusalem Post* which begins:

We have lost our son Moshe. He fell in a clash while leading a patrol inside the Lebanon to ferret out and destroy terrorists before they could enter Israel and carry out more massacres like those at Kiryat Shmona, Maalot, Shamir and Kfar Yuval. He paid with his life so that all of us can live free from terror and sudden death. The pain of his death is something that only a parent who has lost a child can comprehend. But ... Moshe and many like him have given us a perspective which in these dark days we desperately need ... Through our son and his comrades we can still retain the pristine vision.

Indirectly, Mr Whartman was expressing the dichotomy which most Israelis feel — a profound regret at the need for fighting forces and equally profound pride in their prowess. More than anything else, the forces — and particularly the Army — have unified the Israeli nation.

David Ben-Gurion saw this clearly and expressed it succinctly when he gave a lecture to the Army High Command in April 1970. 'The Israeli Army is obliged to become the creative force of the nation's pioneers, and the cultural instrument for the assimilation of returnees, for their integration and for their advancement ... It is incumbent upon the army to implant within the youth under its influence the basic values of cleanliness — physical and moral — knowledge ... physical and mental dexterity ... creative initiative ...'[1]

Through Hagana, the underground defence force which protected the Yishuv before the establishment of the Jewish state, all these virtues had been nurtured for a long time. Inadequately protected by the Turkish overlords of Palestine and later by the British, the Jews had no option but to organize their own defence against marauding Arabs.

In the early days of the kibbutz movement the Jewish population was protected largely by civil defence units and each settlement had to take care of itself in the face of an almost full-time emergency. The mobilization of women was an absolute necessity and women all over the country wanted to share with men the responsibility and burden of defence.

In the thirties, the newly-established Hagana accepted a few women and trained them to use revolvers and shotguns, mainly for personal defence. Women were used to transport arms on the assumption — which proved to be correct — that the British police would not search them for hidden weapons. But women kept up their pressure for membership of fighting units and gradually the Hagana command gave way. In 1937 it organized the first training course for women commanders, in Kibbutz Gvat, and the first commando groups included a woman leader. The activities of the Palmach — Hanaga's commando arm — demanded a high level of fitness and taxed the human body to its utmost. Among the 1,200 Palmachi soldiers who fell during the organization's eight years of existence were 19 women. The most famous was Bracha Fold, who died in 1946 in the defence of Tel Aviv.

Women took part in one of the most daring of Hagana projects during the Second World War. Among the parachutists sent to organize Jewish self-defence and revolt in Nazi-occupied countries were two female officers of the kibbutz — Haviva Reick and Hannah Senech.Both were captured by the Nazis and killed.

At the start of the War of Independence in 1948 Hagana had 10,000 female soldiers and 50,000 men. In the first phase of the war women shared in both the active and defensive battle activities. They were especially efficient in the defence of border kibbutzim, such as Nirim, Yad Mordechai, Negba, Mishmar Haemek and Degania. Many fell in battle and some were taken prisoner.

If I have emphasized the role of women fighters it is only to show part of the unique nature of Israel's problems of defence. Not a single person is unaffected. I know of one family — that of General Avraham Yaffe — which contributed 15 of its 21 members to active service in the Six-Day War.

After independence had been achieved with the defeat of the Arab armies in 1949, a good many Israelis hoped, perhaps naively, that it would no longer be necessary to fight the Arabs. For centuries the Jewish nation had prided itself on being 'the people of the book' and it had studiously avoided any vestige of militarism. There was no love at first sight between the people of Israel and their Army. The great majority disliked it; they had, after all, been the victims of Hitler's war machine. Others had served with the British or American armies and they had seen enough of life in uniform.

As usual, Ben-Gurion was realistic.[2] 'We do not believe in physical superiority, in the superiority of physical power, but the denial of the superiority of physical power does not imply a denial of its value.'

The Defence Service Law of 1949 laid the foundation for the Army to play an important educational role. The Army undertook to teach conscripts the language, topography and history of the country as part of their military training. It was hoped also to generate pioneering sentiment among the young conscripts who had had no preparation for life in their new society. The Army provided special courses during their period of service for all who had no previous elementary education. Hagana had been egalitarian and this was maintained by the Army in spite of the introduction of normal insignia and hierarchical ranks. Officers and men shared the same conditions and were on intimate terms. The Army's democratic atmosphere did much to hasten the confident intermingling of a young people with unequal civilian social status and to create a sense of unity which was not only of military value but also contributed to dissolving social barriers on the return to civilian life.

By western standards the non-military functions of the Army are extensive. Its role in agricultural development, particularly in the border areas, is notable; the Army also provides girl soldiers for teaching jobs in new settlements where the Ministry of Education often encounters difficulty in attracting sufficient civilian staff. At one time every girl who qualified at a teachers training college was drafted into the forces. These girls not only teach school and adult education classes but take part in youth club organization and in a range of cultural activities.

The wars of 1956, 1967, 1969-71 (the war of attrition along the Suez Canal) and 1973, together with the constant need to prevent terrorist raids, or the wish to retaliate after they had been made, established the armed forces as the basis on which Israel exists. In most countries of the western alliance the quality of the army is important but not vital. Possession of an army provides political influence, prestige, a say in N.A.T.O. conferences — but national existence does not depend on it. In Israel the armed services are the difference between life and death for every Israeli.

Military service has thus become the embodiment of Israel's very existence. As a result, personal prestige and high social status are attached not only to those who fulfil the compulsory conscription period of three years but also to those who choose to remain in the Army for a further period.

The highest prestige is enjoyed by fighter pilots in the Air Force. They earn this prestige. Selection for the corps is stringent, even ruthless; admission is difficult and even up to the morning of the ceremony of awarding wings candidates may be dropped. So great is the pilots' prestige that families of non-kibbutz fliers somehow manage to provide them with small cars during their service and fighter pilots from kibbutzim are given cars paid for with kibbutz funds. Nothing could more clearly indicate the status of fighter pilots and the general attitude towards military excellence.

Not all Israelis want to go into the Army — but every boy says he does. A doctor in Jerusalem told me, 'We Army doctors are probably the only ones in the world who find ourselves trying to detect sick boys who claim to be healthy, rather than the other way round.'

Insistence on getting into the Army — or the Navy or Air Force — is understandable for many reasons. One of the most important is that a boy who does not have service experience carries a stigma which is difficult to erase. So some young men go to extraordinary lengths to gain entry. Yudin Ya'akov is a good example. He was turned down because his hearing was defective, but as this defect was not evident to others he became the subject of malicious gossip. Ya'akov sued the Army, claiming that his partial deafness did not make him unfit for Army service and that his 4F status caused him 'unjustifiable shame and visited disgrace' upon his family. The Supreme Court upheld his claim and ordered that he be inducted at once.

Even the young male dropouts of Tel Aviv, the youths who become delinquents, want to be accepted by the Army. If the Army decides that it cannot absorb them these boys are bitterly disappointed and turn into even more 'wild ones'.

The armed forces have not been content to follow the rules established by other armies. Take the matter of water discipline, a subject of rigorous training along rigidly traditional lines in most armies. The Israelis always like to find out — they are a nation of researchers — so on several occasions Army doctors sent three different battalions of paratroopers on a forced march through the desert to the shores of the Red Sea. The first battalion marched on a canteen of water a day; the second with as much water as each man wanted; the third was provided not only with water but coffee, tea, soft drinks and light alcohol. On all occasions the second battalion made the best time and its members were invariably in better health. The experiment proved that a man cannot get used to drinking less — those who had their water rationed for a longer time succumbed first when cut off from water. This finding is contrary to the old idea that men trained to live and fight on a small amount of water are somehow tougher and can stand the pace longer.

The Israelis do not have, in the European tradition, a military staff of conformists perpetually fighting the previous war.

Israel's top military talent has repeatedly gone on to distinguish itself in the academic world, law, politics, diplomacy, business, kibbutz life, or technology. Often these diverse fields have in turn supplied Israel with its military leaders. In almost every full-time Israeli military man there lies a highly qualified and capable civilian.

Israel is geographically too small to be able to make distinctions between a civilian and a military population. The civilian character of Israel's fighting forces is a visible reminder of the need for each citizen to convert into combatant at short notice. The relative absence of battle fatigue or battle breakdown among Israeli soldiers is one indication of the capacity of many citizens to face up to the relentless continuance of military as well as civilian demands. The citizen soldier must accept the pressures of battle and then return to his family and cope with his wife's loneliness, the children's problems, money difficulties, business interruptions.

I found that tank crews who served in the 1967 and 1973 wars came from highly diverse backgrounds. For instance, one tank crew of 1973 consisted of a Tel-Aviv lawyer, originally from Germany; a baker from Jerusalem born in Algeria; two Sabras, one a bank clerk and another a kibbutznik; an electrician recently emigrated from Salonika. The officer happened to be the electrician — military talent takes precedence over social standing, Sabra-birth and formal education.

Public response to war emergencies is immediate and uncompromising. When the 1973 war broke out large numbers of the population were at once busy donating blood, volunteering personal services to the Army, using their cars to carry goods or service personnel. Some volunteers worked with the families of missing servicemen, a harrowing job; families needed information and this could involve helpless waiting for as long as four months, and it was the job of the volunteers to comfort and advise them.

A lot of foreigners believe that as soldiers the Israelis, are unemotional, crisp and entirely military in their demeanour. In fact, they can become excitable and emotional. Tough in action, they are quick to relax and talk; no foreign war correspondent has ever found Israeli soldiers reticent.

As the fighting forces of the hostile Arab states have grown, so Israel has been compelled to strengthen its own Army, Navy and Air Force. With men in short supply women are even more indispensable than before. As weapons become more sophisticated and the requirements of advanced techology more urgent, the number of laboratory jobs rise — jobs which are increasingly being filled by women in uniform. Gone are the days when a girl enlisting in the armed forces could hope for little better than operating a typewriter or filing forms for the duration of her service. Now there are women aboard ships and several have completed the standard naval captain's course. On top of that almost the entire giant military bureaucracy is handled by women.

Certainly, some girls try to wriggle out of Army service. One who convinced the special exemptions tribunal that she could not uphold her high standards of modesty in the Army later competed in a Miss Israel contest clad in nothing but a bikini.

Girls are trained in the Cheil Nashim — 'Women's Army'. It is commonly known by its abbreviation Chen, which also is a Hebrew word meaning 'grace'. There is not too much grace in the girls' basic training, under a staff of women officers and instructors. The training day lasts from 5 a.m. until 9 p.m. and it is physically and mentally tough. No concession is made to the girls' sex and they use live ammunition in training. As if to show that they are genuine combat soldiers, the girls perform no menial tasks during this period of basic training. Kitchen duty, guard duty and other routine tasks are carried out by men.

But the combat tasks have disappeared; women would not be used in front-line battle except in an 'ultimate crisis'. The girls' skills and talents are put to better use. Many become clerks and typists; secretaries of regimental commanders accompany their chief everywhere. Women also run telephone centres, teleprinters, radio communications and equipment laboratories. They perform cultural and welfare tasks, they listen to soldiers' welfare problems, visit soldiers' homes and try to help soldiers' families. As cultural officers, they teach in special schools for soldiers who have not had elementary education. Women are also part of the military police. Important members of the air force, they work in control towers and with electronic equipment. A sought-after job is that of folding parachutes — heavy work and a great responsibility. It is considered a glamour job, probably because of the link it gives the girls with the élite paratroopers.

Some girl soldiers still carry weapons; they are members of Nahal, a special unit of the Army recruited from graduates of youth movements. The Nahal combines military training and service with agricultural and settlement activities; boys and girls share all the work, including armed night-watch duty.

In 1978 the first four female instructors began work at a male training camp in the Judean Hills. They teach recruits how to handle arms and dismantle sub-machine guns and rifles, target shooting, marching drill and physical exercise. Their results impress their superiors but to psychologists there is no secret to their success. A man taught by a girl instructor how to dismantle an FN rifle in three seconds cannot allow himself to be slower than the girl. And when the girl instructor takes her platoon on a 15-mile march with full equipment no man will fail to complete the trip. Yet other girl instructors teach soldiers how to handle heavy tanks.

By contrast the Israeli Navy has some strict rules to 'protect' itself and its ratings from women: Women must be a minority of the crew, they must have separate quarters and there must be 'no lapse from discipline' in interpersonal relations.

Israel has been called a great natural laboratory for research into stress. It is a tragic and pathetic label but accurate enough. The amount of research on war stress is remarkable, unique in international military medicine for Israel must make the greatest possible use of its slender manpower resources. The Yom Kippur War of 1973 gave the Israeli medical researchers much experience and expertise in the effects of war on men, particularly in their search for ways of rapidly repairing mental and nervous damage so that a soldier can return to the fighting. Some of the symptoms observed in the field — and for which treatment had been devised — include delayed reactions, over-sensitivity to noise, inability to concentrate, difficulties in remembering, physical shakiness, hysterical symptoms such as paralysed leg or blindness of one eye, impotence, nightmares, depression, loss of appetite — especially a revulsion to meat — and a sensitivity to nylon; nylon was used to pick up bodies and parts of bodies on the battlefield.

Immediately after the 1973 war a group of soldiers from kibbutzim recorded their innermost feelings as they went into battle. We read of their revulsion against death and carnage. They reflect on their change of role from agricultural workers in a kibbutz to soldiers in a bloody battle. They dare to analyse their feelings towards the Arab soldiers. The result is an intimate disclosure of how these young kibbutznik soldiers felt about war and about their enemy in battle. These remarkable battle conversations were first of all mimeographed and were immediately widely acclaimed in Israel. They had the obvious attraction of an unusual and direct access into these soldiers' minds and feelings. The critics rightly pointed out that these young kibbutznik soldiers did not hate because this had been their first experience of combat and luckily it was very brief. What, however, is revealing is that the kibbutz produced such extraordinarily honest young men, who, while not shrinking from combat, refused to take it for granted and agonised over their need to wound and kill. Israelis loathe war and refuse to hate.

The most salient fact of all in assessing the influence of the Army and Army life on the Israeli mind is this: the Israeli individual cannot easily define himself as a citizen unless he fulfils a role as a soldier. Each Israeli is living a paradox: he wants to create a society which affirms peace but he faces the threat of recurrent, acute and erratic wars.

The courage of Israeli fighting men is now legendary. An analysis of citations for bravery show that Israelis are much like the servicemen of most other nations which value individual valour. Compare Israeli citations with those for the Victoria Cross of the British Commonwealth, the Congressional Medal of Honor of the United States, the *Légion d'Honneur* of France and you find the same qualities of leadership, gallantry and self-sacrifice. Until recent years, the Israel Defence Forces awarded no decorations, apart from the National Hero Decoration given to 12 men after the War of Independence. After this brief excursion into the world of awards, the government restricted recognition of outstanding bravery to a citation called in Hebrew 'Tziyun Leshevah' or 'Tzalash'. The first Tzalash was awarded in 1950.

Comparison of Tzalash citations with foreign citations will show similarities. The differences show up more clearly when one studies what the Israelis themselves consider outstanding among the outstanding. A book published in 1970, *Above and Beyond* by Yehuda Harel, states that a private soldier named Nathan Albaz demonstrated 'the greatest heroism in Jewish military history'.

Nathan was a Moroccan Jew, driven out of his home country by savage anti-Jewish riots in 1950, when he was 17 years of age. In Israel his only home was his army camp, his only possessions his tent and bed. On 11 February, 1954, Nathan and a friend volunteered to defuse grenades, not a particularly dangerous job but in any case one which these two soldiers preferred to cleaning up the camp. According to Albaz's official citation for bravery, he and his friend took a box to each tent to collect the grenades which were on the beds next to the rifles. During an alert the previous night each soldier had primed a grenade by inserting the fuse; having disarmed the grenades Nathan would return them to the camp magazine. The two boys spent an hour collecting the grenades, then went to an empty tent at one end of the camp where they sat with the grenade box in front of them, and began to remove the fuses. Suddenly there was a minor explosion. The pin on one of Nathan's grenades had come out and fired the cap which lit the fuse. In four seconds the detonator would explode the grenade. Nathan Albaz could do one of three things. He could throw the grenade through the tent flap, he could run out of the tent leaving the grenade behind, or he could run out of the tent with it.

As the official citation explains, people were working near the tent so tossing out the bomb was risky; if he left it and ran it would kill his friend and probably set off other grenades. He yelled 'Grenade!' and startled soldiers dropped flat on the ground. Then Nathan came bursting out of the tent, apparently intending to throw the grenade, but other soldiers were all around. He ran for the trench around the camp but he must have known he could never reach it. He pressed the grenade to his body and threw himself down on top of it. The explosion killed him instantly.

Private soldier Albaz became a legend, songs were written in his honour and his sacrifice was extolled as an example to Israeli youth. His courage gave pride to a good many of the North African immigrants who at that time felt that the Sabras and European Jews looked down on them.

Albaz's particular form of courage exemplifies certain aspects of the Israeli mind. The first is that every Israeli is part of a unified society in which mutual help is vital. The second is that a man must live or die by his own actions, even when they are mistakes. Most probably Nathan Albaz was careless in handling the grenade whose pin came out; if so, it was his obligation to accept the consequences. This in no way lessens his courage; on the contrary it enhances it, for it then becomes cold-blooded and deliberate.

One of Israel's best soldiers — by popular consensus — was Sa'adia Elkayam, commonly known by his Palmach *nom de guerre* of Supapo. A consistently courageous soldier and an inspiring junior officer, at the age of 25 Supapo was killed in action in 1955, during a raid against terrorists at Gaza. He was born to die on the battlefield, a friend said in a graveside eulogy. Such a notion, in itself alien to the general Israeli hope for a peaceful, productive life, is now more commonly accepted in Israel.

According to Moshe Dayan, Israel's finest soldier is Meir Har-Zion, a captain in the prestigious 101st Unit 'There has not been a more courageous fighter in Israel than Meir Har-Zion since the days of Bar Kochba' [in the first century AD], said

Dayan in 1967, soon after the Six-Day War. A big, fast-walking man, the Kibbutz-reared Har-Zion worked his way up through the ranks and took part in many operations in the 1950s. An advocate of the dictum that 'sweat saves blood', he introduced rigorous training methods for his men. Greatly distressed by the death of his sister, killed while fighting Jordanian Bedouin who ambushed her in the hills, Har-Zion made an unauthorized personal raid on the Bedouin camp and shot dead his sister's killers. After narrowly escaping trial for this action — which he did not try to conceal — Har-Zion was in action in Gaza and later on the Syrian frontier. Then, in an attack on a Jordanian Arab Legion post he was shot in the throat and arm. After a painful, protracted recovery he was officially considered 80 per cent disabled, yet he served in a headquarters unit during the Sinai campaign of 1956.

His crowning glory came during the Six-Day War of June 1967. A farmer by that time, Har-Zion was a captain in the reserves. Because of his incapacity — he could not hold a rifle — nothing much was expected of him but on the night of 5 June he turned up in Jerusalem among Israeli paratroops who were preparing for their historic assault on the Arab Legion troops holding the Old City. With him he had a bag of grenades, the only weapon he could use with one good hand. His colonel, Motta Gur, later Israeli chief-of-staff, gave him a command. His exploits are too numerous to be described here but one episode should be related. An Arab sniper had taken up position on the roof of a house in Arab Jerusalem and was shooting men in the street below. The Israeli attack was held up for an hour, despite several attempts to knock out the sniper. Har-Zion stalked the man through dangerous streets, climbed walls and finally appeared on a roof, from where he sprang on to the sniper's roof and killed him. Only he knows how he managed to do all this with a paralysed hand. With Jerusalem secured, Har-Zion rushed off by himself to the Golan Heights where he took part in the deciding battle on the last day of the war.

Moshe Dayan coined the term 'Har-Zionism' to describe the type of spirit and morale which he believed permeated the Israel

99

Defence Forces after the Six-Day War. Har-Zion lives today with his wife and children on his farm, Ahuzat Shoshana — named for his murdered sister — which overlooks the Jordan Valley. 'Har-Zionism' might also be used to label an important part of the Israeli mind — the will to win.

Writing in the *New York Times* on 2 July, 1967 (after the Six-Day War) Ammon Rubinstein summed up his impression of the army which had won such a remarkable victory:

> While I write the men are making an evening meal of their rations. As I watch them from my tent I keep thinking, 'Surely this is the strangest of armies. Its face is that of our whole people. It is an army of individuals but there is hardly any need for disciplinary action. It is an army which always wants to go home but which can fight like lions if necessary. Surely, there have never been soldiers like these civilians'.

I began this chapter with an extract from a memorial article by Eliezer Whartman for his soldier son. To underline the Israeli attitude to war and defence I can do not better than to quote Mr Whartman again:

> How can one convey some idea of the inner conflict that tears our children apart — as it does our nation? How does one get the world to understand the tragic dichotomy that forces our children to lead the kind of lives they don't want: that our sons loathe war and yearn for meaningful lives touched with joy; that this generation, even in wartime, sang hymns to peace, not odes to victory? How does one get across the ungraspable fact that even after 27 years of bloodshed, this generation never learned to hate the enemy, that they hated war, hated killing, even though they were forced to kill.

8 People of the Family

Jewish society has always been family-oriented and Israeli society is different only that it is more so. While tensions and conflicts exist within families, as they do almost everywhere in the world, Israeli families have less of a generation gap; this is because all members of the family have shared so much adversity. In most countries each generation normally passes on its experiences to the next — verbally; but in Israel all generations have had the same experiences since 1948. An older person might have lived through more wars but only the youngest of infants have seen no war at all. It is natural that this shared adversity has produced a marked degree of family unity and sympathy for one another's problems.

I have always been intrigued by this because the Israeli way of life — as I have already explained in my account of kibbutzim — is incompatible with privacy, which might be expected to cause acute tensions. For one thing, most people live in apartment complexes and are thus accessible to their neighbours, who might want to borrow anything — sugar, the telephone, or an ear into which to pour personal or political troubles. For another thing, inside the home it is rare for any member of the family, except mama, to have a place in which to hide secrets from prying eyes. Again, not many rooms have locks or bolts. Only the toilet may have some locking device, if it is separate from the bathroom, and this is where the Israeli head of the house will retreat — but his occupation of this sanctuary is usually time-limited.

101

In most cases apartments are bought rather than rented, so there is a need for co-operation among apartment owners in such matters as central utilities; this can lead to conflict at times but co-operation is more typical. The apartment may consist of a sitting-room, sometimes with a balcony, one or two bedrooms, kitchen with balcony, toilet and bathroom. Flexibility of room arrangements results in multiple use of rooms with total floor space of 60 to 80 square meters. Proximity to good schools and living in a 'good' neighbourhood takes precedence over spaciousness or modernity of the dwellings. Closeness to central shopping areas is also relevant, since transport is expensive and often uncomfortable.

Home furnishings are plain, tending towards functional Scandinavian design. As the sitting-room is likely to double as a bedroom or at least as a guest room, the sofa is almost invariably a convertible bed. In addition, there may be a rug or two on the polished wood floor, occasional chairs, a formica-topped coffee table and assorted ornaments. Bookshelves piled high are a universal feature of the Israeli apartment. Lighting fixtures are rarely elaborate and it is not unusual to see a bare light bulb hanging in an otherwise well-appointed room.

Many families have no room in their small apartments which serves exclusively as a bedroom. In these places the arrangements are often ingenious; a beautiful sitting room and dining room may, in the evening, be converted into bedrooms. Privacy under such conditions is minimal and socialization must include the learning of ways to make the most of privacy.

Balconies are a special feature of the Israeli apartment. The kitchen balcony is an integral part of the kitchen itself. Depending on its size, it serves as a place for a washing machine, a clothes-line, storage shelves for extra kitchenware and container food items, and general storage. The refrigerator and/or oven are sometimes placed on the kitchen balcony — to provide eating room in the kitchen.

Eating is an important family activity which reaches the level of ritual on a Sabbath eve, with the traditional candles — even in non-orthodox homes — and the ceremonial breaking of bread.

The custom which most appeals to the gentile is that of family members wishing one another, and any guests, 'Shalom Shabbat' — 'Peace on the Sabbath'. Jewish mamas have long been known as good cooks and Israeli housewives are no less capable. The main difference in Israeli diets rests primarily on a cultural basis rather than on availability of produce. European-Israelis are the main meat and potato eaters, whereas oriental-Israelis prefer rice, vegetables, salads and oily fried food.

The stubborn love for life which is ingrained in Israelis is evident in their food. Surely only the Jews could have made a gastronomic monstrosity called 'cholent' into a popular dish. It is made of lengths of entrail and intestine, which are cleaned and then stuffed with a mass of cholesterol better not described. The types of bread include the flat oriental pitta or the Jewish matzohs, and dark and light European varieties. Wheat is also used in burghul or parboiled wheat, chiefly by oriental Israelis Chick peas (houmous), another oriental staple, have become universally popular in a dish called felafel, consisting of chick-pea paste fried in small cakes and served in a pitta roll with a dressing of oil and salad. This has become Israel's typical snack.

Except in orthodox homes, dietary restrictions are not as strictly observed as they used to be in Jewish homes of the diaspora. I have had some of my best bacon meals in kibbutz dining rooms and from the kibbutzniks' enjoyment of the flesh of the pig it is obvious that they are not conscious of any dietary sin.

The cost of eating — and of living generally — has had an effect on limiting family size. The average family in the late 1970s is 3.7 but this hides the fact that some Israeli couples have large families, up to 8, 11 or 13 children. The greater number of these families are orthodox — the truly observant orthodox Jew does not practise contraception. These large families seem to be remarkably tension-free, even in the generally cramped conditions of their homes. I know of one family of 13 — all 11 children were born within 16 years — which lives in five rooms and an alcove in the Jewish Quarter of the Old City of Jerusalem. Yet the family runs so well that the mother, Leah, who is still only 40, manages to go out two nights a week to study for a degree.

Eastern European and Near Eastern Jewish societies developed cultures which required that extended families assume much responsibility for their members. Physical danger was ever-present from hostile surrounding communities, while poverty required that families pool resources to survive. This pooling has gone on into Israeli life and is evident in Leah's family, where older children care for the younger ones.

Despite the crowded conditions of his apartment the Israeli invites home strangers as well as acquaintances, people he has simply bumped into in the street. He does this because he is innately friendly; because he is passionately interested in what is going on elsewhere in the country or in the world and he hopes that his guest will be able to tell him; because he is proud of his home; perhaps because he likes to have an audience and to be an audience. Tradesmen and others who come to the door are apt to be invited in for coffee or a cold fruit drink, and with justifiable trust since doorstep confidence tricksters are rare in Israel.

Child educators in other countries are deeply interested about child care in Israel, since its unique problems have required inventive and dedicated efforts in the care of children. It is remarkable that in the midst of pressing national problems so great a proportion of Israel's resources have been devoted to children.*

In order to understand the mind of the adult Israeli it is useful to study what happens to him as a four-year-old during a day's activities. Let us follow a day in the life of Gilard — which happens to be the name of a little boy I know. By four he is probably more independent-minded than his counterparts in Europe, the Americas, and Australia and he is treated as a trusted family member. Mother is not too concerned about Gilard's vagaries in eating; she is more on the look out for

*For a scholarly study of young Israeli children, see *Early Child Care in Israel,* Chanan Rapaport, Joseph Marcus, et al., Gordon and Breach, 1976. I have found it particularly useful.

indications of mental alertness and ability to take care of himself among children of his own age. If he says something bright or perceptive or uses interesting words for his age his parents are delighted — and the child's development will be appreciated by family, neighbours and friends. He is expected to stand up for his rights and if another child breaks his toy he will not be punished if he punches the offender. The parents of the punched child will not object; serves him right.

Gilard, having started at the nursery school or kindergarten at three, is now a veteran. He arrives just before 8 a.m. complete with the regulation clean towel and snack bag. The nursery school teacher wants to see Gilard develop as a member of a group. She emphasizes comradeship, helps him to work with other children and encourages him to speak well. She will not punish him for aggression, provided she assesses it as retaliatory.

Birthday celebrations are important, and celebrated differently from other countries with a western life-style. On Gilard's birthday it is *he* who brings presents and sweets for his classmates. He still has certain privileges — such as being the one to serve the snacks, give out the napkins and choose the games.

With his classmates, Gilard is taken for hikes into the country when the children collect stones, flowers and leaves which are later used for craft activities or classroom instruction. Much teaching emphasis is devoted to environmental studies and field work. Even at the early ages of three and four Israeli children are taught an appreciation of nature.

The nursery teacher is no mere child-minder; she is constantly explaining, questioning, demonstrating and talking, and the school day is very full. The teacher is alert for the difficulties a child may experience; she encourages him to search for causes, and when necessary she assists him, but she does not solve the child's problems for him. There is nothing uniquely Israeli about this — the policy is part of the Froebel, Montessori, Decroly and Isaacs theories — but together with all the other strands of child care, this early insistence on solving your own problems is at the root of the young adult's self-reliance.

At 10 a.m. Gilard and his friends have a supervised hand-washing, then sit at a table to eat their snack of sandwich, fruit and biscuits. Table discipline is enforced — there is no disorder — though there is considerable latitude about 'correct' table manners. At one in the afternoon, after more structured school activity, Gilard is picked up by his grandmother — mother is likely to be at work — and taken home for an afternoon sleep.

Mother is still Gilard's main adult model but gradually his peers become the major socializing agents. Gilard's school friends are his home friends, too; many of his classmates will live in his apartment house so, after the general afternoon nap, groups of these children will join in play on the lawns of the apartment building or at the nearby juvenile playground with its interesting and adventurous slides, climbing bars, and obstacle courses. Children are expected to be adventurous. The traits considered most undesirable are weakness, sentimentality, 'femininity', 'sissyness'. Surprisingly, this holds good for girls. It is also considered bad to be a 'stray cat', to shun company, to develop a taste for loneliness or misanthropic moods. Displays of individualism will be tolerated whenever one claims one's rights but not when they are intended to impress others. There is a notable dislike of pretence and phony behaviour.

Uncertainty in regard to some values has had important consequences in the marked tolerance for behaviour which other cultures would punish. For instance, educators — in kibbutzim at least — do not interfere with masturbation or infantile genital play. The same tolerance applies to infantile aggression and some observers, especially of the kibbutzim, believe that the child is actually encouraged in aggressiveness. Again, the child is sometimes not conditioned to be courteous or personally unobtrusive.

Father's main family activities are providing financial security, direction for leisure time and performance of family rituals. He is unlikely to interfere with the management of domestic activities and he is not likely to contribute much to home maintenance — do-it-yourself activities are expensive. Medical problems and contacts with the school are the responsibilities of mother. Father may advise and he will be warm and solicitous with the children, but decisions about their health and education are mother's alone.

Father's activities revolve around leisure time. He arranges the details of outings and when the family goes on a camping trip — as many middle-class Israeli families do — father will be leader, director and instructor. If the family is religiously observant the children will attend synagogue with him and at home they will observe father's performance of religious rituals. All children see their father as defender of the country. He is often enough in uniform for young boys to identify with him in the role of soldier.

Israeli parents appear to be exceptionally permissive. It is rare to see a parent strike a child even when the child has been grossly disobedient and has pushed his parents' patience to the limit. According to the highly-regarded Israeli researchers into child care, Rapaport and Marcus, 'Children are expected and even encouraged to act without restraint ... Aggression, physical as well as verbal, is, if not actively rewarded rarely punished.' Certainly, individual play activities, especially of young children, include much aggression — but it should be stated that street or gang fighting is extremely rare. Children are too individualistic to form gangs.

Many a Western observer would consider the Israeli child excessively indulged. If this is so the reason is not difficult to find. Parents are painfully aware that life is going to be difficult for their children in comparison with life for young people in other countries. So while their children are young they tend to lavish affection on them, an affection often underlined with gifts, 'special treats' and much indulgence about behaviour. No Israeli parent whose child may be killed in war at the age of 18 wants to look back and think that he denied that child something as an infant.

An essential and fascinating aspect of the socialization of Israeli children is the influence of those outside the nuclear family, even outside the extended family. Neighbours and passers-by play a positive part in bringing up children which is not usually resented. Adults regard it as a direct responsibility to participate in the life of any and every child with whom they have even casual contact. Mothers get a stream of information, guidance, instruction and directions. I was sitting with a young Israeli mother and her three-year-old son in a Jerusalem park when a middle-aged woman joined us on the park bench and told the mother that the little boy should be put into different shoes so that his feet would not be stunted. 'Thank you,' the younger woman said and the older one left.

I said, 'A relative of yours?'

'I haven't the faintest idea who she is,' my friend told me. She was not offended by the gratuitous advice — advice which my wife would not presume to give her own daughter-in-law. Hostility and resentment about 'interference' is extremely rare; indeed, it is common for younger women to accept advice from their elders. Advice from grandparents is specially heeded and it is not unusual for the maternal grandmother to take over running the household and even complete charge of an infant's care during the first few months after its birth.

Family consciousness spreads in all directions. Three-quarters of the adult population of Israel (whose parents are alive) visit their parents at least once a week and parents visit their married children with equal frequency. Education and social class make no difference. In one survey, when people were asked to speculate on what they would do if the five-day working week came to pass, the most frequent answer was, 'I would spend the time with my family.' Family time is warm and relaxed and there is much talking, joking, playing of games and quiet, companionable reading.

Despite the great emphasis on family and family life fewer Israelis are getting married; in 1975 there were 32,000 marriages, in 1976 29,500 and in 1977, 27,000. At the same time divorces have been going up by about 10 per cent a year —2,621 (1975), 2,857 (1976), and 3,500 (1977). The average family size dropped to its present 3.7 from 3.9 in the late 1960s.[1]

In family planning, three sometimes conflicting factors are at work: a general wish to increase the population of the country; a concern over the excessive size of some families in socially deprived areas coupled with the small size of families in prosperous areas; strong opposition to family planning on religious grounds by a considerable number of people.

More than 500 Arab-Jewish couples are known to be living in Israel. In 425 cases Moslem men (Arabs, Bedouin, Circassians) are married to Jewish women; seven Moslem or Christian women are married to Jewish men and 68 Druse (members of a Moslem sect) and Christian men are married to Jewish women. The total figure is small and may have been even smaller but in a good number of cases the Jewish woman had not known she was dating a non-Jew until after she was emotionally and physically involved. Most of the women who have married non-Jews are from the oriental communities and were high school dropouts from broken or unhappy homes.The new marriages are generally stable but few of the Jewish women, all of whom speak Arabic, like living among Arabs. In the evening all the men get together in the local coffee house and discuss the world while the women sit at home alone. Such women cannot get a job, they cannot go to a cinema, they cannot be friends with anyone who is not a member of the family. Many of them must live in their mother-in-law's home. Jewish society is much more tolerant of the Druse-Jewish mixed marriage than of others. For one thing, the Druse serve in the Israel defence forces, the families tend to live among Ashkenazis and most bring up their children as Jewish, even in cases where the father has not converted.

Since Israeli society is couples-oriented, Israel can be a depressing place for those who do not marry. Walter Ruby, who carried out a survey on the problems of being single for *The Jerusalem Post,*[2] quotes a 29-year-old single man as saying, 'Unmarried women over 25 often go a bit crazy in this country. They are subjected to thoughtless teasing by their peers because they haven't found a man, and have to fend off questions about their prospects from well-meaning parents.'

The housing situation for single people is difficult and in some areas Israeli-born single people are not eligible to rent apartments. In other places they can acquire apartments only if suffering from family tensions under the parental roof or if they are members of 'preferred professions' such as medicine, nursing and teaching. Single immigrants who solve their housing problems — perhaps living in a hostel — still have to face loneliness and alienation. The same problems confront Sabra singles.

Desperate for company, some single people have organized singles social groups, which attract not only the unmarried but the divorced and widowed. These clubs are not for swingers — that American aberration is detested in Israel — but for serious-minded people who want to share such social experiences as conversation, discussion, lectures and outings. Romance might bloom in such a club but it is not organized for that purpose. Most group members are probably looking for a mate, but friendship and company comes first. Physical attraction tends to follow shared interest. Most members of these clubs are from middle-class or kibbutz backgrounds and each club consists of about 40 people aged from mid-twenties to late-forties. The clubs — the Israelis call them 'hug lehehedim' — help a lot of people but in a sense they increase the isolation of the singles because they are even less likely to come into social contact with couples.

Israel has no secluded love-nests in the hills or on the beaches, around the lakes or in remote corners of the country. If a man does take a woman to some out of the way place at least 50 per cent of their attention is devoted to watching in case friends or acquaintances should turn up — Israel is such a small country, it is just about impossible to have an illicit liaison.

Oriental Israeli women have particular problems and an increasing number are actively trying to become better parents, an ambition provoked by difficulties they are having with their children. As these women see their difficulties they are serious. For instance, many do not feel they are receiving from their children the respect they are entitled to. With government encouragement, clubs have been established to enable these women to discuss their troubles with a counsellor and with one another. Young oriental mothers often complain that their children are treating them more like friends than parents, a notion acceptable to most parents with Western backgrounds. Others find their children disobedient, perhaps in refusing to go to bed.

Several organizations have involved themselves in the widespread desire of many people — not all of them of oriental background — to raise their children more efficiently and make their family life more satisfying. Chief among these groups are the Religious Women's Organization, the Adler Institute, Na'amat (a women's organization) and Women's International Zionist Organization. Jerusalem University runs an M.A. course for parent group leaders and Ben Gurion University Behaviour Science Department has a degree course in counselling of parents and children.

A principal technique is to build up the parents' self-image, pride in their ethnic roots and confidence in their ability to educate their children. The methods used increase the physical contact between parents and their children. Mothers particularly have been taught how to develop their children's mental skills, play with them, talk with them, get them to talk about what happened in the classroom — and to get the father involved in all this.

The overall aim is to improve the quality of family life, which Israeli political and educational leaders believe strengthens society as a whole. Most adult Israelis do not need to be taught this; they accept it as fundamental.

9 Hunger for Learning

The Jewish people were always preoccupied with teaching and learning, rather as if they had a commitment to study for its own sake. In the world at large in earlier times literacy was limited to groups of the social élite, to the aristocracy and to the clergy — particularly in Christian countries. But in traditional Jewish society literacy was everybody's legacy.

More pragmatic considerations have modified the modern Israelis' approach to education but their commitment to it is even stronger than among the Jews of the old diaspora. The profound seriousness with which the aims of the educational process are defined in the law of the land speaks volumes. State education, according to clause 2 of the Education Law, 1953, is based 'on the values of Jewish culture and the achievements of science; on love of the homeland and devotion to the State of Israel and the Jewish people; on training in agricultural labour and handicrafts; on fulfilment of pioneering principles; on the aspiration to a society built on liberty, equality, tolerance, mutual assistance and love of fellow-man.' This is as much a condensed version of the aspirations of the Israeli people as a programme for educational development.

During the Yishuv and the early days of the state, education was not seen only as a training of the mind as a suitable basis for some future but unspecified task. It was also the straightforward acquisition of knowledge and of facts for practical use.

Two of the first things which Israeli children are taught is to respect knowledge and to *want* to learn. The educators have realized, probably more than most people, that the best education system in the world is useless unless children have a taste for learning. To create this taste among people from vastly different cultures, to evolve a system of education which would provide hope for the illiterate and satisfaction for the literate and to find a balance between practical needs and more speculative education was a monumental task.

One of the great successes of the Israeli school system is in instilling an interest in the country, its history and its geography, which is expressed in constant travel and exploration. This early conditioning is regularly reinforced — in the youth movement, the Army, associations and organizations of all kinds, the mass media, even in institutions for the aged.

But education is by no means parochial or insular. The eclecticism and internationality of the Israelis' devotion to education was summed up — one might almost say, pronounced — by Ben-Gurion in a speech in April 1950. 'We will translate the spiritual, philosophical, scientific and political treasures of all nations and all generations into our language so that the spiritual bequest of all of mankind will be our national property.'[1]

This was a tremendously ambitious aim in 1950 for the teaching of the Hebrew language, as of arithmetic, geography and history, involved difficulties for pupils coming from an environment where abstract study and historical understanding were not an integral part of their cultural heritage. A few far-sighted men had long before seen the need for a 'new' Hebrew; Israel's first great educator died 26 years before the establishment of the state. He was Eliezer Ben-Yehuda and his achievement was the revitalizing and modernizing of the Hebrew language, thus providing a basis of Israeli education.

Ben-Yehuda revived words under the influence of Hebrew's sister language, Arabic, or he just invented words, such as 'ofna' — fashion. Slowly, Jews in the new settlements began to speak Hebrew and hundreds of children began studying in the language. Teachers published textbooks in Hebrew and succeeded in expressing complicated scientific concepts. So the ancient language began to flourish as a medium of everyday communication.

There were, however, poets and authors who wrote in Hebrew, but believed it could never be an everyday language. They

113

mocked Ben-Yehuda and tried to undermine his innovations. In order to prove his point, to show that Hebrew was taking root among the people, and displacing Yiddish, Ben-Yehuda wrote an editorial in his small Hebrew newspaper proclaiming: 'This is the first time in 2,000 years that the words "I love you" were spoken in Hebrew' [in everday life]. Then he told the following story: 'A young boy coming from Russia met a Sephardi* girl in Jerusalem from a family that had lived for many generations in Palestine. The two fell in love. Since they had no other common language, they were compelled to speak only Hebrew [which both were then learning]. The day of their wedding was a day of great celebration in Jerusalem; they had to say "I love you" in Hebrew — a great step forward for the language.'

Hebrew has unified the speakers of 70 languages — in Israel it is not too far-fetched to assume that in any crowded shop you will find 20 languages to every 40 square feet. The fact that Hebrew is *the* language may have contributed to the feeling of detachment from the rest of the world, but it has also been Israel's prime cohesive force. Had the Jews chosen English or German for the national tongue the image of the nation would be very different.

Journalist Ruth Bondy says that 'No one can argue that Hebrew cannot be the everyday language of a vibrant people. When all is said and done we can play volleyball in Hebrew and run a brothel in Hebrew and repair tanks in Hebrew'.[2]

It will be appreciated that the Bible is limited as a linguistic source; in fact, it uses less than 8,000 different words. The Prophets, who wrote their great works in Hebrew, did not need such words as 'garbayim' — socks; 'misrad' — office; 'roveh' — rifle; 'rackevet' — train. Words such as these and hundreds of others did not exist in Hebrew until recently. Those who wanted to express these concepts had to use a foreign language. Ben-Yehuda created these words and many others, such as 'rishmi' — official, 'shiamum' — boredom, 'mimchata' —

---

*Plural Sephardim. Jews of Spain and Portugal and their descendants, wherever resident.

handkerchief, 'magevet' — towel, 'tizmoret' — orchestra, 'mivreshet' — brush, 'timron' — manoeuvre, and 'tekes' — ceremony.

Since Ben-Yehuda's time etymological innovation has become as much a national hobby as discussing politics or hunting bargains. The Hebrew Language Academy meets regularly and helps produce and approve new words and phrases, general and special, according to requirements. Some words find acceptance at once, such as the word for garage, 'musuch', which has been in use for 30 years. It comes from the Second Book of Kings, where it used to mean a covering roof in a part of Solomon's palace.

The Israel Defence Forces had, until recently, their own language committee which was responsible for a number of creations which have passed into ordinary speech. Some new words have failed to pass the test of popular acceptance. Seven different words for 'match' failed to strike until someone came up with 'gafrur' — a word based on 'gofrit' (sulphur).

In Israel, 'old' and 'elderly' as designations of advanced age are considered crude. Most people use the word 'parents' as a euphemism for older people. And there is no 'Home for the Aged'. It is a 'Parents' Residence'.

Euphemism is generally only used when it is necessary to be kind or courteous. The Sabras value the simple, direct vernacular. A man carried away with words is regarded with suspicion. Facts are the things, not words. Those Israelis concerned with the purity of their language are apprehensive lest Hebrew absorb too many foreign words from English or Arabic or Yiddish, or in case spoken Hebrew and literary Hebrew should take different courses, as happened to Arabic.

Names have been Hebraized — another unifying factor. A new name may be an expression of willingness to start out in the Jewish homeland completely anew or it may show resentment towards the old names, which were mostly German in origin. In biblical times, Jews were called by the names of their fathers — Meir ben Joseph was Meir the son of Joseph. The Jew who achieved fame was honoured with a nickname, as Maimonidev was called the 'Rambam', and this name gradually became the proper name. To make the census easier and identification more complete, gentile authorities in the early Middle Ages decreed that all Jews needed a family name. A family which lived in a house decorated by a red shield became Rothschild. The Rappoports are the descendants of Rofe miPorto, the physician from Porto. Some Jews fashioned their names from their professions — the Sattlers had been saddle-makers or saddle merchants. Others took their names from their size — so the Klein and Gross families prospered. And there were Jews who selected colour — hence Green, Braun, Gelb (yellow) or Blau. The case of a Jew named Green, who was born in the Russian town of Plonsk, is interesting. He emigrated to Palestine as a young man and became the pioneer of Hebraizing names. He himself chose Ben-Gurion. His successors as prime minister changed their names too — Shertok became Prime Minister Sharet, Skolnick became Levi Eshkol, and Miss Myerson became Golda Meir.

The Hebrew Academy has issued a booklet which lists all the Hebrew family and first names from the Bible. Some people look for names aggressively Hebrew, or parents want the name of one of King David's generals for a newborn son or the name of King Solomon's most beloved wife for a girl.

Diplomatic representatives of the Ministry of Foreign Affairs must Hebraize their names before taking up posts abroad. For others the decision to do so is a strictly personal affair. A change of name is significant, for it represents a person's attempt to change his entire personality, his image in the eyes of others, his children's future. Some changes are drastic — from Abdallah Ramzi to Ami Yisraeli, from Zorel Hershke to David Ben-Zvi, Diamantoni Koroptva to Dina Shamir.

Those Israelis who need to mix a lot with Gentiles tend to choose a name with an unmistakably Israeli sound but which will not scare a Gentile away. They go for five-letter names such as Givon, Naton, Ribon, Rabin, Perak. Many names have only three letters, — Gat, Gan, Bar, Dan, Gal, Mor, Rom, Kol, Ziv, Niv and Nir, Paz.

A popular mode of Hebraizing a name, advocated by Moshe Sharett when prime minister, is to arrange the letters of the original name so as to obtain a similar sounding Hebrew name. English Jews who are friends of mine changed their names when they became Israelis from Marie to Miriam and from Bernard to Benad.

It is probably easier to change a name in Israel than anywhere else in the world. You fill out a questionnaire, pay one pound at an office of the Department of the Interior and from that moment you are not Toria Sa'id but Nurit Shimoni. The second name is merely a convenient label; first names are used everywhere, even between pupils and teacher, students and professor, for education in Israel is not only an enlightening process but a levelling one.

I have spent a good part of my life among students of various nationalities and generally under agreeable circumstances. Still, I usually have some niggling reservation, mostly to do with the students not being serious enough. Nobody could make this criticism of Israeli students. To them the B.A. is only the 'first degree'. A 'first degree' is needed just to get a job as a secretary or a clerk. The number of university graduates is estimated at 20 per cent and none of them finds it difficult to get a job.

The fundamental reason for the application of Israeli students is that they are older and, because of military service, are beginning their advanced education at an age when most Americans and Frenchmen are finishing theirs. This maturity makes them more difficult students in one way — the lecturers and professors must be that much better. When Israeli students make demands they have good, sound reasons for them. They want more concentration on practical living than on theory because in an Israeli context you do not survive on theory. They ask for courses in modern philosophy, as being more relevant to their needs, than the work of ancient, medieval and romantic philosophers. Education is expensive in Israel — another reason for the serious approach. A large majority of students must live at home and work to afford their degrees. The universities have beautiful campuses but virtually no campus life — so much a part of college education for most Americans. A lot of Americans who go to Israel for a year at Jerusalem or Tel Aviv or Haifa universities are disappointed.

With some envy and even more contempt the Israeli student watches the foreign students, 'children' to him, who can cut class with impunity, read for pleasure, explore wider horizons and seek alternative life styles. Even the girls, who may dabble in 'chuppahlogy' — the hunt for a husband — harness their intellectual curiosity in pursuit of a profession. The Israeli student, after Army service, may have spent an additional year or two working to earn money for his tuition. Adult in every sense of the word, he may be married with family obligations so he fills the six-day work week with between 25 and 38 hours of study and generally a full-time job as well. The Army still influences him because men are liable for duty approximately two months of every year. He may be called in the middle of the term but would not be excused from normal completion of his studies and examinations.

Israeli students cannot afford the luxury of a three or four-year escape from reality — and that is what university education amounts to for many people in other parts of the world. They keep their sexual activity strictly private, and while hashish and marijuana can be found on the campus there is no drug-culture. Students generally seem to indulge their curiosity once and, satisfied with the knowledge, leave drug-taking at that point. It is yet another reflection of the desire to live life and not escape from it. Any difference between the Israeli student and society in generally is coincidental. The campus reflects the national pressures of building a country surrounded by hostile nations, of raising inflation, taxation...

The Israeli campus is a peaceful place — about the last place you would expect to find a demonstration. There is no such thing as a student opposition — the protest faction so prominent in most western universities in the 1960s. This may be partly because the Israeli university tradition is so short; in the fifties and sixties there was nothing much to change. In any case, everybody's energies went into survival. After the shock of the

Yom Kippur War outlooks changed and students began to ask questions. The most significant are, 'Have we placed too much faith in the wisdom and competence of our elders to keep Israel safe?'; 'What is the best way to be safe?'; 'Can we ever be safe?'; 'How do we convince the Arabs that we have a right to a place in the sun?'

Even German heads of state have arrived without being harrassed by picketing students. Who has time to waste on picket duty? To my knowledge, the university of Jerusalem has known only one demonstration — and that did obliquely involve a German head of state, Konrad Adenauer. When Adenauer was due to visit the university a few students paraded with placards with fairly innocuous slogans — OLD NAZI GO HOME or DID YOU BRING YOUR GAS CHAMBER? The university administrators could not induce the handful of students to disperse and called in the police; the policemen unwisely used their clubs on a few of the students. Within seconds this news spread throughout the university and dozens of classrooms emptied in a hurry. Within minutes the police were in flight, out-thought and out-fought by the students — 90 per cent of whom had completed their military training as officers or non-commissioned officers. The university officials and the police had been guilty of gross ignorance in assuming that they could bludgeon university students of all people into submission. Israeli students will always listen to argument; that's what university life is all about, they say. They are contemptuous of assertion, dogma and force.

Students from religious colleges occasionally get involved in demonstrations when they are worked up about some contentious issue. For instance, many extreme orthodox Jews believe that post mortems are wrong — or for that matter any medical work on a corpse. On one occasion six students from a yeshiva (a religious college) tried to disrupt a conference of pathologists at Tel Aviv university and put red-painted slogans on university walls — DRIVER BEWARE — THE PATHOLOGIST IS HUNGRY. DOWN WITH HEART TRANSPLANTS, END AUTOPSIES NOW!

119

They finished up in court, where they attempted to convince the judge that their actions constituted prayer — and prayer could not be disruptive. As a show of strength another 100 yeshiva students sat in the court alternately muttering, glowering, and calling for their friends' release. The judge was unimpressed and as the Court Proceedings show his sentence was succinct: 'Sixty pounds or 30 days in prison.'

The ultra orthodox groups, which opted out of the state system, have maintained a high degree of separateness in education, with teaching devoted largely to the study of Jewish traditional writings. The major part of their budgets is controlled by the state, however, and a recent innovation is the combination of modern subjects with religious studies. Harmonizing the scientific and technological spirit of the twentieth century with rules and laws fashioned several thousand years ago is a formidable task. It is interesting that applications for places in the religious schools exceed the number they can offer; in 1977 enrolment exceeded 18,400. Many schools receive endowments from Europe and the United States which enable them to offer free board and lodging to pupils. The majority of orthodox schools are in Jerusalem, from which students emerge with qualifications for further training as rabbis or religious teachers.

There was a time when mature foreign students used to flock to Israel to attend the Afro-Asian Institute, a graduate school for people from countries as far apart as Burma, Indonesia, Nigeria, and Uruguay. You could find government officials, trade union leaders, university lecturers and corporation executives — all staying for four or five months to study courses they themselves had requested — computer technology, moshav farming, handicrafts in village life, education in a multi-ethnic society. Sponsored by the Histadrut, the giant Israeli labour organization, the Afro-Asian Institute was an inter-continental bridge of knowledge, a place for the exchange of ideas. The whole of Israel was the laboratory in which these students worked. The Institute was spectacularly successful — until Arab propaganda convinced the Third World that Israel was exploiting them, though precisely how this was supposed to be happening it is hard to see.

A new college is being established near Jerusalem for the education of gifted children from Israel and the diaspora. In the process, it is hoped, future community leaders in Israel and the far-flung Jewish outposts will be brought together in close understanding and friendship. All the 480 boys and girls, aged between 14 and 17, will be boarders and the staff will live on the campus. The brainfather of this project is Rabbi Herbert Friedman, an American Israeli, who founded the Jerusalem Society for the Advancement of Education and Culture. The college, at Tsur Hadassah in the Judean Hills about 15 miles from Jerusalem, will be largely patterned on good English or American schools, with demanding educational, sport and cultural commitments. Compulsory courses will include English, science, mathematics, human and economic geography, art appreciation, music appreciation and great books and ideas. Graduates will qualify for the matriculation certificate in Israel, the C.E.E.B. in America and Advanced Level G.C.E. in England, so that they can enter for Oxford, Harvard or the University of Jerusalem. The visionary Rabbi Friedman told me that his students 'must master a course of humanism and science to be leaders in the twenty-first century'. He hopes that the four-year course will establish lifelong ties among the young people. 'I visualise our graduates becoming mayors of Manchester and Rosh Pinna and keeping in close contact with each other'. If the plan seems to be an attempt to create an élite, Rabbi Friedman would agree: 'But it would be an élite in the best sense of the word, I see nothing wrong with training youngsters to believe in noblesse oblige, in fulfilling their obligations to society and their nation and their people'.

The Israelis are impressed by the Open University in Britain and use it as the model for their own Everyman's University. Largely financed by the Rothschild Foundation, the university was delayed by the Yom Kippur War but it got under way in 1976 with 2,500 candidates. The low response among manual workers — only four per cent of the foundation course — was a great disappointment. The sponsors had dreamt, like so many educators of other countries, of reaching the people who need education most. Another disappointment was that only 20 per cent came from North African and Middle Eastern families.

The Everyman's University student has to work to a strict timetable, which demands a minimum of 10 hours work each week; a course lasts 12-14 weeks and the student needs credits for 18 courses to qualify for a first degree. The 18 courses will cost him about 8,000 Israeli pounds which is about half what a student pays in fees at a regular university.

Unforgettable experiences come in various forms and for anybody interested in peace in the Middle East, as I am, observation of an educational experiment in peace is memorable. In the summer of 1977, exceptionally hot even by eastern Mediterranean standards, I arrived by chance at Neve Shalom (Habitation of Peace), a communal settlement for people of all cultures and religions, just getting under way opposite Latrun on the Jerusalem-Tel Aviv road.

Neve Shalom is only a camp with a few pre-fabricated buildings and tents. The few full-time residents live in shacks and the visitors use tents, all of them going to the bamboo shelter for meetings and poetry readings, among other activities. The dusty land on which the settlement stands has been leased for a token price from the monastery at Latrun, scene of bitter and bloody fighting in 1949 during the War of Independence. The settlement exists to promote meetings between Arabs and Jews throughout the year, mostly for a week's 'course' built around a loose, often extempore schedule. Between 40 and 80 youths and adults attend each course, searching for mutual understanding. Even given the bi-lingual or tri-lingual (Hebrew, Arabic, English) abilities of the people involved, the search was bound to be difficult and during my visit I heard no problem solved, though I did hear a lot of argument, sometimes rapid and heated. It seemed to me that neither Arabs nor Jews were convinced by what the other had to say. Israeli attempts to explain that people were more important than land were no more successful than Arab attempts to explain why the Arab poet was 'being forced' to write historical documents rather than poetry. To me, this lack of agreement did not mean lack of success for the mission of Neve Shalom, because nearly all of the people attending were listening. That seemed a healthy sign. Even healthier was that the songs, in Arabic and Hebrew, were being sung by inter-racial groups.

It goes without saying that the settlement is organized by the Israelis; no Arab would dare arrange such a get-together for fear of punishment by agents of the Palestine Liberation Organization. The Arabs at Neve Shalom were known only by their first names or by a *nom-de-guerre*.

While a third of Israelis study regularly, it has to be admitted that, according to figures from the Education Department, 37 per cent of Israeli adults have only a primary school education, and 14 per cent have less than that; and that 8 per cent have never been to school. In practical terms, this means that in the late 1970s about 40 per cent of the adult population do not understand radio or television news because such concepts as 'inflation' and 'energy crisis' are beyond them.

The latter figure may be no higher than in European countries but it alarmed better educated Israelis when first published. The education system is not to blame. Hereditary lack of regard for education is the basis of the difficulty. Illiteracy is not merely a result of poverty or material deprivation. Many oriental-Jewish parents prefer to set their children up in a profitable business rather than have them spend years in institutions or secondary or higher education for doubtful financial rewards.

People from the ghettoes and caves of North Africa need to develop for generations before they want education. Attempts to solve the illiteracy problem have been frustrated by apathy among potential students, lack of qualified people willing to teach adults, lack of suitable teaching materials and a chronic shortage of funds. In 1978 Israel Television introduced a schools programme for adults. Called 'Ma Ha'Inyanim' (What's up) it is aimed at adults who are unable to understand the main news at 9 p.m.

Sometimes older people only need stimulation, as Rachel Inbar, an active and unconventional teacher and editor, showed in 1977. With the help of the Department of Adult Education, she organized a seminar for 60 women, aged between 35 and 55. All were mothers of large families and all had been living and working in various moshavim in the Negev Desert for 20 years, since being driven out of Morocco, Tunisia, Yemen and Kurdistan. Their educational background was poor, none having reached secondary level in any basic educational skill. Rachel Inbar's five day course gave them insight and instruction in reading and writing, household budget arithmetic, discussions on current affairs, guidance in creative play and children's literature, hygiene, cooking, home decorating and cosmetics. The aim, to give the women a taste for education, was successful and more seminars have been held, but their impact must be limited until more Rachel Inbars are available.

While it is not the aim of Israeli education to produce flocks of intellectuals, since the days of the Yishuv the intellectual has had a prominent place in Israeli society. Initially it was an ideological society created by intellectuals who, in their participation in the Zionist movement and in pioneering groups, epitomized the traditional role of the intellectual as a rebel against the established order.

The tradition of intellectual protest had been directed 'outside' — in relation to the British or capitalist society, or the diaspora. As the state developed it was much more difficult to express protest, since the intellectuals had created the society by their own rebellion.

A great variety of intellectual types now appeared among the ideologically committed — the bureaucratic intellectual, the professional, the academic, and a good many freelance writers and journalists. Some criticized but a good many conformed — a new notion among Israeli intellectuals. Nor was this all. There also appeared many non-ideological intellectuals, quite uncommitted to any particular party, as well as many apathetic intellectuals wholly consumed with their professional functions.

As the state of Israel became increasingly complex and competitive, less idealistic and more materialistic — as is the way of emergent states — the first group, the pioneering intellectuals, again found a cause for existence: they could now protest against the established order. Some of them are still doing this, as are second-generation intellectuals.

Any nation's education system and the standard of its teaching must have a profound effect on the minds with which it works. Education in Israel has succeeded in inspiring youth with love for their country and with an aspiration to rebuild it. The youth are fully aware that the country is poor in natural resources, but this realization does not result in attitudes of dislike towards the poor land. On the contrary, young people are imbued with the determination and conviction that their task is to rebuild and beautify it. This determination is expressed in a typical Israeli song: 'We shall dress thee in a garment of cement and we shall clothe thee with a carpet of gardens'.

10 People of the Book

In the reading of books the Jews anteceded many western peoples by hundreds of years. As early as the seventeenth century, the bookcases in the bet hamidrash (the 'house of study') attached to the synagogue were accessible to the poorest Jew in town; he could sit and read there in light and warmth at no cost. This was at a time when the Christian world had no concept of a public library and when even reading the Bible was forbidden to the lower classes of continental Europe unless an authorized overseer was present.

The hard-working farmers of the Yishuv liked to read and the early kibbutzniks spent precious money on books rather than on creature comforts. The Jews who came to Israel from abroad brought with them a love of reading. With all this background it is hardly surprising that relative to other countries Israelis spend more of their leisure time reading books. For most of them a book supplies not only enlightenment, information and entertainment but pure pleasure. Surveys show that reading is ahead of any activity connected with the arts or the media in the list of things which Israelis say they would do with more time.

Israel has 2,000 libraries, which collectively contain about 14 million books. Eighty per cent of the entire population reads at least one book a year — a higher percentage than in all western European countries. UNESCO statistics show that the percentage of 'active' readers — those who read at least eight books a year — is also higher than in all European countries except Britain. And, again, Israel holds the highest percentage of those who read more than 50 books a year.[1]

Almost all homes have some books — only four per cent do not. About one in five homes has over 200 books, a high figure by any standard. It is not surprising that 93 per cent of homes own the Bible and that three in every four have a picture album on the Six-Day War. It is common to see soldiers with books of poems in their packs and to come across groups of kibbutz members discussing a recent novel.

In every year since 1962 Israel has been first, second or third in the number of books published per capita; only Denmark and Switzerland have outdistanced her. With such an avid reading public and a thriving publishing industry it follows almost automatically that Israeli writers feels encouraged to write. In the western world poets are expected to be penniless. In Israel some poets — Nathan Alterman, Avraham Shlonsky, Uri Zvi Greenburg, Leah Goldberg — can sell 15,000 copies of a volume of poetry in a population of three-and-a-half million. In Britain, with a population of 55 million, the chances of any volume of poetry selling 3,000 copies is slender. A poet would have to sell 250,000 copies to equal the Israeli sale, on a population basis. Israelis enjoy poetry because they are a sensitive people. They have a desire to express eloquently what they feel but, since relatively few people possess this faculty, they make use of their poets, those individuals who can perceive a truth and express it. More than this, Israelis are taught from early childhood to love language; from this comes their delight in linguistic imagery. To them poetry is not only something to be enjoyed alone but in company when read or recited aloud. It is accepted as one of the least expensive joys of life.

The pre-occupations of the novelists and poets reveal much about the conditions and environment in which they write, and about the society for which they write. Some scholars have studied this exhaustively, notably Leon Yudkin.[2] Yudkin believes that Israeli writers have 'escaped into siege'. Most of those with whom I have discussed his concept dispute it, some vehemently, but Yudkin argues persuasively that the images and developments of a narrative line often reflect a siege mentality. He stresses other characteristics common in younger Israeli

127

fiction: the sense of threat and terror that is present in life and nature; the external world is often seen in terms of 'lands of the jackal'.

Certainly a sense of loneliness and despair frequently pervades modern literature; the hero is estranged from his social environment and needs to re-establish contact with a new order of personal truth.

In this book it is possible to look only at some of the more important considerations affecting the Israeli writer. To do this closely it is necessary to go back to some Jewish roots. Jewish culture in the dispersion was complete, even in time of great oppression. It was a complex amalgam of customs and habits, popular beliefs and mystical associations, rituals and traditions — a gold mine for writers. They did their writing in Yiddish or perhaps in the language of the country in which they were born and reared; in any case, the language was adequate. Most of the old culture was not taken to Israel; those parts of it which were taken could not survive the realities of climate, weariness from hard labour, tension from Arab enmities, the sheer inability to obtain many of the things traditionally used by Jews in their ancient customs. On top of that, Hebrew was at first too limited.

Israeli writers have had problems which writers of other nations never had to face. The author Aharon Megged relates[3] how a much younger writer once lamented to him how distressed he was when writing stories that he didn't have a grandmother: thus, he was ignorant about the extended family. 'Most of us Israelis do not have grandmothers', Megged wrote. 'Many of us do not even have mothers. They were left behind in Europe or North Africa or America. They died or perished or were abandoned. The little we know of them is from stories and memories. We lost touch with them, and the silver thread of continuity of generations has been cut off'.

The Israeli writer has another problem: his vision may be blurred because he lives incessantly in a state of insecurity, of threats of war, siege, and hostility. His writing is dictated by outside pressures. Rarely can he indulge himself in literary luxuries, such as love, beauty, fantasy and the contemplation of abstract ideas. One Israeli short story writer has told me that though he would like to experiment with the boy-meets-girl theme it would seem flippant in an environment where survival is at stake.

At the Hebrew Writers' Association conference celebrating Israel's twentieth anniversary in 1968 the novelist Haim Hazaz presented something of a blueprint for Israeli literature and Israeli writers.[4] '... Israeli literature should be a responsible literature ... one concerned above all with the people and the country, the people and their neighbours, the people and the diaspora, and similar subjects requiring seriousness, courage and honesty ... Above all ... writers shouldn't be ... lukewarm, comfortable people ... [but] heroes of a national struggle, of a class-war, of culture; people of conviction and responsibility.'

But many Israeli writers knew by 1968 that a free literature must abandon ideological commitment. Early Israeli writers were concerned with 'collective' themes; those of the 1960s and 1970s were concerned with the individual.

An interesting case to study is that of the novelist Amos Oz, born in Jerusalem in 1939. Inner violence is a demonic power which permeates his stories; women possess it, men suffer it and animals symbolize it.

This private violence is closely interwoven with Israel's threatened military position. In a story written in 1975,[5] Oz writes of Dr Hans Kipnis, who has an enlightened vision of a 'decent' state and pleasant family life, and his wife Ruth, a respectable housewife. Ruth elopes with a British admiral at the time of the British mandate, and Russian ladies from next door rape her child. The drives which motivate these characters are closely related to the politics of the Kipnis' sub-tenant, a member of a dissenting terrorist organization on the eve of the 1948 war. Dr Kipnis' vision founders on sexual and political rocks.

For the Jew, throughout his history, there was no distinction made between his nation — be it English, Dutch, or Russian — and religion, and in his writing he rarely made a distinction between himself as an individual and as part of his nation. Now, with the Jews of Israel, there are two differences: the writer shows his consciousness of being an Israeli, though he can make the distinction between himself as an individual and the nation of which he is part. Yudkin believes that 'Even the ideological links between Israel and the diaspora have been evaded by some writers'.[6]

Some Sabra writers have indeed abandoned the diaspora foundations of modern Israel and A.B. Yehoshua and Oz, have challenged the idea of indebtedness to the society from which they originated. What was significant to the writers of the diaspora — the breakup of Jewish culture and faith — is not significant to the Sabra writers.

In Yiddish, the language spoken for years by occidental Jews, the content of ghetto literature and poetry had emphasized 'troubles', prayer and praise of God. By the early 1950s Israeli literature and poetry stressed the national concepts of land, water, work, immigration and defence. The melodies of the old songs were those suggestive of praying and crying, the new were dynamic, confident and martial. Moshe Shamir, one of Israel's best-known authors, has said that when he started to write his feeling that he had something vital to say sprang mainly from a sense of belonging to a generation that spoke a language different from that of its predecessors.

Israeli characters are different from those to be found in a Jewish novel in Europe. For instance, it is unusual to find in Israeli fiction rabbis, shopkeepers, holy men and scholars — all commonplace in Jewish fiction. The main characters are soldiers, workers, farmers, settlers. Another difference is that the background is rural rather than urban. The language, quite apart from the change from Yiddish to Hebrew, is more colloquial and secular. Megged has identified the biggest change as the myth source; writers whose roots were in the diaspora drew from the myth of the people, while Israeli-born writers draw from the myth of the land. As he puts it, 'The shift has taken place from the myth of a people in search of a land to the myth of a land in search of a people'.[7]

This land, Israel, was from the first an active, closed society, concerned with establishing itself. Not surprisingly then, the writer too tried to justify his own existence. Thus most Israeli literature takes itself and the world seriously. Realism is what counts.

Many modern Israeli writers began their careers as road builders and workers on the land; so it was only natural that the earlier generation of writers should stress their national and social commitment while a younger generation, which emerged in the late fifties and early sixties, rejected this kind of commitment in the belief — mistaken I think — that it impairs the writer's freedom and individuality.

At its best, contemporary Israeli literature reflects the tensions in society and the inner conflicts of the individual. There is so much doubt, irony and bitterness in the Israeli mind and society that these things find their way into literature. When mixed with passion and conviction the whole compound is one of great strength.

One novel in particular has been represented to me as typically Israeli — though there might well be other novels which vividly show Israeliness. It is Ehud Ben Ezer's novel *Nor the Battle to the Strong*,[8] which tells the story of the life and death of a young Israeli, Fullik Shomron, a student of philosophy at the University of Jerusalem. It is written in a naturalistic manner with a partly documentary background of Jerusalem and Tel Aviv during the autumn of 1960. The more Fullik gets involved in his desperate love affair with Ofra, a fellow student, the more he tends to interpret political events in the country as his own personal affair. The following summer, while on reserve duty with his military unit, an inner rebellion causes him to run towards the place from which enemy shots are being fired. He is mortally wounded. In his last moments his thoughts are concentrated on the necessity to break down the wall of Arab hatred. 'You are killing me by allowing me to kill you,' he appeals to Arabs in his mind.

In the late 1950s and early 1960s Israeli fiction changed; it became less Israeli and began to show the characteristics and tone of contemporary European literature. The typical hero is now not so much a figure within collective Israel as an individual

131

at odds with his society, trying to work out a personal solution for his own unique problems. This new fiction deals with man in general, and not specifically with local conditions. Contemporary Israeli literature shares the mood of the world. It looks for freedom as well as for new directions, but its search is not determined by the history of past ideologies or certainties. Much greater stress is being placed in current Israeli fiction on the need for roots, national and personal. Naturally, the Holocaust is a significant element at the base of the contemporary situation.

In one important way the Israeli novel is traditional and conventional — in keeping with what world literary criticism expects of the novel; it examines and assesses the individual in his society.

It is interesting that many an Israeli novel reaches the point, in its plot, where the hero is in flight. Yudkin sees this as an expression of dissatisfaction with current circumstances, 'a sense of oppression and claustrophobia that forces the hero to grasp at any straw in searching for his own authentic freedom'.[9] Other fictional heroes are given the task of 'finding themselves' — a motive common in any literature. But the Israeli hero on such a quest goes to the limit in his search for truth and meaning. Like Daniel Dror in Y. Orpaz's novel *Daniel's Voyage* (published in 1969), his function is part messianic in that he seeks a prophetic vision. He does not find it. This is to me indicates that Orpaz did not find the Six-Day War (two years earlier) the answer or even a pointer towards the solution of Israel's problems.

Orpaz is typical of Israeli writers in his directness. Here are the first lines of one of his stories:[10] 'The destruction of the world will almost certainly begin like its creation — with the movement of a tiny grain from its place.'

The work of three novelists in particular claims international attention. They are David Shahar, A.B. Yehoshua and Amos Oz. Oz is the most characteristically Israeli. His novels and stories are written in a realistic vein and focus on kibbutz life and the struggles and pleasures of a pioneer people. Less conventional are the writings of Yehoshua and Shahar. Yehoshua's novels have been written in styles ranging from surrealism to naturalism. Shahar has created a style uniquely his own and is perhaps the most promising of current Israeli novelists.

Another fine writer is Shulamith Hareven who, in her *City of Many Days* published in 1974, creates a vivid picture of Jerusalem during the days of the British Mandate. Writing with a lyrical quality that elevates parts of her novel to poetry, Mrs Hareven describes Jerusalem as:

> a veiled lady on a still, torrid day, feminine, forlorn, softly dreaming, self-absorbed, sucking time sweetly like an old sugar candy, her sons gathered under the many folds of her robe, picking rockrose and herbs. Other days she was a man, fierce, dry and ancient, smelling of thyme and wild goat, his head covered with a sack against the wind, bare feet viny-veined ... sniffing the slippery scent of sin in abandoned alleys, the odor of prophecy in public squares ... Put your hand on a wall and you feel the stone pulse ...

Like her fellow Israeli novelists, Mrs Hareven is imbued with a sense of the dynamism and vitality of the land of Israel, qualities which are transmitted to her writing.

Israeli poetry is revealing, as all poetry should be, and sensitive, as it must be. To quote entire poems in translation is difficult, unfair to the poet and unsatisfying to the reader. It is enough here to quote a few lines from several poems to show the compulsions of Israeli poets and to indicate the beautiful and rather baroque nature of their poems.

Abba Kovner:

Naked soil is the way to my beloved.
I come to her like someone coming to a tryst.
I quietly try to rebuild
a city, transparent.

From 'It's Late'
translated by Shirley Kaufman.

Y. Ratosh:

Why does God not favour and have mercy
On the soul of man

133

Which is small
When you call Him.

From 'Poems of Calculation'
translated by Leon Yudkin.

H.N. Bialik:

Let the hands be strong of our brethren who tend
the dust of our land, wherever they may be;
May your spirit not fall, be glad, exult.
Come with one shoulder to the help of the people.

From 'People's Blessing'
translated by Leon Yudkin.

Hayim Be'er:

I am a child
of six generations here
under the sun of lower Syria.

From 'The Sequence of
Generations' translated by
Stephen Mitchell.

Uzi Shavit:

Blossoms appeared in the land, and
The neglected grapevines climbing in the ruins of Kuneitra
Gave forth fragrance.

From 'Two Variations of Spring 1974'
translated by Arthur C. Jacobs.

Yehuda Amichai:

On the Day of Atonement 1967 I put on
My dark festival clothes and went to the Old City of
Jerusalem.

From 'On the Day of Atonement'
translated by Arthur C. Jacobs.

Anton Shammas:

Sitting on a Tel Aviv rooftop in the sun
On a cold day.

From 'Sitting on the Rail'
translated by Betsy Rosenberg.

Samith El-Kassim:

In my aloneness I'll let the sadnesses
Shake the ashes of my sorrows ...

From 'Cinerama' translated by
Sasson Somekh and Richard Flautz.

Yehuda Amichai:

The best time to meet a new love
Is the time most amenable
For those who place bombs.
— At the conjunction
Between two seasons
In a brown study,
A slight confusion during the changing of the guard,
In the fold.

I dip my dry look
like bread into the softening death
that is always on the table before me.

From 'Spring 1970' translated by Leon Yudkin.

Avot Yeshurun:

Yeho' bless us
In the Middle East.
Not a man with us
In the Middle East.

From 'Not a Man
With Us' translator
unknown.

135

THE ISRAELI MIND

Amir Gilboa:

I am the slain one, my son,
My blood is already on the leaves,
And my father held back his voice
And his face was pale.

From 'Blue and Red' translator unknown.

I go on disappearing from myself and suddenly I see
myself walking ahead of me. If only I could cry.

*From 'Three Poems' translated
by Shirley Kaufman.*

David Avidan:

Now it may already be said:
Second World War Jewry
has no more monopoly on death —
the local industry has been making marked progress.

From 'Antitear Gas' translated by the poet.

Nathan Zach:

When God said, for the first time: Let there be light —
His intention was to rid himself of the dark.

Avner Treinin:

The age of the first crocus will never
return. Always move on.

*From 'The Day is Coming'
translated by Shirley Kaufman.*

Arnold Sherman:

he looked for god
god found him
he searched for truth

truth was there
he desired beauty
his eyes were opened
he called for love
she awaited
he cried for peace
death came.

'Simplicity' translated
by the poet and
reproduced here in full with
his permission.

Considering the popularity, success and relative prosperity of
the Israeli writer it is significant that in Israeli society the status
of authors and poets has dropped. At one time Hebrew writers
were the glory, pride, inspiration and leaders of the community.
Today, their influence on what goes on in the country is slight.
This may be changing slowly, as it is changing in other parts of
the world; people appear to be looking to the writer to supply
what the church and priests can no longer supply — meaning to
life.

Within roughly half a century Hebrew literature has begun to
find its place in world literature. The award of the Nobel Prize
to the late J.S. Agnon was not only a mark of honour but also a
sign that this fact had been recognized. Many Hebrew books and
plays have been translated into European and other languages.
Since modern Hebrew literature is accessible to the outside
world in translation only, the quality of the translation must be
high. With the foundation of the Institute for Translation,
Israeli work available for readers outside the country has
improved in quality and increased in quantity.

Perhaps foreign political leaders should study Israeli literature
as a guide ·to contemporary thought. Such knowledge would
help them to understand what makes Israelis tick. For instance,
in one brief paragraph the poet Nathan Alterman crystallized
the importance to the Israeli people of the Six-Day War:

The storm of the times seemed to sweep all that was secondary and irrelevant from our image and essence, leaving only
that which counted. And what counted was faith and discipline, and a quiet, tense readiness and a specific and practical
courage ... The character of the nation that has been revealed
to us these days is one of the greatest sources of wealth that
has come to us ....[11]

If the novelists and poets take themselves seriously the
humourists do not — though their theme is often serious. Generally, they are an irreverent group, capable of biting cynicism and
sarcasm, especially when it is directed towards the United
Nations. Most Israeli humourists seem to see themselves first of
all as social commentators and they are merciless in exposing
what they consider the deficiencies and vanities of people in
public life and the dictatorial nature of bureaucrats. Some
humourists pose in their writings as the typical Israeli, and
recount real or imagined brushes with authority.

Nearly all the Israeli humourists and satirists write with an
undercurrent of conflict or antagonism. The topics of their
articles and poems are against bureaucracy or inhumanity or
government policy; the tone is one of exasperation or frustration
or irritation — with the Arabs for not wanting peace, with the
United Nations for their consistent condemnation of Israel, with
'the system' for its inflexibility. In *Israeli Humour and Satire,* a
collection of 24 pieces by 10 different humourists published in
1974, every contribution contains an element of conflict. The
contributors are probably the best of Israeli humour writers —
Ephraim Kishon, Dan Ben-Amotz, Amos Kenan, Adam Baruch,
Ya'akov Rotblit, Danny Raveh, Menachem Talmi, Eliyahu Sal-
peter, Amnon Zakov, and the novelist Aharon Megged.

The best-known humourist is Ephraim Kishon, whose work is
said to appear in more publications than any other humourist in
the world. He can even be humourous about the Palestine Liberation Organization, a body dedicated to the destruction of his
country. 'Dear inflexible P.L.O., a truthful terrorist organization, the only reliable party among all this treacherous lot', he
once wrote in a Tel Aviv newspaper. As Kishon tells it, the

P.L.O. is the only party to the Middle East conflict which does not hide its intention to crush every last Israeli underfoot; the others plan to do just that but they prevaricate and dissemble about it. You know where you are with the P.L.O.

Kishon evolved the Eskimo Law for Quality Preservation. It goes like this: the number of Eskimoes in the Arctic is growing every year but the number of seals is at best static. When an Eskimo discovers a new seal colony he keeps it himself and sends other hunters off in the wrong direction. So if you come across something desirable, don't broadcast it, but tell people how lousy it is. As Kishon tells it, the law can backfire. His favourite restaurant went out of business because everybody in Tel Aviv was giving it a bad name, so no one ever turned up — though it was the best restaurant in the city.

Kishon explains the meaning of the Jewish interjection 'Nu!' which is rather like the English 'Well!' According to a superficial estimate, says Kishon, it has 680 meanings, depending on the speaker's facial expression and the time of day. Here are a few meanings picked at random:

'Come on!'

'Please, leave me alone, can't you?'

'I didn't understand a word of what you said. What are you driving at?'

'All right, suppose things are as you say, though mind you I don't say so. Is that reason enough to start shouting as if I had trod on your corns? Bloody fool! Yes. You. Really ...'[12]

Generally, Israeli humour is like Jewish humour with politics added. Sometimes funny stories of some age are resurrected to fit a current political situation. During the Six-Day War, Haim Hertzog, later Israeli ambassador to the United Nations, was official government spokesman, and he told this story on Israeli Radio:

> Nasser's promise to destroy Israel this time brings to mind a story from that apocryphal centre of Jewish folklore, Chelm. A large river divided Chelm in two and when the inhabitants wanted to cross from one side to the other, they were tied to a tree trunk and pushed across. On one occasion, the tree trunk turned over in mid-stream and the unfortunate

139

individual tied to it was suspended with his head in the water and his feet in the air. The wise citizens of Chelm stood on the bank and said to one another, 'See what a fool he is! He hasn't crossed the river yet and already he is drying his stockings.

Jokes about the Arabs are wry and often exasperated, but they are never vicious. I cannot count how many Israelis have told me the joke about Abdullah — though the name varies. Abdullah is having an afternoon sleep when the nearby play of children disturbs him. He goes onto his balcony and calls to the children, 'Why are you wasting your time here? On the other side of town Mohammed Ali is handing out free figs.' The children run to get their share of the fruit. Abdullah goes back to his couch but he cannot settle down to sleep. Finally he gets up with a start and puts on his shoes quickly. 'Why am *I* wasting my time here sleeping when Mohammed Ali is handing out free figs?'

Some of the best and most pungent humour appears in the cartoons of the English-language *Jerusalem Post*, whose cartoonist is Yaacov Kirschen. A typical *Post* cartoon published in 1977 has two Israelis talking:

First Israeli: Egypt says that we tried to flood their country with worthless phony money in an attempt to collapse their economy.

Second Israeli: What an outrageous obvious lie! We've had worthless phony money for years ... and *our* economy hasn't collapsed!

And another example:

First Israeli: It's simple. We let the Israeli pound fall in value, allow free exchange of dollars, Israeli exports become dirt cheap and in the long run the economy is strengthened.

Second Israeli: And in the short run?

First Israeli: We starve.

Significantly Israelis really laugh at such humour, I suspect because it contains more than a grain of truth.

11 The Serious Business of Spare Times

Traditional Jewish culture did not tolerate vacuums — and this has carried over into Israeli life.·

It is one of humanity's ironies that the Jews invented leisure — in the institution of the Sabbath — and then took it back again by minutely describing how to spend it. Jewish-Israeli culture sanctifies activities governing the round of life — prayers, eating, sleeping, leisure...

Israelis need to feel that leisure is being spent constructively and while the outings of youth are probably more aimless than the outings of their elders they are nevertheless approached with a certain amount of dedication. I noticed this particularly one Sabbath when, in the July heat, I visited the Ein Gedi nature reserve, in the brown hills facing the Dead Sea. In the almost tropical vegetation of this strange, narrow valley is a mixture of wildlife found nowhere else in Israel. Even in summer a spring-fed stream tumbles down the rocks and at one place becomes a short waterfall. Here Solomon had a palace, and here, in this unusual oasis, he wrote love poems.

The bleak country surrounding the oasis is where David took refuge from Saul, and later the oasis' spring was named for David, his Fountain. The oasis' grapes must have been famous even then for they were spoken of in the Song of Solomon, 'My beloved is unto me as a cluster of grapes in the vineyards of En-gedi'. The love-song's praise in an apt reference. The grapes and peaches of Ein Gedi kibbutz are among the earliest of the season's produce to appear on the market.

THE ISRAELI MIND

One of the most appealing sights is that of the wild deer who come down from the Judean Hills to drink and rest in the shady grounds of the natural history museum. And here, every Sabbath, crowds of mostly young Israelis come for picnics. I walked less than half a mile in the fierce heat before I found a pool where I was content to sit and bathe my feet. Troops of robust, vigorous Israelis carrying refrigerated picnic hampers, clambered past me, talkatively enjoying themselves yet with expressions which said, 'I'm going to the end of this trail, no matter how steep and how hot'.

Much of this zest is the result of good health. Israel is the one country in the Middle East free from the ravaging epidemics of its neighbours — malaria, typhus, typhoid, tuberculosis, bilharzia. The country has a doctor for every 430 inhabitants — the highest ratio in the world — and it has 1,100 clinics, 500 hospitals, 600 mother and child centres.

With all this medical care, as well as public and family emphasis on plenty of exercise and a balanced diet, Israelis have energy for all kinds of cultural and recreational activities. The success of the health service can be measured by life expectancy, which is now higher than most western countries. It averages 69.5 for men and 73.2 for women, compared with 67.3 and 72.4 in Britain and 66.6 and 72.7 in the United States. These figures are remarkable, for throughout the earlier years of the state a large number of newcomers were ill, at least 13 per cent chronically so. Those from the Arab world were plagued by malaria and trachoma and had little idea of basic hygiene. Many from Europe needed mental care after their dreadful suffering in the Nazi prison camps.

Hiking is almost the national sport of Israel. In the vacations, almost every boy and girl will be on some hike organized by school or youth movement, the younger children for a day or two, the older ones for the better part of a week. Adults, too, commonly take a day or two off for a walk in the Negev, Galilee or the Judean Hills. Before Passover there is a publicly-organized four-day march to Jerusalem, with 20,000 hikers from the quite young to the elderly. The National Committee for the

Friends of Nature organizes a number of long-distance walks and other annual events.

Israeli recreational habits vary, as elsewhere, with age, education, finances and the season. And I do mean 'recreational' instead of spare-time activities. Israelis have no spare time; they are always doing something. Even when they visit somebody it is something they *must* do, as they must write letters or read the newspapers. The only non-time is the Sabbath afternoon nap, which is partly a leftover from the diaspora and partly a Mediterranean custom. At any time of the year the Israeli will rest, supine and silent, between two-thirty and four on the Sabbath. I have been out for a Sabbath with non-religious Israelis and have had them whisk me back to the apartment at dangerous speed to be sure of lying down by two-thirty.

Since most Israelis work a six-day week public and religious holidays are important. The significant holidays, after Independence Day which heads the list, are Passover, Purim, Rosh Hashana and Hannukah. Passover (April) celebrates the ideals and miracles of the redemption from slavery and the coming of spring. Purim (March) commemorates the overthrow of the wicked Haman who was the victim of his own plot to destroy the Jews. Hannukah (December) celebrates the triumph of the Maccabean revolt against the Greeks and the miracle of the flask of oil which burned for seven days. Rosh Hashana (September-October) the Jewish New Year, signals that the summer is over and that a new year is about to begin. It may or may not be significant — but it is certainly interesting — that three of these holidays, Passover, Purim and Hannukah, celebrate victories. In each, the weak Jews, with the help of God and a hero — Moses, Esther, the Maccabees — emerge triumphant. So with Independence Day, in 1948.

Internal tourism is a major integrating mechanism and a great deal of travelling goes on. A survey has shown that more than two-thirds of the population have visited Caesarea, Hebron, Safed, the Negev. Three-quarters have visited a kibbutz and half the population have visited the Israel museum in Jerusalem. The country meets itself on the road and at historical and national sites. Israel abounds in places to visit, and because of the country's small size, these places are accessible. Also, the same places can be seen over and over from different points of view. Caesarea is an example. An informed visitor can see Caesarea as a Crusader, a Patriarch, as early Christian, a Roman, a Zionist, or as a tourist surfer or golfer.

A steady stream of Israelis makes its way to Eilat on the Red Sea coast and the serenity and solitude to be found along a 240-kilometre stretch of Sinai Desert coastline. This is the Israeli Riviera, and Eilat is its centre. Israelis drive there but foreigners mostly arrive by jet, the planes screaming to a stop just metres from a row of luxury hotels along the edge of the Red Sea. Eilat may be the only community in the world with its international airfield almost down the town's main street. The Israelis are proud of Eilat and its development. The town's real attraction is scuba-diving among the coral reefs and fish shoals of the Red Sea.

The most adventurous way to travel from Eilat to Sharm el-Sheikh at the southern tip of the Sinai is to go by the amphibious craft operated by one of the tourist companies. It is all rough and ready and instructions for the tourists undertaking the desert odyssey are candid. Toilet facilities: 'None'. In the desert you do as the Bedouin do.

For all their liking for the great outdoors Israelis spend most of the time that can be called leisure inside their own or somebody else's home. A recent survey[1] expressed this fact in simple statistics: 'Discretionary' time (excluding work, household, sleep, meals, prayer) is 31 hours a week; 25-30 per cent of this time is spent outside the home, of which only a small proportion, 5 per cent, is spent in cinema, theatre, coffee house, discothèque. Half of the home time is spent in visiting and conversation, the other half with the media. That most leisure is spent at home, and that so much out of home leisure is spent visiting other homes, is significant.

The Israelis are devoted to music. The fact that 23 per cent of the population own a musical instrument confirms the high interest in musical expression. The Israelis are as knowledgeable about classical and serious music as they are about the Bible.

Tickets for concerts of the Israel Philharmonic Orchestra are at a premium and are sometimes sold years in advance. One would think that with the orchestra presenting three or four programmes a week there would be seats for everybody, but the demand cannot be satisfied. Israelis collect conductors as well as performances and want to hear the orchestra perform under every one of the several conductors officiating during the season.

Cultivated by the German Jewish migrants to Israel in the 1930s, symphonic and chamber music in Israel quickly achieved international fame and generated a myth that subscription tickets are obtainable only through inheritance. Here the ethnic gap, the generation gap and the education gap are larger than in other areas of Israel's social life but younger conductors and imaginative impresarios are reducing the gap and many younger people can be seen at symphony concerts.

In its 1977 season the Israel Philharmonic Orchestra performed 220 concerts, an incredible number by international comparison. The Orchestra earns about 64 per cent of its budget from its ticket sales and subscriptions; the government contributes only 25 per cent. It has 37,500 subscribers, another remarkably high figure. As one of the most sought-after orchestras, the IPO has crowded programmes; during a month in Australia it performed 16 concerts. Another interesting orchestra is the Kibbutz Chamber Orchestra, with its 29 members. Founded in 1974 by Noam Sheriff, the KCO meets every week for practice and gives concerts all over the country.

Israel is as rich in public art as in music. Art objects and statuary can be seen on all the campuses, and at memorial sites such as Yad Vashem, in the city squares, at the airport, opposite beaches and along the main highways you come across large abstract sculptures. No Jerusalem school is without sculptures, fountains and murals; one per cent of building construction funds are apportioned by law from the education budget for school public art.

There are sculptured playgrounds, 'environments' and memorials, from Karavan's Negev Brigade memorial at Beersheba to the 'tank graveyard' at Yamit and the splendidly evocative infantry memorial north of Jericho in the Jordan Valley. Functional buildings and even spaces assume sculptural forms, like Rechter's Kikar Atarim on the Tel Aviv beachfront, Hecker's polyhedral synagogues and Kiesler's Shrine of the Book. Landscaping also takes on sculptural aspects, as do Noguchi's garden at the Israel Museum and Plebsner's Liberty Bell Garden. Among the most interesting and controversial — 'What's it supposed to be?' — is Kadishman's 'Three Discs' which dominate the Mann Auditorium square and the Habimah Theatre circle in Tel Aviv. And one of the most dominating is Tumatkin's Holocaust Memorial in another Tel Aviv square.

Kadishman's 'Three Discs', one atop the other set at a 45 degree angle as if defying gravity, looms above a main road and blocks a view of the Mann Auditorium. It is a fine sculpture in the wrong place but the placing is understandable; Israeli sculptors and their patrons, who are often municipal councils, want their work to be seen not only at a distance but by a regular procession of people on foot and in vehicles. These works say, 'Look at me! I'm worth noticing!' Just like Israelis themselves.

The Holocaust Memorial (Tumatkin) in Tel Aviv's biggest public square is an ingenious inverted pyramid of metal and glass with inner lighting at night. It descends to a tabernacle housing a twisted metal assemblage symbolizing the Holocaust destructions. The closer you draw to the sculpture the more you respond and when you are inside it you react the way most Israelis would want you to — you feel revolted by the hideous waste of the Holocaust. Unfortunately, the sculpture clashes with its city background, including fair booths; the square cannot tolerate the memorial and the booths.

Israeli public statues cannot be ignored; they provoke, they intrigue, they entertain, perhaps occasionally they exasperate. The best-loved and most photographed work in Jerusalem is a sentimental sculpture of a woman and two children by Haim Gross outside the maternity wing of Hadassah Hospital in Ein Karem. It entices children into its satisfying shapes and the smaller ones fold themselves comfortably into the mother's arms.

A piece of statuary which I find appealing is the non-sculpture of a woman carrying a dead child. Composed by Ilana Goor, it is a sculptural compound of apparently unrelated pieces and a first reaction is to say 'It doesn't look a bit like a woman carrying a dead child'. That's the point. The piece is in the grounds of the Holocaust Memorial Museum, Yad Vashem, where an actual woman figure carrying a child figure would be too brutal and stark, too cruelly identifiable. So the sculptor has left its identification to the imagination of the viewer. Elsewhere, one can find the traditional neo-classic sculpture of Nathan Rappaport, with its human figures ranging from childhood to old age, all of them victims.

Occasionally real controversy erupts around a piece of sculpture as it did in 1976 with Ilana Goor's 'Woman in the Wind', a large expressionist bronze in Yarkon Street park, Tel Aviv. Perhaps the civil authorities were trying to compete with Tel Aviv's red light district, just behind the statue. The statue's subject is recognizable, if with difficulty, but this has not appeased Tel Aviv's ratepayers, some of whom have promised unrelenting hostility until the great bronze is removed.

One of the most influential public artists was Yitzhak Danziger, who was killed in a car accident in the summer of 1977. Not only a sculptor but a draughtsman, artist, landscape gardener, ecologist, teacher and thinker, Danziger understood that a piece of sculpture should be part of its background. When acting as a judge for a competition for a monument to the fallen of the Six-Day War on the Golan Heights, he saw with a peculiarly Israeli sense of vision, that the chosen site did not need a monument. With a sacred grove on one side and Mount Hermon on the other, he asked for a 'landscaped sculpture' where Israelis on pilgrimage could rest and find peace. In 1970 he made the most unusual contribution to a 'Concept and Information' exhibition at the Israel Museum; it was 60 square meters of chicken wire covered with layers of jute, newsprint and plastic containing perforated pipes and on this artificial eco-system Danziger created a living painting of green shoots that flourished as the show progressed.

147

His major work was on the rehabilitation of the Nesher Quarry on Mount Carmel, to transform the ravaged site into a garden — mostly planted in soil contained in wire baskets and in niches on the quarry face.

Statistics are supposed to show that Israelis attend cinemas more often than any people on earth. I would have thought that the Hong Kong Chinese and the Indians might hold the record, but no, the Israelis do. Each Israeli sees at least 25 films a year. The figure could be higher because kibbutzniks view at least one film a week and in army camps, youth clubs and cultural groups, where films are shown free, no statistics are available but they are probably high. A brief explanation is probably that the Israelis go to the cinema to ease their tension and to relax. But there are other reasons. Young people go because they have few places where they can get together in private — the cinema is blessedly dark. Many people attend because films are the sole outside-the-home evening entertainment which is cheap. Again Israel is so small and the besieged Israelis are so hungry for the big world outside that they believe that they find it in films. Their appetite is undiscriminating and virtually insatiable; they gobble up whatever is offered in any langauge. They prefer Hebrew sub-titles but they will cope with any language without complaint.

The main achievement of the Israeli national film industry has been in developing the Israel-Jewish image. Significantly, Jews from abroad are often depicted as figures of fun. Sex scenes are rare in Israeli-made films. Israeli actors are notoriously camera-shy when it comes to love-making. They will lie apparently nude in bed with a blanket pulled up to their noses but directors find it next to impossible to induce them to kiss passionately. These actors are worried about offending their families and are concerned that other people might think less of them. This attitude underlines the tiny size of the country.

Radio in Israel is closely tied to the need to be alert. Before the advent of day-time television in Britain, radio-listening in Israel outdistanced radio-listening in Britain by at least 15 per cent at any hour of an average day. A rise in tension in the country is at once reflected in a rise in attention to news bulletins. The radio is the important link between the individual and the nerve centre of society. Information programmes have the highest proportion of regular listeners — two daily news-magazines, at noon and in the evening, head the list.

Television arrived in Israel in 1968, after more than a decade of debate over whether it should be introduced at all. The arguments of its opponents are interesting. They said that it would debase the effort to revive Hebrew culture; that it would impose criteria of personality and charisma on the conduct of politics; that it would replace the goals of productivity with the values of leisure and consumerism; that it would make the people passive. The arguments of the pro-television group were more compelling but it was not until Ben-Gurion stepped down from the premiership that television became a practical possibility. Then by June 1970 fully 58 per cent of Israeli adults had television in their homes. Few Israelis are now without access to a television set.

It is ironic, perhaps, that television is most popular on Friday night — the beginning of the Sabbath. For some people television provides the only recreational facility on a Friday night and for a good many, I suspect, it is the only alternative to loneliness. On an evening in which a high premium is traditionally placed on cultural uplift and social recreation — and yet a time when most means of public entertainment are closed down — the opportunities afforded by television become dramatic. The single most popular television programme is the news magazine, attracting, according to the Israeli Television Authority, about 70 per cent of the population. This stresses the Israeli hunger for news. If Israeli television has any unique quality, it is the programming in Arabic. This is an attempt to combine politics, entertainment and information for presentation to Israeli Arabs and the million Arabs in the occupied territories.

Television has not adversely affected theatre attendance. Israel's theatre productions attract about 3.3 million spectators each year — a figure which could well be the highest in the world for the size of population. In May one year I counted 30 plays in Hebrew, (including two by Shakespeare), four in Yiddish and

149

two in English. I probably missed a few others. The quality of the plays is high — Miller, Molière, Strindberg, Gogol, Pinter. The Israelis are hungry for theatre but not so hungry that they will buy tickets for anything.

Light entertainment has several distinctly different facets. One style is produced by electronic western-type rock groups. Another has its roots in Army entertainment troupes, small groups of spirited young men and girls singing and pantomiming ballads and songs. A third type involves a solo singer backed by a group of musicians and singers.

Israel has its rock artists, talented and often angry young performers like Danny Litani, Danny Sanderson and Ariel Zilber. Their songs used to deal largely with politics and the conditions of life in Israel, but personal themes have become more typical. Litani says he sings 'window songs' — the view he gets from his kitchen window.

Collectively, the amount of culture and entertainment offered to Israelis is impressive. The four largest cities — Tel Aviv, Jerusalem, Haifa, Ramat-Gan — each provides its people with 200 to 300 different events in the course of a month. Some are multiple performances, as in the cinema, but many are once-only events, such as a lecture or meeting.

While swimming is popular as an individual or family activity only one sport in Israel can be classified as mass entertainment — soccer. On most Saturdays outside the worst heat of summer about 300 adult games take place, attracting perhaps 160,000 spectators. On a Saturday when games are played as part of a tournament or league as many as 200,000 Israelis will watch. Apart from this activity lesser soccer games are taking place all over the country. Soccer is played with vigour bordering on combat training roughness and sometimes with a skill comparable to top level European football. The game has a benefit which probably never crosses the minds of those who play or watch it: it provides a means of integrating Jews of different racial origins that nothing else could equal.

It is possible to find a game of cricket on some of the Anglo-Saxon kibbutzim — though the umpiring and its language might confuse an English cricketer. When I heard a kibbutznik umpire talking about 'ell pee topple you' it took me all of a minute to comprehend — and I am a long-time cricketer.

Sports lotteries are a popular activity in Israel, together with other publicly managed lotteries. The most popular of all is the national lottery, Payis. Over 40 per cent of the population invest at least once a month in one or more lotteries.

Surveys of Israelis and their hobbies produce some puzzling results. For instance, the emancipated Israeli woman does not come strongly to light; she is busy with the 'hobbies' of baking, cooking and knitting! The image of cerebral preoccupation is also not supported; men are playing chess, but this is a stereo-typed activity. Hobby surveys do not even begin to glimpse the outdoor physically fit Israeli. Still, about six in 10 Israelis have more or less regular hobbies, with age and education the domi-nant factors. The higher the education, the more hobbyists; the younger the person, the more hobbies. Men's hobbies are collecting, sports, chess, raising pets. Men and women list art and music — but more men than women.

As a rule, Israelis collect nothing bigger than postage stamps. They would like to do so but they have neither money nor the time to indulge in collecting. And if they did, mama would quickly point out that they do not have the space. I am excluding records, and perhaps I shouldn't, for the stereo record-player is ubiquitous and a good selection of records can be found in most homes.

The Israeli taste in art is discriminating and the people as a whole delight in light, bright colours. The country has plenty of galleries — new ones open each month — and they are well patronized. I have visited galleries in many countries and have often found myself alone; this does not happen in Israel. There is also no strained hush as if in the presence of death; Israelis do not conceal their enjoyment of galleries.

But what is one to say about Israeli painting? The work on display is varied, competent and interesting but it does not appear to be peculiarly Israeli in genre. Nearly every art form that has developed has been based on cultures and approaches that have evolved in Europe and America. Some Israeli artists are well known — Louise Schatz, Yosl Bergner, Napthali Bezem — for example, but the only one I know whose work is derived from local sources is Shalom Moscovitz, now known as Shalom of Safad. He began painting in his sixties, specializing in illustrations of biblical themes. His style is derived from that of eighteenth- and nineteenth- century Jewish folk artists of Safad who painted on glass.

The best known art critic, Meir Ronnen, writing in *The Jerusalem Post* in 1978, said that, 'It is inevitable as it is desirable that Israeli artists seek to discover universal truths rather than conditional local ones.' Noting that the Holocaust still overshadows all Israeli experiences, Ronnen believes that artists trying to give the Holocaust direct expression have failed.

Whatever the finer criticisms, Israeli art is aesthetically and intellectually satisfying. Avigdor Arikha's 'En Silence' is an evocative multi-coloured splurge, rather as if a bomb had gone off on a palette and the blast had given fire and form to the thrown paint. Mordecai Levanon's 'Jerusalem Landscape' captures the entire essence of Jerusalem without his scene looking conventionally like Jerusalem. Holocaust themes are introspective but, surprisingly perhaps, introspection is otherwise rare. Pessimism does not appear to afflict Israeli artists and possibly in this they are reflecting the Israeli outlook. When they become 'universal' in theme — hardly to be expected of artists in a country only a few decades old — they will find their work more universally appreciated.

12 Settlement and Stress

The Israelis are self evidently not a homogeneous people in origin; nearly half are of Asian and African stock, and are totally different from the Europeans. But today, the principal distinction is not between the various traditional communities but between all these and the increasing number of Hebrew youth, embodied in the Sabra, the Israeli-born youth, who is particularly non-Jewish in appearance, outlook and horizons.

It would have been so easy for Israel to develop as 'two nations' — occidental and oriental, well-off and poor, educated and ignorant, the self-satisfied and the socially resentful. Perhaps it is surprising that three nations did not develop — the Sabras, the European Jews and the oriental Jews.

From the beginning the state-builders — the 'proud doers' as Ian McIntyre called them[1] — saw the dangers. To avoid the divisions they set out to mould relatively traditional societies into a specific modern pattern, as the U.S.S.R., Yugoslavia and Mexico did in their own ways. The four basic tools in this moulding have been, probably in ascending order of importance, the schools, religious institutions, the Hebrew language and the Army. Virtually all immigrants have gone on entry to an absorption centre for a basic course in Hebrew langauge and Israeliness. This training provides a blueprint; the various institutions transform the blueprint into the finished article.

The Histadrut — the great labour organization — must be given some of the credit for the unifying process. From the beginning it was the most important organization of the many which affected the life of the Israeli citizen. It controlled areas of

153

work, and for a long time access to work through the various labour exchanges, health services and a large part of the access to housing and other basic necessities. Everyone in Israel, salaried or self-employed executive or labourer, receives complete medical security from spectacles to heart surgery, for himself and his family, for as little as a few dollars a month. These benefits held in common have heightened the sense of unity.

Israel has always had a remarkable number of voluntary community service organizations. In Jerusalem alone, at the end of the mandatory period, there were 1,146 different organizations, ranging from simple philanthropic aid societies for local children to countrywide associations of different kinds. Most workers' organizations are closely related to and often form part of various general social movements and political parties. Others perform, or used to perform, vital community functions, such as guard duty and defence, medical aid, social welfare, propagation of the Hebrew language, help for co-operative settlements, furthering the consumption of local products, developing various professional and cultural activities.

Israeli society shares important characteristics with other pioneering egalitarian societies such as the United States, Australia, Canada and New Zealand. First, it has a strong emphasis on equality and the consequent lack of any strong, hereditary, feudal, aristocratic landowner class. Second, it shares the development of a strong concentration of various types of economic and administrative activities within broad, unified, organizational frameworks. And, again in common with other pioneering societies, Zionist settlement emphasized the conquest of wasteland through work — as shown in the expansion of productive, primary occupations.

While it is true that Israelis tend to live in ethnic groups this has little if anything to do with class distinctions. Anywhere in the world most people are happier among people they understand, so Yemenite Jews prefer to live in a suburb or settlement of Yemenites, just as English-speaking Israelis prefer to live in clusters. As the state grows older and mobility and integration increases the ethnic residential grouping will become much weaker, especially under impetus of mixed marriage. There used to be a distinct pecking order among Israel's ethnic groups, both old and new. The Jewish writer, Chaim Bermant, said, 'The Russians look down on the Poles, the Poles on the Hungarians, the Hungarians on the Rumanians; everybody looks down on the North Africans, and the English look down on everybody else.'[2]

The difficulties of turning Russians, Poles, Hungarians, Rumanians, North Africans, Englishmen, Yemenites and Iraqis into Israelis in an Israeli society can hardly be overemphasized. For instance, Yemenite children once married between the age of nine and 11, and the father ruled supreme over the family group. This situation no longer applies but puberty is dificult for the Yemenite girl because her mother serves neither as an example nor as a counsellor and her father finds his traditional role weakened when his sons pick up a new set of attitudes in school.

The relative helplessness among orientals and their dependence on the state is shown by a single statistic: about 80 per cent of the people living on welfare or supported by it are orientals.

Again, life is initially hard for immigrants from communist countries with no experience in competing for work in a democratic world. Communist countries provide jobs, even dictate them, and the fact than an employer in Israel is free to hire or not at his own discretion — and that they themselves have a choice of jobs — is a mind-boggling concept for these communist-world immigrants.

An extensive folklore exists about the real or ascribed attributes of the various groups. The Rumanians, for instance, are held to be untrustworthy and light-fingered. Ian McIntyre reports that a man said to him, 'Beersheba means the town of seven walls, but since so many Rumanians came to live here it's had to be amended to three'.[3]

The columns of the Israeli newspaper used to be full of articles and letters which demonstrate the contrasting attitudes to immigration of the western Jew and the Sabra, 'Let the people come here who want to be like us, others should stay away', a young university-educated Israeli pronounced. 'I like the Yemenite immigrants because whatever you do for them, they appreciate it. Give them a new home, a job, a loan — they appreciate it. Not like the Americans who only come and complain — who get everything and then demand still more. If the Americans don't like it here and don't want to live our way they shouldn't come. We don't need them.'[4]

But Israel does need Americans. I believe that the quality that has drawn American Jews to Israel is that in Israel the individual still counts for something, whereas in the amorphous American society he counts for little. Israel needs immigrants from wherever they can be found among the twelve million Jews of the diaspora. Many of them will go to live in the new towns, as Tel Aviv is already too big and Jerusalem, by its nature, is limited in the number of jobs it can provide. Land for new kibbutzim is also limited while that for individual farmers is even more difficult to find. So, as any Israeli handbook will tell you, Israel has become an urbanized society with 30 per cent of the population living in the three major cities, Tel Aviv, Jerusalem, and Haifa; 52 per cent in other towns and cities and 18 per cent in the countryside. The equality-based rural communes, while retaining great political influence, and while playing a disproportionately important role in the nation's economy, comprise less than five per cent of the population.

Brought up on problems, the Israeli mind is always seeking solutions to a multitude of clamant crises. One enormous social problem was how to prevent a drift from the small country towns to the large cities, especially of younger people seeking a wider range of stimulation. One part-solution was the creation of the Israel Community Centre Corporation, a classic exercise in self-help. Each of the 75 centres is based on the assumption that a clientele for community services must be cultivated, especially among disadvantaged populations.

An Israeli community centre is like an English one only in that it has a games and play area; other facilities include a laundry with washing machines, a well-stocked library, art studio, practice kitchens, white-tiled bathrooms, meeting and lecture rooms, workshops for carpentry and metalwork, a music room, and perhaps a museum. The lovely biblical city of Safad has three centres, one of them made from a building which had at various times been a Turkish administrative headquarters, a British gaol and a Jewish old-age home.

In England and other countries a community centre is used or it isn't — little attempt is made to 'sell' it. The Israeli approach is more positive; workers from the centre go out and bring in the people through soft-sell techniques. In Kiryat Shemona the community centre staff realized that many people among the 16,000 population did not know what the centre had to offer, so they trained seven women as para-professional community workers to go to the outlying areas and work with people of their own background, be it Moroccan, Syrian or East European. In many cases the first job of the centre's girl is to induce the woman of the family just to leave the house for a while; then she will build on this breakthrough to interest the woman in exhibitions, talks and finally some participation. But the community worker's functions go much further than this: she strives to bring children into the centre's activities, perhaps through a branch clubhouse, and she gives advice on problems which her 'clients' would not reveal to 'official' social or welfare workers. Perhaps the most important task of the centre's girl is to encourage the people of her area to take the lead, to operate the activities she has set up — the housewives' club or the children's play group, for instance.

Israel's community centres are not financed by the government but by various private benefactors and organizations. The newest Safad centre was one-third paid for by the Wolfson Trust in England.

Some visiting experts is community relations, as well as Israelis with a more academic approach, say that no community centre should be opened until a trained staff is available to operate it. The workers already involved with the centres say, 'Yes, that would be ideal' and go on with their labours, for they found out long ago, as have Israelis in other fields, that you don't have to know how to swim before you can dive. If you go in head first you will come to the surface and somehow it will work out.

Ordinary Israeli society can be seen at work in the unprepossessing suburb of Katamon in south Jerusalem. Katamon, built in a hurry in the 1960s, suffers from what more affluent Israelis call the 'social gap'. and has become an area of intense sociological, demographic and ethnic research. About half of Katamon's oriental population is of Kurdish origin and the atmosphere generally is restive, critical and suspicious, especially among the younger generation made so sceptical by the Yom Kippur War: the hint of defeat weakened their trust in Israel's leaders.

Katamon has many 'disadvantaged' people, though their deprivation lies in various fields. Some are unskilled labourers who keep their large families above the poverty line with the help of National Insurance children's allowances. Some are poor, large 'problem' families, constantly in need of help from the welfare officers and the police. Yet others have educational problems. A major problem in Katamon is that many parents feel that their children should be getting an academic education rather than a vocational one, though the latter would probably be more suitable. This creates social tensions. These particular Israelis do not know much about foreign attitudes to Israel beyond the inescapable fact that 'They are against us'. They are too caught up in the mechanics of survival to delve into reasons for Arab hostility and world indifference and ignorance. Family-centred and suburb-oriented, they live in general misery despite the efforts of many other Israelis to solve their problems. In one part of Katamon families with up to 13 children live in apartments ranging from 42 to 65 square metres and the father is out of work. He could have a job, but he probably comes from an Arab or Kurdish background where men do not consider work as part of life.

An extraordinary settlement — extraordinary because it really should not be where it is — is Mitzpe Ramon. It lies in the heart of naked Negev Desert and it is 35 kilometers from Sde Boker, the nearest habitation. The Negev capital, Beersheba, is 90 kilometers distant. Mitzpe Ramon is also improbably placed on the edge of a cliff which drops steeply into a depression. For a long time there had been a small town at Mitzpe Ramon, its reason for existence being that it served as a halfway house on the long road to Eilat, 162 kilometers away. When a new highway was built, nowhere near Mitzpe Ramon, the town lost its reason for existence and most of its inhabitants moved away. But the Israeli mind is capable of defying economic logic and some enterprising town planners, encouraged by the Ministry of the Interior, decided to build a new type of town, best described to me by one of its creators. 'We are building in the most isolated and completely undeveloped part of the desert a town which will offer its inhabitants a quality of life, both physical and spiritual, that they will not find anywhere else. Whatever we add will be designed to maintain the unique and dramatic environment with its unpopulated atmosphere. We hope to attract people who want to leave the closely settled and overcrowded centre of the country.'

The plan is to bring in 10,000 people, many of them to work in industries attracted by subsides, generous loan and other assistance. Typically, the apartment buildings are planned around gardens, parks, tree-groves, and playgrounds. In every empty space is a small garden or park with coloured benches and sandpits.

As clean as a Swiss village, Mitzpe Ramon is heavily committed to the quality of life, so one of its first public buildings was the cultural centre and sports complex. The cultural programme includes twice-weekly public music lessons and performances in the auditorium by actors from Tel Aviv and Haifa. The air is crystal clear and the sky is ever blue, but the very existence of the town leaves a foreign visitor dumbfounded. How can a settlement prosper in a landscape where even Bedouin do not live and where rain is virtually unknown? One good practical reason is that the Israelis know better than anybody else how to coax water from deep underground. The other reason is less easy to analyze but its existence is proven by the success of Mitzpe Ramon — the will to make the improbable come true.

The new towns on the Golan Heights — all built since 1967 — are dull as towns but in terms of their people they show an interesting side of the Israeli mind. One such town is Katzrin, founded on the tenth anniversary of Israeli settlement on the Golan. Named after a Jewish town in ancient Palestine, Katzrin is in the middle of a plateau of black soil and greyish basalt and was built as a link in the overall strategy to hold the plateau against Syrian encroachment; it is 12 miles from the cease-fire lines with Syria. The vision behind Katzrin is immense. The town is planned around eight self-contained neighbourhoods, each with 650 dwelling units. Each neighbourhood is to have its own shopping centre, school and other institutions. A green belt separates an industrial estate from the residential areas. Prospective settlers must be approved by an admissions committee, which wants to know if the settler and his family stand a good chance of making a living in the early stages of the town's development. The last thing a town like Katzrin needs are social problems which would burden it with welfare cases.

The settlers here range in age from 20 to 40, though I found an enterprising couple of 60. What motivates Israelis — most of them well established in the country and not recent arrivals — to want to found a place like Katzrin? One finds an interesting link between people's personal and national needs. 'We came to fulfil a national need', more than one couple told me. Personal opportunity is equally important. In the case of one couple the husband is an agronomist and his wife an agricultural economist, and in Katzrin there are jobs for both.

Building a new town and a new life from scratch can be exhilarating, especially in the clear air and the great views of the Golan — you can see the Jordan River and the Sea of Galilee. And here we come to official if not personal motivation about the existence of Katzrin. When the Syrians dominated these heights they too could see the Israeli farms below, and they attacked them. Once again, the Israelis' desperate need for security becomes evident.

But Israelis have more in common than a security consciousness. Landscape has a special importance for a people returned

160

from exile and there seems to be a relationship between this and the Israeli passion for archaeology. It is just about impossible to find a parallel of the same degree in the western world. Tens of thousands of Israelis dig enthusiastically. For them, digging up the past is a form of self-assertion because it is their own past, their Jewish past. To unearth Herod's palaces at Masada or the remains of a Canaanite city destroyed by Joshua is an affirmation of their right to be there today, a symbolic title to the legitimacy of the state. Archaeology provides physical proof of their existence in Israel as a people. When the Israelis see mosaics with Hebrew inscriptions, coins, Solomon's stables in Megiddo they are moved. I think they project the present both back into the past and forward into the future.

Despite the shared dedication to making Israel work as a society and as an economic unit, stress is evident to the professional observer. Indeed, with the rapid expansion of settlement and increase in mobility in Israel stress can be seen in almost every aspect of life. It becomes noticeable, for instance, in a variety of daily occurrences — as in the great congestion on the roads and the number of road accidents, due both to the inadequacy of the roads and to the impatience and lack of courtesy among drivers. Stress is also evident in the general impatience of people and the lack of basic manners.

Foreigners on a first visit take more exception to an Israeli's lack of courtesy than other Israelis do. They do not mean to be discourteous; it is just that they are preoccupied with their problems and in a hurry. Also, they are on the defensive because they tend to assume that a gentile is critical of them or against them — until he proves otherwise. This is an historical hangover made worse by the general anti-Israel plotting carried out by some countries at the United Nations.

Some stress situations are serious and most are annoying but some diminish with time and all can be explained as manifestations of Israeli dynamism. The foreign visitor soon senses the stress on the roads. Israel is a country of road users and the growth of motorized vehicles since 1948 has been spectacular. In 1978 the number of privately-owned cars was 220,000, plus

85,000 trucks and trailers, 45,000 motor cycles and scooters, 5,300 buses and 4,000 taxis.[5] This works out at roughly one vehicle for 14 Israelis and 47 vehicles to every kilometre of highway. All 47 usually chase and overtake me, except when I am driving in the lovely Jordan Valley, the Negev or on the back road from Jerusalem to the Tel Aviv interchange near Nachshon.

The Egged Company, with a fleet of well over 2,500 buses, is surpassed in size only by Greyhound in the U.S.A. and London Transport in England. As bus drivers, the Egged drivers handle their buses as if they were tanks; not one of them seems to have noticed that their passengers are made of flesh and bone and blood, all three of which are at risk aboard an Egged bus.

The sherut taxi is an Israeli idea which other countries might do well to copy to ease traffic congestion and reduce the cost of owning private cars. The sherut, a leftover from the early years of statehood when public transport was in short supply, is a large car fitted to take up to seven passengers. They operate between the larger city centres and between almost all sizeable towns on fixed routes and fairly regular schedules; generally the driver leaves base when he has a full load. On some popular runs sheruts may be hailed from the kerbside but they tend to operate from fixed addresses which vary according to the destinations involved. Sheruts do a flourishing business late at night and on Friday evenings and Saturdays when other forms of public transport are scarce. Fares are about 10 to 30 per cent higher than those of buses but much cheaper than an ordinary taxi.

Another kind of stress is evident in Mea Shearim, the orthodox suburb of Jerusalem. Clinging fiercely to their Jewishness in dress, personal appearance, life-style and values, the people of Mea Shearim sometimes seem to be practically at war with their fellow Israelis. Authority is patriarchal and forbidding, as is shown by a sign in the market place. In Hebrew, Yiddish and English it reads: 'Jewish daughters, the Torah obliges you to dress with modesty. We do not tolerate people passing through our streets immodestly dressed. *Committee for Guarding Modesty*.' The committee can bite as well as bark. Women passing through Mea Shearim's streets on the Sabbath wearing shorts or short-sleeved blouses will be chased out by stone-throwing orthodox vigilantes. The Israelis generally know better than to make this mistake but every so often an 'indecently clad' woman tourist becomes a target for stones. Drivers careless or ignorant enough to enter Mea Shearim on the Sabbath will have their cars stoned.

In another orthodox area near Tel Aviv the guardians of the Sabbath string heavy chains across the main road to keep out unwelcome traffic; a young Israeli driver was killed when he ran into a chain. Normally, these orthodox Israelis are mild mannered enough, keeping themselves to themselves, but the Sabbath seems to arouse a mean streak.

Financial tensions have brought about some changes in the Israeli way of life. For years the Israeli haughtily refused tips. Tourists helped to foster the acceptance of tips and the high cost of living made it almost imperative. Still, the tip must be offered; the demanding outstretched hand, so common in other Middle Eastern countries, has not yet appeared in Israel.

Crime is another tension — or the result of tension — and the rate is growing — a steady seven per cent per annum increase in crimes against the person, against property, and in economic crime. It should be said, though, that Israel, like France, has never been a country in which respect for laws, rules and bye-laws, has reigned supreme. This applied equally to the old pre-state Yishuv. Casual attitudes to the law are a hangover from the past. The Jews of the Yishuv broke British laws which they felt put them at a disadvantage compared with the Arabs; the Jews of Europe and of oriental countries could hardly have existed had they obeyed the law implicity. There remains a suspicion that the law is oppressive and coercive even when it is purely administrative. For reasons which seemed sound at the time Jewish leaders encouraged their followers to break laws, so it is not surprising that the Israel community as a whole has only gradually approached a complete acceptance of administrative law.

Israeli police are tough and clever but they do not beat up suspects in order to get confessions. Police have cultivated the anonymous telephone call and although most of what they hear in these calls is slanderous and abusive some information is valuable in trapping criminals. Shaul Rosalio, just before he retired from the position of Inspector General of the Israel Police Force, told me that Israel has no organized crime in the international sense. 'I've never heard of a protection-operator who tried to take over an entire street, let alone an entire quarter, or an entire chain of businesses. Sometimes you find crime with sophistication but people who talk loosely about syndicates are doing a great injustice to the country. The Israeli public is not prepared to tolerate that sort of system.'

Nevertheless, organized crime does exist, as the Shimron Committee revealed in its Report on Organized Crime in 1978. It is not exactly in the model of the Mafia but some crimes need large-scale organising and financing. The Committee named 16 men as leaders of the underworld, involved in drugs, smuggling and thefts from ports, and 'black money' — funds gained illegally or without taxes being paid on them, often through illicit diamond trading. Organized extortion and protection rackets are notably absent; as Shaul Rosalio says, Israelis do not tolerate bullying.

A reporter writing in *The Jerusalem Post* (7 August, 1978) noted that while crime in Israel is less than in many western countries, 'We must not ignore the fact that crime and disrespect for the law have seriously affected the quality of our life, our national economy, and, most serious of all, the inner fibre of our society.'

Among juveniles there are almost no cases of robbery, murder, arson or extortion; rape is virtually non-existent and even minor sex offences occur only on a small scale. Another phenomenon is that there are practically no gangs among delinquents. Juveniles might commit an offence together but they do not constitute a gang. The basic elements of a gang — an offender with leadership qualities exercising his influence on a group of others for the purpose of committing delinquent acts — are conspicuously lacking.

Sadly, drug abuse has become widespread since the Six-Day War of 1967. Volunteer workers and students from abroad who are accustomed to using drugs continue to use them in Israel. Israel is situated on the crossroads between the great hashish producers, and since the Six-Day War and the breaking down of many barriers illegal traffic in drugs has increased considerably. Drugs have become rather cheap and easily obtainable. In addition, the urge to imitate, the need to ease stress and the desire to conform to cosmopolitan ideas have been responsible for an easy penetration of drugs.

Neither the police nor any other governmental agency has been able to stem the rising tide of drug usage. One official survey puts the number of addicts at 4,000, most of them in Tel Aviv. This might not be a large number in itself but a similar report in 1976 gave a figure of only 1,600. Doctors and other medical workers may be unwittingly to blame, in that they tend to prescribe barbiturates and tranquillisers without much reflection on their possibly addictive effects. According to the Buchner Report on drug abuse, published in February 1978, about 600 individuals in Israel are engaged in smuggling and distributing drugs, including 50 independent importers, wholesalers and financiers. Opium from Turkey or Iran, like hashish from Lebanon, is brought to Israel by way of Jordan and Saudi Arabia. Bedouin in the Sinai transport the drugs to the occupied territories where Arabs take over and pass on the narcotics to their Israeli connections.

Drug-taking might be increasing but abuse of alcohol is not. Drunkenness has no place in Israeli life. You never meet a drunk in an Israeli play, novel or short story; such a character would be unrealistic. The Jews of Israel, as of the diaspora, have a great aversion to the indignity, shame and crudity of drunkenness. You will never see drunken Israeli soldiers or sailors. On ceremonial occasions in the army the tables are stacked with bottles of lemonade, orangeade and grapefruit juice. If an Israeli officer were to get drunk his career would be finished; everybody who knew him would be ashamed for him. The Jewish religion does not forbid strong drink, as Islam does, and the Bible has many precedents for drinking fermented liquour, but the people seem to have applied an unwritten law.

165

An Israeli drinking in the family circle is particularly careful not to step across the border of sobriety; he wants his character to be impeccable in his children's eyes.

But Israel cannot claim uniqueness in the matter of prostitution. It has its harlots and accepts them as a fact of life; their numbers are officially estimated at somewhere between 1,500 and 2,000, (including a good many Arab women) not a high figure for a population of 3,500,000.

There could well be more girls on the street but for a counselling service introduced by the Welfare Ministry in 1970 as a way of rehabilitating 2,000 girls between the ages of 13 and 21 considered to be morally at risk. A pilot project — a club for teenage girls which combines individual counselling with group work — has been successful. The club was established in the northern development town of Migdal Ha'emek where a co-operative municipality provided an empty apartment and a budget for two young youth workers, Mazal, a Yemenite and Rachel, a Moroccan. They furnished the living room with couches, easy chairs, colourful rugs and posters, magazines, a tape recorder, a small stereo and records, and games; the kitchen was equipped with everything needed for cooking and baking. One bedroom became an office, the other an activity centre. As with so much that is Israeli, the youth workers did not wait for customers — they went looking for them. Frequenting the town's coffee houses and teenage hangouts, they soon found the 28 girls whose names appeared on a list compiled by local probation officers, policemen, teachers and social workers. Most were girls in conflict with their parents and had run away to spend days or weeks wandering around Eilat or the Tel Aviv central bus station. They were promiscuous and often took money or gifts for sexual intercourse but did not consider this prostitution. Mazal and Rachel, who dressed much like the girls they sought to contact, told anyone who was interested that they were available for 'just talking' and that the clubhouse was open from morning till night. Seventeen girls began to turn up regularly, as well as 18 non-problem girls who were invited to be members in order to ensure that no stigma would be attached to Beitenu (Our House).

Classes were arranged in home economics and drama, a psychologist gave regular talks and a nurse dropped in to chat about menstruation, pregnancy and venereal disease. There were group discussions or daughter-parents relations, dating conflicts, the meaning of 'boyfriend', how to avoid provocative situations. Rachel and Mazal never worked with a girl unless they had consulted her parents; it was important for families to understand what they were trying to achieve and why things had gone wrong in the family. 'The intentions of parents are usually good but their backgrounds didn't prepare them for raising their children in a modern secular society,' Rachel told me.

The club was successful and others have been started, with methods and environments adapted to particular localities. The youth workers, all women aged 30 or less, have done what many people considered impossible because they reached the impressionable, rebellious and confused girls before their deterioration had gone too far and before vice as a way of life had become fixed. Over a two-year period, Beitenu had only two or three 'failures' out of 65 girls in distress and other such clubs report a similar success rate.

13 Civil Religion Orthodox Judaism

Anybody who grew up in the cruel reality of the Palestine-Israel of the late 1940s and who had to fight, and kill, see others die and bury many bodies, has difficulty in recognizing the traditional God — the personal, loving God, the God at the source of Jewish tradition, a God full of mercy. After that bitter period came other wars and, even worse, the ruthless cruelty of terrorism. Religion stands out as potentially the sharpest dividing line in Israeli society. Religious people, who are concentrated in the lower educational groups, not only differ from the non-religious in their outlook and behaviour on many things, they are also more cohesive among themselves than the non-religious population.

The sharpest part of the dividing line concerns the attitude of non-observant Israelis towards the orthodox young people who obtain exemption from conscript service. Boys are able to get this exemption on presentation of a letter to the effect that they have been enrolled at a recognized yeshiva or religious school since at least the age of 16. Girls obtain exemption on their own declaration that they are 'religious'. Some of the youths go through the motions of putting in token appearances at a yeshiva for as many years as necessary while they devote the greater part of their time to their own secular careers and private lives. Some girls carry out a form of substitute conscription in the voluntary National Service, serving from one to two years in various capacities in the newer development towns, hospitals and poor areas. Other girls, having declared themselves religious, pursue their private careers, which often have no religious connection; some attend general universities rather than the orthodox Bar-Ilan University. The conscription-evaders among the orthodox Israelis arouse resentment among the great majority who do their service, and even greater resentment among the parents. Some middle-aged orthodox leaders, such as Knesset member Menahem Porush, who is leader of the Agudat Yisrael Party, have said in the Knesset that the Army is no place for a 'true Jewish boy'. Such a comment does great harm to the cause of orthodoxy, since it makes the public infer that Mr Porush and his followers are not doing enough to make the Israel Defence Forces a true Jewish army. The same type of comment also implies that military service is for second-class Israelis who have not the wit to find themselves an escape clause. After Agudat Yisrael became a partner in the Begin coalition government in 1977 the number of exemptions for girls increased sharply. So few girls were available for service, compared with before, that not enough could be spared for Hiba — the women's auxiliary police force. Members of parliament complained that Agudat Yisrael officers were advising girls on stratagems and methods to avoid military service — and so successfully that the exemption rate for 1978 was as much as 50 per cent higher than before the 1977 elections.

It seems to me that unless a good proportion of Orthodox youths, boys and girls, do readily accept military service the orthodox community will find itself held in less and less respect and influence in Israeli public affairs.

Religious issues constitute an important and continuous focus of political debate, as can be seen as early as 1948 when the drafting of the Declaration of Independence caused differences of opinion between the religious representatives and the secular majority. The religious leaders demanded that the Declaration include some religious legitimation of the state. The compromise solution adopted, which quotes 'The Rock Of Israel' instead of 'God', is typical of the many compromises which mark the relationship between state and religion. For a great many Israelis the ties between the two were never strong; a University of Jerusalem survey made in 1978 showed that 85 per cent of them never

169

attend a synagogue. Yet Judaism and the Jewishness of the Jewish State cannot be measured by surveys or synagogue attendance and perhaps is best assessed by the tensions it produces and the compromises it forces.

The desire to return to Israel was largely a movement of non-observant Jews and, with some notable exceptions, religious Jewry only really began to get involved in this national movement when Israel became a state. While the non-observant Zionist movement had about 80 years to adjust to the implications of statehood, the religious bodies have had a much shorter time. The apparent gap may be not so much a religious difference as one based on a time divide.

The rabbinate or Judaistic authority makes its power felt in many ways. For instance, during the summer of 1969 the Broadcasting Authority, a government agency, announced that it would soon schedule programmes seven evenings a week. To obviate religious criticism of working on the Sabbath, Friday evening programmes would carry the prominent notice PREPARED ON WEEKDAYS. At this time there was a general election and Golda Meir's party was five seats short of a majority, which meant a coalition with the National Religious Party. One part of the deal was that the cabinet would order the Broadcasting Authority to cancel its plans for Friday night television. A private citizen took the issue to law and the Supreme Court asked the cabinet to show cause for its decision on no Friday night television. In effect, the 'show cause' order permitted the showing of *The Forsyte Saga*, as well as a weekly review which included belly dancers. A great row blew up between Golda Meir and the chief rabbis — and Golda, with the court's help, won. There was a bonus: road casualties dropped 80 per cent during the Friday television hours.

Advertisers are supposed to submit all proposed advertisements to the rabbinate. One company wished to use an ad based on a picture of a wife sitting on her husband's lap. The rabbi censor rejected it and refused to discuss the matter. The company then showed husband and wife holding hands in the kitchen. This, too, was rejected as too suggestive. The censor finally settled for husband and wife looking at each other in a sorrowful . way while a valentine heart reflected their love.

Because of such absurd situations, many secular Israelis are critical of orthodox rabbis. A leading member of the Kibbutz Religious Movement, Dov Rappel, considers the average rabbi is unable to answer quite simple questions about the Hebrew language and Jewish history and 'does not even know much about such purely religious matters as Bible, religious philosophy and the meaning of prayers ... he is also incapable of giving a religious interpretation to problems of modern life.'[1] Rappel claims that few rabbis set an example in visiting the sick or in trying to make peace among quarrelling neighbours. Nowhere in the world is the position of the rabbi as lowly as it is in Israel, except among the 15-20 per cent of the population which constitutes the religious community.*

The character of the Sabbath is an active issue in Israeli society. Trains and buses do not run except in Haifa and anybody without his own car must rely on taxis. Some religious extremists picket bus stations to see that buses are not taken out too early on Saturday night before the Sabbath ends. To remain open on the Sabbath industries must prove that their continuous operation is vital to national security or economy or that shutting down would do serious damage to the plant. Most theatres are closed as are most coffee houses and restaurants. The newspapers publish supplements on Fridays to tide their customers over until Sunday, and a double ration of milk is delivered on Friday.

There is a strong consensus concerning how people 'ought' to behave on the Sabbath. Most of the population feel that it is

---

*It is significant that though, as a church, Judaism is disorganized and decentralized, it is more uniform in doctrine and observance than the various sects of Christianity and Islam. Judaism has no dogmas and the basis of its belief is the incessant struggle to serve the will of God (Yahweh) in all things. The rules for believers are contained in the Jews' Holy Scripture, the Torah (law) attributed to Moses — the five books of Moses or the Pentateuch. In addition there are the commandments laid down in the collections, Mishna (A.D.200) and Gemera (A.D.500). Mishna and Gemera collectively form the Talmud.

more than just a day of rest; even the non-religious seem to agree that it is also a day of spiritual communion, although the 'spiritual' is often translated into 'cultural'.

Bnei Brak, a town of 90,000, provides an interesting study of Sabbath observance. In fact, it begins to ready itself for the Sabbath somewhere in mid-week, when festive meals are planned and provisions purchased. On Fridays, hectic preparations come to a climax and the streets hustle with activity as young, bewigged mothers wheeling prams rush about for last-minute shopping. The intent large-scale shopping might lead a stranger to think that a long strike was about to commence. Later, the male population hurries out for the ritual cleansing. At nightfall, to the sound of sirens and the light of candles, the Sabbath is ushered in. The transition is both spiritual and palpable. The outside, everyday world is banished from Bnei Brak. Radios are silenced, telephones do not ring and cars do not run. No wallets may be carried and no money handled. Whole families, attired in holiday best, stroll leisurely in mid-street as if the motor car did not exist.

Juvenile delinquency is almost unheard of in Bnei Brak. The small side-curled boys and the giggling little girls who wear long sleeves and long stockings even on the hottest of summer days, are unaware of the generation gap for their parents make extreme attempts to keep the children's minds closed. In 1977 a new community centre was built and included the city's first public library. The decision to have a library was reached after a bitter fight; many Bnei Brak parents claimed that children might be tempted to read secular books or waste precious time filling their minds with 'trivia'. In other ways Bnei Brak shows flexibility. For instance, driving schools in Bnei Brak advertise that they employ women teachers, with whom young girls learning to drive may feel totally safe and at ease.

To a stranger the sight and sound of street barriers, dangerous chains across the roads, demonstrations and angry fights against transgressors of the Sabbath is disquieting and distressing. On the other hand, much can be said for the idea of having one day a week totally quiet.

The religious bigotry of Bnei Brak, Mea Shearim and other orthodox neighbourhoods is better understood in the light of the persecution endured over the centuries and can be seen as bravery when one realizes that the Jews' stubborn clinging to their faith meant even greater persecution.

The elections of 1977 once again brought to the fore the issues of the Jewishness of Israel and the position of religion and halacha (religious law). These issues are highly sensitive, for even moderate parties are fearful of being called anti-religious. In the modern world four basic approaches are evident in defining the relationship between religion and the state. The state can either oppose religion, be neutral to it, encourage it, or enforce it. In Israel the last approach predominates, partly because certain matters of public and family status are enforced by the state. In addition, the existence of an official rabbinate, and of official religious councils, places all those who wish to participate in Jewish religious life under the control of a single system of authority.

It has come to be taken for granted that it is the duty of the state of Israel to enforce halachic norms in such matters as conversion, marriage and divorce. This means not to permit Jews within territorial borders to marry or divorce, or non-Jews to be officially converted, or anyone to be legally recognized as Jewish unless the state-appointed agencies, the chief rabbinate and religious councils, so agree. The argument most frequently used is that the holiness, purity or wholeness of the Jewish people would be endangered if things were allowed to be otherwise.

Rabbi Reuven Hammer, Assistant Professor of Philosophies of Judaism at the Jewish Theological Seminary in Jerusalem, is representative of the large number of thinking Israelis who oppose the sweeping powers of the rabbinate. He asks,[2]

> Would it not be possible for the State of Israel to move from the enforcement to the encouragement of religion, and for even the staunchest Orthodox Jew to recognize the legitimacy of this kind of arrangement in a democratic state? State neutrality towards religion, on the U.S. model, may not be

suitable for Israel. But why should the Orthodox not be satisfied with state support of all religious efforts, without trying
to lay down arbitrary criteria of religious legitimacy? Since
Israel is a Jewish State, it is neither possible nor desirable to
separate the state totally from Jewish matters. And to separate the secular from the religious within Judaism would be
equally impractical. In matters such as the calendar, holidays,
and at least semi-observance of the Sabbath, kashrut [Jewish
dietary laws] and the holy days, the state cannot be totally
neutral if its Jewish character is to be retained. Beyond that
Jews in Israel should be allowed to run their own religious
affairs, with the Government supporting them in this but not
dictating the manner of their practice.

As Hammer sees it, there is something 'inherently obnoxious'
in the thought that the Jewish state exists in order to enforce a
code that could not otherwise be enforced. He believes that there
is nothing to justify the fear that Judaism in Israel, with the
encouragement of the state, would die if exposed to more freedom. On the contrary, the present situation cannot continue
without further alienating the majority of Israelis who have
already accepted Israel as a secular state.

The constructive and human side of Israel's orthodox religion
is exemplified in the work of Rabbi Ze'ev Chaim Lifschitz, who
is an exception to the generalization that rabbis are held in low
esteem by non-orthodox Jews. Rabbi Lifschitz, a psychologist,
is one of the few men in Israel respected equally among the ultra-
orthodox communities, in the academic world, and by ordinary
people. He has achieved this respect through his work in
advising, counselling and treating people suffering from psychological and psychosomatic problems. He is in so much demand
that he has founded in Jerusalem the Sadnat Enosh (Human
Workshop) Tora Centre for Spiritual Guidance, which has
branches in London, New York and Cape Town.

Most of his clients — Lifschitz avoids the term patient — are
educated people and many are yeshiva students with fears,
neuroses and complexes. His main interest and skill is in treating
people with a 'sickness of the soul or spirit'. In a sense, Rabbi

Lifschitz de-confuses people by drawing out their problems and helping them to look at these difficulties. His methods have been so successful that he has trained a score of assistants to help him. People believe in him. One of these believers — himself non-religious — gave Lifschitz a large property near Emek Elah, 18 miles west of Jerusalem. Here the rabbi is establishing a high-level intellectual centre with a resident staff of 50 and their families. Lifschitz refers to it as 'a super-yeshiva, the Eton of Jewish studies'. Known as Beitaynu Village, the institution's aim is to develop intelligence to help solve the problems of Israeli, world Jewry and the world itself.

Such an ambition is expensive but Lifschitz, like a good many Israelis, has given up worrying about money, even though he has a wife and 12 children to support. His attitude is that God provides. Since the Rabbi makes no formal charge for his services, and because he is not subsidized by any government, political or religious institution, God apparently does provide — through donations from some of Lifschitz's thousands of grateful patients and their families. The label of 'Human Workshop' for Lifschitz's Jerusalem centre is one which could in many ways be applied to Israel as a whole, with its great variety of experiments, exercises and projects into life and living.

I have great faith that Israeli common sense will find compromises with religious restrictions as with other parts of life. I saw this common sense at work with the shrimp industry. Jewish dietary laws prohibit the eating of shellfish — lobsters, shrimp, clams. Yet Israel has a large fishing industry. So when shrimp swam into the nets the fishermen were for many years compelled to throw this catch away. This waste hurt, since, with its expanding population, Israel is always in need of new industry. Someone in authority decided that it was not the fisherman's fault if shrimp swim into his net. Israel needs exports — and other countries could not care less about Jewish dietary laws. So the government financed a cannery for freezing and packaging shrimp — with large signs everywhere FOR EXPORT ONLY. The rabbinate was satisfied.

175

An Israeli funeral seems to me to be another demonstration of common sense. It takes place soon after death and it is simple and moving. The corpse is buried on a plank rather than decked out in a casket, so that the outline of the body is readily discernible beneath the draped black cloth. There is no cult of the dead — this would be considered infantile and insulting. Tombstones are practically identical and are always functional and unsentimental.

Privately, mourning lasts a long time but Israelis finish with public mourning in a week after a death. In that week the principal next-of-kin and the family of the deceased person receive in their home visits from other relations and friends offering condolences. After that concentrated week public mourning and displays of grief cease, and usually outsiders make no further mention of the loss suffered by the family. It is considered unfair and heartless for people to go on reminding them of their bereavement. There is great dignity and compassion in this custom.

Israeli military cemeteries are as beautifully kept — with flower gardens, lawns and tree-lined walks — as are those of the British Commonwealth War Graves Commission and they are frequently visited. The Israelis have a touching habit of placing a few small stones on a serviceman's grave; this is to say 'We have been here and leave these pebbles as a token'. Much inspiration has gone into investing the military cemeteries with religious sentiment and symbolism. In the Jerusalem cemetery I particularly like the commemorative stones set under shallow water in a pool. Each stone is for a serviceman drowned on service whose body was not recovered. On various anniversaries religious services are held in the service cemeteries by the survivors of military units.

For me, as a gentile, Israel has a civil religion which is more impressive than its official synagogue-state religion. I refer to the set of *beliefs* which joins one Israeli to another. It is a religion of common purpose. The great exponent of civil religion was David Ben-Gurion, who linked together ancient Israel and the Bible and modern Israel. This produced a mingling of cultures and ideas which have the force of a religion quite different from traditional Judaism — this, after all, mostly developed in the 2,000 year gap between ancient and modern Israel. From the beginning the new civil religion depended heavily on Jewish symbolism — the blue-white flag with the shield of David, for instance; the national anthem, the Temple candelabrum or menora as the state emblem, the insignia of the Israel Defence Forces.

Israel's civil religion is partly founded on the Masada legend, which stresses military courage and steadfastness; the fact that the Masada defenders lived religious lives was also important. Another aspect of civil religion is the idea of the Jews as 'the people that dwells alone', forced to depend on their own resources. This aloneness is felt in Israel in a uniquely religious way. How Israelis feel about the Holocaust is also religious. It is generally accepted that the Holocaust is the central political force of Israeli society; it is also a profound religious force since it gives Israelis the subject of their most heartfelt prayer — that a second Holocaust will never occur. Yad Vashem is second only to the Western Wall as the most sacred place in Israeli civil religion. It is maintained as a shrine and it has the feeling of one; religion becomes almost palpable in this remarkable place, with all its reminders of the Holocaust and its perpetually burning flame to symbolize unfailing memory of the period.

The Western Wall is not only the most sacred place in Israeli civil religion but also the most sentimental. When the nation is aroused by some emotion or alarm or when it wishes to display some value, its people congregate at the wall. Some élite Army units take their oath of allegiance there; demonstrations or fasts on behalf of suffering Jews elsewhere in the world, such as those in captivity in Syria, are also held at the Wall. This Western Wall of the ancient temple symbolizes everything that is Jewish-Israeli. The fact that early Christians called it the Wailing Wall, from the loud laments of the praying Jews, is itself suggestive of the force of feeling to be found there.

Nobody appears to have yet conducted a survey on civil religion, and it would be a difficult exercise. But its place in the

Israeli mind should not be underestimated. Most of the 85 per cent of Israelis who never attend a synagogue pray, in one way or another, at the military cemeteries, and at Masada, Yad Vashem and the Western Wall. This is a fact which bears a lot of thinking about, for why and where a whole people prays is a window into their soul.

14 Politics – Painful Pragmatism

'Israelis have a world view so charged with desolation of the past and the anguish of living memory that all sense of trust has been eradicated. Many Jews are tormented by the past, troubled by the present and fearful of survival in the future.' So wrote Donald Neff, in a despatch to *Time* (6 March, 1978) from Jerusalem. In this assessment he indirectly crystallizes the philosophical basis of Israeli politics, of Israelis' attitudes towards the world political scene and of their own rather complex internal affairs.

Perhaps the worst handicap the Israelis suffer is their difficulty in belonging to any particular group. Israel is not a member of the Third World because it is too advanced. It does not have full membership of the western world because so many western politicians see Israel as an upstart and because Israelis are impatient with what they consider lack of dynamism in western nations. Again, Israel cannot belong to the communist bloc because of Soviet hostility towards Israel as 'an outpost of American imperialism.' Finally, Israel cannot yet belong to the Middle East fraternity because it is the one modern democratic state in the region.

The Israelis have a mission. They want to make their land the philosophical centre of the world, as a hub of educational and scientific exchange, and as an international workshop of ideas in a dozen fields. There is no suggestion of domination or of wanting to control events; the Israelis merely volunteer the setting and environment in which work can be done.

179

They are disappointed in the malfunctioning of the United Nations organization, which they see as feeble, frivolous and unreliable. In the early years of Israel's existence as a state, the U.N. was a forum in which Israel had to fend off innumerable attacks; later it became a place in which to bait Israel.

Israelis' view of the U.N. has been coloured not only by what goes on in New York but by the performance in the Middle East of such U.N. bodies as the Truce Supervisory Organization, U.N.W.R.A. and the U.N. Emergency Force. The events that led up to the Six-Day War of 1967 confirmed the Israelis' worst suspicions about the efficacy of the U.N. Terrorist raids had not been punished or even condemned — but Israeli retaliatory raids had been censured. Then the U.N. Emergency Force was withdrawn from the Israel-Egypt borders when it was most needed. The Security Council was ineffective; when the Egyptians imposed a blockade some Security Council delegates claimed that they could see no reason for having a meeting at all. The Council decided little and did nothing.

Gradually conditions for the Israelis became worse at the U.N. The Arab delegates induced Third World delegates to walk out when the Israeli representative rose to speak. No terrorist attack was condemned in open session — but every Israeli military response was damned. Various U.N. bodies either refused to co-operate with Israel or demanded her expulsion. Understandably, Israelis became cynical about the U.N. and cannot bring themselves to trust the organization.

A good many Israelis resent foreign criticism on the grounds that their critics do not understand Israel's unique problems. At a seminar in Tel Aviv University in December 1974, an Israeli writer said to me bitterly, 'In none of the countries which presume to pass judgment on Israel and to decide its fate, do citizens become accustomed to death at so early an age.' A significant exception to this resentment of criticism is one-time Foreign Minister Abba Eban who says, 'I am disturbed less than most of my countrymen by the fact that some appraisals of Israeli policy are critical, because I don't believe that criticism of a policy is inherently an unfriendly act.'

The U.N. attitude seems to be a continuation of the extraordinary anomalies and inconsistencies shown in foreign attitudes to the Jews. The Germans likened them to Bolsheviks and Freemasons; the Bolsheviks said they were Trotskyists; the French paired them with Protestants and the Czechs coupled them with the Germans. The Negroes said they were 'Whites', using all the obloquy which that word can hold for Negroes. The English included Jews among Levantines, and the Ku-Klux Klan lumped them in with the Catholics and Negroes. They have been labelled, with grotesque perversion of reason, 'Nazi Zionists'. Also, as Stalinists, imperialists, capitalists, reactionaries, racists, fascists and militarists, and communists. No historical or etymological absurdity has been too bizarre to apply to the Jews and to the modern Israelis.

International condemnation puzzles the Israelis, for they believe, perhaps naively, that as conquerors they are more enlightened than the British, more trustworthy custodians of the Holy Places than the Arabs, and that their administration is more democratic than that of the French. Objective study appears to support these views. Historically-minded Israelis remember with a mixture of exasperation and amusement some of the information published in textbooks for the use of administrators of the British Palestine Mandate.[1] For instance, the key British word for the self-respecting Arab was 'proud' — since he was hospitable, rode a noble steed and kept his women strictly in their place. The code word for the self-respecting Jew was 'arrogant' — because (while no less hospitable) he used four wheels whenever he could, disliked being bullied and treated his women as equals.

Many British people have seen Israel with a more visionary clarity than the bureaucrats did. One was Miss Pamela Fitten, who went to live in the country, as 'a Christian of Zionist persuasion'. On 25 November, 1970, at a lecture in London, she explained why she lived in Israel.[2] The most significant part of her explanation was this:

I would ike to say that this is not in the least a change of loyalties. I am English. I am a British citizen and I am no less loyal to the country of my birth now than I ever was, and this loyalty to Israel is an extension of loyalty; it really is a loyalty to something bigger than one's own country. *It is a loyalty to humanity*, as I see it. But since I think one should take not only the privileges but also rights and duties in a land where one lives, I hope, when I am eligible, to apply for Israeli citizenship while retaining my British citizenship. [Author's italics].

In recent years the Vatican, as if conscious of its tragic failure to protect Jews from Hitler, has made more responsible gestures. In 1969 it published a document which recommended that Catholics should recognize the significance of the state of Israel for the Jews and that the Jewish religion should not be seen as a stepping stone to Christianity.[3] Also, Catholics should understand that Judaism was not a religion of 'justice alone', and that it too possesses a law of love and freedom.

The Jerusalem-based 'Rainbow Group' — an organization largely composed of Christian clerics — has been equally forthright and in a recent publication, *To Be or Not to Be,* stated that, 'We believe that one of the greatest disservices that Christians have rendered to the Arab peoples and States in the last twenty years is in not having helped them to face the comprehensive Jewish reality, particularly the Jewish link with the land.'

Arab attitudes to Israel do not anger the Israelis — but they are puzzled, exasperated, frustrated and worried. There is a general feeling of resignation, for the average Israeli cannot understand what the Arabs want of him. I have become accustomed to the plaintive question, 'Why can't they just leave us alone?' If any resentment exists it is that Arab propaganda put an end to the powerful Israeli pioneering urge which used to find expression in doing work for the developing nations in Africa and Asia. Confused by this propaganda, many Third World countries cannot now fit Israel into either one of the two standard roles — Israel is neither a co-object of sympathy nor a dispenser of largesse. Israel's problem is that it is too advanced technologically to qualify as a developing nation and not sufficiently helpless to merit a patronizing protection.

Despite the incessant hostility, many Israelis do not hate the Arabs, or, as Golda Meir told a group of journalists, (including myself) during the Yom Kippur War, 'We Jews only hate the Arabs because they made our boys killers'.

It seems to me absurd for the Arabs to be worrying that Israel is 'a European outpost' in their midst. This belief merely shows Arab ignorance about Israel. The fact is that year by year Israel grows more and more like the rest of the Levant. Having seen both the beaches of Alexandria in Egypt and those of Tel Aviv in Israel, I am struck by the similarity of the people and their behaviour. Eating, swimming, arguing and laughing, each could be in the place of the other. The youth are especially inter-changeable; in both cities machismo-minded young men strut along trying to impress girls in bikinis. The comparison cannot be taken too far — the Israeli girls are free to respond while the Arab girls are not — but essentially there is enough similarity to indicate the possibility of a growing together.

Israelis understand Arabs better than Arabs understand Israelis. As far back as the 1920s Zionists in Palestine were making an intensive study of Arab history, religion and politics because it had been forced on them that the Arabs were different from the Jews in behavioural patterns. By Western standards Arab behaviour was irrational and the Jews saw the importance of anticipating Arab responses.

It is easy for the Israelis to know the Arabs, as any inquiring visitor can find out at the Shiloah Institute in Tel Aviv. It is the academic business of the Shiloah to study the Arabs and its publication *Middle East Record* is one proof of that study. The Israeli analysts have found out that there are no secrets in the Arab world, that sooner or later everything finds its way into the censored press — contradictions, anomalies, inconsistencies and all. The Shiloah staff determine what is actual and what has happened by comparing how contradictions vary from place to place and from time to time. As one of the Shiloah directors told me in 1974, 'You can find the truth no matter how deeply an Arab government might want it hidden, and however censored its press might be'.

He was speaking not of military secrets but social, economic and psychological information. The social scientists at the Shiloah knew that Egypt would have to make some approach to Israel long before President Sadat made his famous mission to Israel in November 1977. Egypt's desperate demographic and economic problems made such an approach inevitable.

Despite their analytical competence, the Israelis can be unexpectedly naive. They expected the Arabs on the West Bank and in Gaza to regard them as benevolent conquerors, bestowing a longer life expectancy, a lower infant mortality rate, and many creature comforts. They were profoundly disappointed when the Arabs rejected these and other benefits. They were naive in thinking that peace would soon follow the so-called Sadat initiative. Wanting peace desperately themselves, the Israelis believed that the Egyptian president would trade concessions for concessions, but he insisted on linking the Egypt-Israel peace treaty to the matter of a homeland for the Palestinians and to Israeli evacuation of the West Bank.

The Israelis were prepared to concede territory for security; they were even ready to give the West Bank and Gaza autonomy provided Israel was given some safeguard to prevent these regions from being taken over by the terrorist Palestine Liberation Organization. The Israelis offer full diplomatic, cultural and economic relations with their Arab neighbours with all the benefits this would give the Arabs. Israel's sole bargaining strength lies in the occupied territories. Its leaders have shown that for a full peace treaty they would give up a great deal; without such a treaty or for the offer only of a condition of 'no war no peace' Israel could never be persuaded to give up anything. In any case, with one leader (Sadat) offering peace and others (of Syria, Libya, Iraq, Yemen) threatening to destroy any peace agreement Israel cannot be blamed for declining to surrender its one bargaining strength — the territories.

Arab pressure makes all Israeli policy bi-partisan because foreign and domestic policy are really one and the same. Foreign policy necessarily dictates domestic policy. For instance, the cost of living is linked with the need for defence spending. That fierce arguments take place between the major political parties, in the Knesset and through the press, does not cancel out the bi-partisan nature of foreign policy. The parties are not at variance about defence or the need to make concessions; they differ only in tactics. The Knesset sits late not because of party wrangling but through worry, despair and sometimes fear.

A fundamental problem is that while Israel is geographically part of the Middle East, politically it is living in another age from that of its neighbours, whose notion of democracy is minimal. Because Israel was just starting decisive commitments about its political philosophy were made in the first years — for instance, to a capitalist economy run by a labour bureaucracy, rather than socialism. Because of the capital needed to finance mass migration there had to be a fully-fledged western orienta-tion, so neutrality was impossible. Arab attitudes meant that there was virtually no option of conciliation with the Arab world so the state had to commit itself to force. An interesting system of contradictions appeared: the Mapai Party talked the language of social democracy while promoting the capitalist economy; the religious parties presented an image of theocracy but indulged in petty clerical politics; the leftist parties presented an elaborate socialist doctrine but protected the market interests of their kibbutzim. In these ways and others the issues of politics were blurred. In the early years it was not a matter of agreeing to differ on a number of well-defined basics; the Israelis had yet to reach agreement on what to differ about. From the very begin-ning voters had a choice of 20 or more parties but the number securing representation in parliament remained steady at about a dozen.

In this book I do not propose to go deeply into modern Israeli internal politics as such, since the members of the various poli-tical parties and factions have, as Israelis, the same mind.

The fundamental political fact of Israel's first three decades is that the Labour Party, which is akin to the British Labour Party in ideology, ruled the land for 29 years. The coalition govern-ment of the Likud Party, the Democratic Movement for Change, and the National Religious Party then took over under the prime ministership of Menachem Begin. The change was salutary but can only be temporary, since Israel is socialist in heart and mind. In putting Labour out of office the electorate was punishing the Labour leadership for certain scandals involving corruption, inept leadership and plain stale leadership. I believe that the people were voting *against* Labour rather than *for* Likud.

Another fundamental but less discernible fact is that successive Israeli governments have found it increasingly difficult to govern. Political leaders tend more and more to follow the people rather than lead them. To be so responsive to public opinion may be good democracy but it is not necessarily good leadership. Such attitudes are forced on Israeli leaders by the nature of group politics — it is virtually impossible for any one party to form a government without help from a smaller party. Shimon Peres, undisputed leader of the Labour Party in the late-1970s, might well find that he has to take the National Religious Party into a coalition, just as Begin did before him.

The Israeli writer Amos Elon describes the Israeli political scene in a single succinct and vivid paragraph:[4]

It is often raucous and noisy with the clatter of endless disagreement, can be exacerbated, stifled, and maimed by tremendous personal rivalries, hatreds, antagonisms and fanatic loyalties. Yet within there is often a strong quality of theatrical drama. For the duration of the show the actors assault and poison each other; at the same time they are animated by a common desire to make the show succeed and hold the public in its spell for long after.

It is inescapable that Israelis and their government neither think nor behave as the world wishes them to. So they are labelled intransigent. One cannot live in Israel without becoming a philosopher contemplating life and death and this produces a realism which permeates politics. It is possible in other countries to indulge in comfortable illusions and for politicians to protect themselves with ambiguities and ambivalences. The Israeli politician can afford no such luxury and must be direct. Ezer Weizmann, appointed Defence Minister in the Begin Government of 1977, exemplified this directness when he said, 'The

Jewish state was formed to solve the Jewish problem, not the Arab problem'.[5]

His meaning was clear. The profound problems of the Arab world are not Israel's fault. With equivalent effort — for the money is certainly available — the Arabs could in time transform their own societies.

15 Scholarly Spies – Minds for Survival

Education and scholarship are highly valued in Israel not only because they result in material prosperity and a satisfying life but in national survival as well.

The intelligence services of Hagana were putting scholarship to work — in language, Arabic history, political science, forgery, psychology — long before the establishment of Israel. After the intelligence services were formalized and developed the use of scholarly spies became more systematic. This is not to say that the intelligence services of Britain, the United States or France are run by ill-educated people, far from it; but most western governments are reluctant to involve their citizens in intelligence unless they are members of the intelligence service itself, or at least members of the Establishment. In Israel, many thousands of people, while neither spies nor employed members of the intelligence services, contribute their expertise to what we might describe as a national pool of intelligence. By the mid-1960s Mossad, the Israeli external security service, was probably using its scholars more enterprisingly than other nations.

Mossad has the advantage of being able to use people who have learned other languages as their mother tongue. Jews driven out of Arab lands brought with them, collectively, the whole vast range of Arabic dialects. Other Israelis speak and read English-English or American-English as their natural tongue. At a moment's notice Mossad can locate an Israeli fluent in any of the world's principal languages and most of the minor ones. The four-language Israeli is commonplace and many Israelis speak, read and write 10 languages. Thinking to test the depth of Israel's linguistic skills, I asked for an interpreter in Welsh when visiting Tel Aviv university. I was given a list of 10 names and told that others were available.

Israeli education produces specialists in everything — a great advantage for a secret service. A Mossad agent preparing for a mission to Norway, for instance, is briefed by somebody who knows all there is to know of Norwegian customs, manners and life-style. One Israeli agent who had never before visited Cairo was sent there on a mission and got a job as a tourist guide, such was his familiarity with the city.

Sabra Israelis and many of western origin are able analysts, for they have perceptive, intuitive, patient and persistent brains. Add thorough training to these qualities and you have a formidable mind to use in solving problems and reaching conclusions. The majority of Mossad's intellectual and operational problems inevitably involve Arabs. What the Arabs are doing, or not doing, saying or not saying, what they are writing and where they are travelling is the substance of intelligence assessments.

Every intelligence agent of any race knows that close study of newspapers, magazines, trade journals and hand-outs by Government departments are valuable material. Mossad and the Foreign Ministry's research units have made the study of openly printed material a fine art. Each day copies of virtually every publication in the Arab world reach Israel, and in the case of the major newspapers, every edition of the day. Most of them are openly bought in the country of origin and posted to a cover address, from where they are airmailed to Israel. Lebanese and Egyptian publications reach Tel Aviv the same day. Some journals take a little longer in the mail but sooner or later even the specialist publications — such as Army magazines, telephone directories and professional medical journals — reach Israel's Intelligence analysts, the 'spies' who work at desks with felt pens and scissors and with instant access to many reference books.

Relatively few scholars are actually on Mossad's payroll but Mossad can call on specialists of all kinds for particular reports or it will make use of work produced by scholars not associated with Mossad.

189

Anything written by the Palestinian-Lebanese Lieut. Colonel Al-Haytham al-Ayyubi interests these analysts. One of his articles in Arabic, 'Future Arab Strategy in the Light of the Fourth War' [Yom Kippur] published in Beirut was picked up and published in English by the Israeli Universities Study Group for Middle Eastern Affairs in 1975. The former head of Israeli military intelligence, Y. Harkabi, himself now a university professor, wrote the introduction and added his professional comments.

Arab strategy as envisaged by al-Ayyubi is readily summarized. It is based ultimately on the assumption that 'the only solution to the tragedy of our times is the establishment [in Palestine] of a democratic Middle Eastern state in which we all live in peace'. The way he proposes to attain this is not by the imposition of a *fait accompli* by military means. Such a step would be unthinkable considering 'the stand taken by the two superpowers who determine the world's political and economic map'. Rather, writes Ayyubi, 'the objective is to erode Israel's morale and ensure the accumulation of emotional shocks and shattering blows, bringing about Israel's eventual collapse through a gradual withering away rather than amputation'. This long-term process of withering away, he argues, is one which 'imperialism' cannot contend with, 'especially once the Israelis come to realise that the country which Zionists intended as a safe and secure home for Jews of the world has become, instead, their most dangerous area'.

Ayyubi notes that his strategy 'does not preclude peace talks'. Indeed, talks, provided they fail, are part of the strategy, since the most favourable results can be achieved only in a climate of 'no peace.'

The Israeli analysts who worked on Ayyubi's article set themselves these questions:

- How influential is al-Ayyubi? Do Presidents Sadat and Assad, King Hussein and King Khalid of Saudi Arabia read his books and articles or does he appeal only to the Palestinian and Syrian terrorist leaders?

- Have any Arab leaders commented on this article about Arab strategy? If not, how can they be induced to do so, in order that we can gauge their reaction?
- For whom is Ayyubi mainly writing? Is he pandering to his own sense of superiority as a military analyst or is he, for some reason, currying favour with the Palestine Liberation Organization chiefs?
- Are the thoughts he expresses his own or is he reflecting those of his P.L.O. or Syrian friends?
- Is the article aimed at Israel, as part of the very strategy Ayyubi proposes?

On this occasion the scholars produced a report which I have condensed here.

Al-Ayyubi is the military analyst of Beirut's leading news magazine, *Al-Usbu al-Arabi*. He writes a kind of running commentary on the political-military aspects of the Middle East, with more stress on military affairs. A Palestinian, he served in the Syrian Army until 1963 and has since been associated with various Palestinian terrorist organizations. He served briefly as chief of the military arm of the Popular Front for the Liberation of Palestine, which he left before June 1967 and is now head of the military affairs section of the Research Centre of the P.L.O.

He has written 10 books and translated 30, all on military strategy ... Sadat and Hussein read Ayyubi, as three recent developments in Arab political strategy indicate ... He represents those elements within P.L.O. who are known to oppose a peaceful settlement of any kind, mainly the Popular Front for the Liberation of Palestine. His strategy is based wholly on the conviction that all attempts at reaching a settlement between Israel and the Arabs will end in failure; a result he considers desirable. His vanity leads him into extreme positions in his efforts to appear more clever than other military commentators. He may not really believe that Israel can be made to 'wither away' but this is the attitude of his friend, George Habash.

The Arab-language newspapers arriving at Mossad's offices or at one of Israel's research institutes are studied for references which could indicate significant military, economic, political, or social information. While the Arab papers are the most fruitful other foreign-language papers can be useful. Alert newspaper reading gave a clue to Egyptian preparations for war three months before the Six-Day War. An agent studying the Yugoslav paper, *Tanyug,* of 29 March, 1967, found a reference to the visit to Cairo of the Soviet Foreign Minister, Alexei Gromyko. As translated by Israeli intelligence, *Tanyug* said: 'Official quarters are reticent as never before ... The only concrete detail which leaked out in Cairo press is that Gromyko will also discuss the problems of the U.N. peacekeeping force in Gaza'. This oblique reference from the well-informed Yugoslav press was read, correctly, as indicating a possible move of the Egyptian Army into Sinai.

Israeli eyes picked up a report in a Beirut newspaper of 21 September, 1973 concerning a meeting in Cairo of President Sadat and heads of the Palestine Liberation Organization. Sadat had told the P.L.O. men, the paper stated, that he had decided to go to war. Mossad referred the report to higher authority but obviously it was not taken seriously enough; war broke out two weeks later.

It is important for an analyst to see all editions of a paper. If a certain item, concerning, say the arrival of a ship in Alexandria appears in the earliest edition of *Al Ahram* but is deleted from all following editions a possible inference is that the item was censored. If this should be so, then that ship is worth investigating — it may be carrying munitions. If an Arab diplomat, especially a Foreign Minister or a Defence Minister, has flown to Moscow and back in one day, what was so urgent about his journey? Perhaps a later edition will amplify the report. On one occasion recorded in Mossad files, an analyst reading the sports pages of a Syrian paper noted that a certain officer, well known as a brilliant horseman, had not been included in a team to ride in an Arab-world competition in Kuwait. This omission was so surprising that an agent in the field was instructed to get information. He found that the officer was attending a secret meeting between Syrian Army officers and terrorist leaders. His involvement with terrorists had not previously been known, so the information was valuable.

192

Mossad's files contain continually up-dated personality assessments of most of the world's leaders. By comparing such an assessment with the political actions of a certain leader, the analysts can see if it is out of character. A prime example of this technique is Fidel Castro, who in September 1973 broke off diplomatic relations with Israel. This rupture was regarded as out of keeping with Castro's character. He had resisted Soviet pressure to break with Israel after the Six-Day War, mostly because he knew that from Israel he could learn many things which could help Cuba. His dossier records that there is scarcely a scientific paper by an Israeli expert at an international conference that he has not studied, especially if it deals with agricultural development. He understands and perhaps envies the spirit that animates Israel. Mossad's scholars decided that Castro had not willingly broken with Israel. They deduced that he had been influenced by Arab propaganda.

For Mossad, Arab propaganda is always worth study for nothing more clearly shows shifts of political opinion or emphasis. Contrasts between propaganda intended for home consumption and that aimed at countries abroad are also valuable. When internal propaganda against Israel becomes more virulent and varied than usual Mossad can be fairly sure that there is an internal political crisis and that the propaganda is the ruling party's way of distracting attention from the crisis. In a major analysis of Arab propaganda made for Israeli government guidance, Mossad's researchers concluded that hatred has been bred so deeply into the Arab masses that even if propaganda were to cease overnight the effects would be felt for a generation.

Arab television also provides useful analytical material. An interesting study was made of General Amin Huweidi when he was chief of Egyptian intelligence, 1968-73. He was interviewed at length on Egyptian television (9 July, 1969) and the telecast was picked up on board an Israeli electronics intelligence ship, video-taped and then studied by scholars.

In their analysis[1] they took into account the effect on Huweidi of the knowledge that his predecessor, Salah Naar, had been

193

sentenced to 15 years' gaol during the purge after the Six-Day War. Would this make Huweidi more cautious in his statements or would he be more outspoken, in an attempt to impress his political superiors with his cleverness and confidence? The Israelis decided that the two factors probably balanced; therefore, Huweidi was neither playing safe nor taking risks during his television interview. If, then, he was being himself what he had to say was particularly interesting.

When the scholars translated Huweidi's Arabic they caught him in an outright lie. He told his interviewer that 'recently in Tel Aviv there was a demonstration in which 3,000 Jews protested over the growing number of casualties on the various fronts' and he gave as his source 'the foreign news agencies'. But the analysts found that none of the 18 foreign news agencies in Israel had sent any such despatch — because no demonstration had taken place.

Finally, the scholars produced this report (in English and Hebrew), which was studied by Foreign Ministry and Secret Services staff:

Huweidi is an intelligent man. He is capable of expressing himself and handles well the information at his disposal. However, he lacks the capacity to form a genuine concept of reality, nor is he capable of an overall estimate of a situation. Instead, he sticks to stereotyped views which are generally accepted in his circle, and is incapable of overcoming them. He shows that general Intelligence in Egypt seeks to confirm propaganda assertions rather than examine a situation comprehensively. In presenting Intelligence estimates Huweidi makes indiscriminate use of unconfirmed reports, false information and forged documents. His staff often quote Israeli publications to give an apparent credibility to biased assessments. Huweidi's attitudes make clear that Egyptian leaders are anxious about the state of public opinion in their country and lack confidence in the capacity of the Egyptian people to face the truth about their situation. Egyptian soldiers are deserting from the Suez front, apparently in large numbers. [Later the Israelis proved this to be so.] The general view that Egyptian Intelligence has of Israel is unreal and shows no knowledge of dynamic processes in the social, cultural, economic and military fields.

Mossad arranged for the Egyptian leaders to see the Israeli report by having it planted it in the diplomatic mail sent to Cairo by Egypt's Rome Embassy. No Intelligence officer of any rank has since appeared on Egyptian television, which seems to confirm that the Israeli study of Huweidi was uncomfortably accurate.

Social conflict within military establishments has great Intelligence value,* hence any such reference is quickly picked up. Discord between politicians and between generals may be worth aggravating while a moderate Arab leader is always worth encouraging in some way.

*For the Arabs as well as for the Israelis. *Sharon's Bridgehead,* by Uri Dan, pubished in 1975, tells the story of factional intrigues and conflicting relations in Israel's High Command. For instance, General Sharon was on bad terms with Moshe Dayan and Ezer Weizman. Arab intelligence services have provided their officers with the book and with a summary of conclusions to be drawn from it.

16 Character and Personality – Warts and All

According to Professor Amnan Rubinstein of Tel Aviv University the male Sabra is popularly regarded as a tall, strong, suntanned man, with an aggressive approach to life and people, conceited and kind-hearted, with an appreciation of humour and with few manners. As a generalization of the Sabra this might just do as raw clay with which to sculpt a more detailed, three-dimensional Israeli, and not just a Sabra.

An author-observer needs to take into consideration so many factors, including viewpoints and half-joking asides — such as that of Ruth Bondy[1] that the Israeli male carries around the character of the region; he is the proprietor of the Mediterranean harem who likes to keep his women on the go between sink and bed. Again, there is some truth in this wry feminine comment.

For the Israeli woman, a popular foreign conception is that she is nubile, full-figured — and, of course, sunbrowned — easy to know, alert in mind and body, eager to marry and have children, and wholeheartedly feminist. There is much more to Israeli women than this but it might serve as a basis on which to build a convincing description.

To get the most accurate picture of an Israeli it might be necessary first to make two different rough drawings — one of the Israeli as he sees himself, the other as a non-Jewish observer sees him. But we need to stress for those who view this portrait that it is of an Israeli, not that of a Jew. Certainly, most Israelis would probably agree that Jewishness is part of their identity; it is much less easy to know in what way they see this as a basic element in their identity as Israelis. For me, the most striking aspect of Israeli self-identity is that it no longer defines *Jewish* identity in terms of a minority group or culture. The problems, uncertainties and anxieties of being a Jew in the diaspora — and these exist even for Jews happily assimilated into the societies of other countries such as Britain — do not affect the Israeli Jew. He is a member of a nation. Each new group of immigrants has contributed to the positiveness of Israel's collective identity. Perhaps because of this richness Israel has escaped many of the problems and uncertainties plaguing the identity problem of other new nations facing modernization.

Israelis have yet to debate — at least in public — some questions which sooner or later will demand an answer. How Jewish should Israel be? Does Jewish mean religious? How much encouragement should be given to the continuity of ethnic cultures? Does Israel want to be a European culture with European values and European arts?

Some pointers to the answers can be discerned in the responses to a questionnaire about Israel-Jewish attitudes prepared by the Israel Institute of Applied Social Research.

For instance:

'I am Jewish because I am in Israel.'

'I am in Israel because I am Jewish.'

'The legitimacy of my being here is explained by the efforts of those who came before me and by those who have yet to come.'

God bless the Israeli obsession with surveys. They reveal more about these complex people than anything else possibly could. In a significant and detailed survey made in 1970[2] about 4,000 Israelis from varying backgrounds and age-groups were given a list of 35 personal, social and other 'needs' and asked to place them in order of importance. The need 'to feel pride that we have a State' easily tops the list. Similarly, Yom Haatzmaut (Independence Day) is the one holiday which has meaning for all Israelis, young or old, religious or non-observant, educated and uneducated. Yom Kippur, the holiest of the religious holidays, is said to have 'no meaning for me' by 16 per cent of the respondents.

197

After the need to feel pride in possession of Statehood, the next 10 most important needs (according to the survey) are:

To understand what goes on in Israel and the world.

To spend time with the family.

To have confidence in the leaders.

To raise my morale.

To feel I am utilising my time well.

To know what the world thinks about us.

To be in a festive mood.

To know myself.

To experience beauty.

To order my day.

The least important need is 'to escape from the reality of everyday life'. I suggest that this comes at the bottom of a list of 35 'needs' because it simply is not possible, in Israel, to escape from everyday reality. The reality of high taxation, Arab enmity, military security, and tensions of many kinds is inescapable.

In another survey[3] several thousand members of the general public were asked to say which of 22 different traits of Israeli people they considered 'very characteristic'. Heading the list is 'Concern over peace among the nations', followed by 'Self-sacrifice for the ideals of the people' (which probably means 'making sacrifices for the common good'); 'attitude of sanctity towards human life'; 'a nation that does not rely on others'; 'emphasis on the importance of family life'. Rather surprisingly, 'ability to laugh at ourselves' is lowest on the list of 22 characteristics. Many foreign observers would put this higher on the list.

Not on the list at all is a trait which is apparent to the foreign observer — acute sensitivity to criticism and slights. Forced onto an exasperated defensive by criticism in the United Nations, most Israelis sometimes see unfriendliness where none is intended.

Ruth Bondy says that, 'Slowly, sooner or later, all of us come to the conclusion that an Israeli is a Jew — only more so.'[4] Indirectly, she attributes more importance to being an Israeli than being a Jew — the sentiments of many Israelis I have met. There is no paradox here. An Israeli post-graduate expressed it this way to me, 'I live in a country surrounded by enemies and do not intend to leave. A Jew can live in any country. Still, it's easier to be a good Jew in Israel.'

What it means to be an Israeli in Israel was well put by Haim Hertzog in 1968, long before he became Israeli ambassador to the U.N.:[5]

> It gives a sense of fulfilment to live here. I enjoy it because I am a Jew in a Jewish state; because I don't have to apologise to anyone for my existence, and because my children are completely uninhibited and completely free psychologically. They don't have to apologise for their existence either, indeed they can't, and that's probably the best vindication of our being here. They just can't understand certain things which exist abroad in regard to Jews. The best example is of the small children here in Israel being taught in school about the Holocaust in Germany and the concentration camps, and their immediate reaction is, 'Where was the Israeli Army?'

This question is full of interest and meaning to the student of Israel and Israelis, if only because it is pathetic in that the children feel so dependent on an army.

The role of the services in shaping character and personality is powerful and it often occurs to me, when in Israel, that just about every soul in the country has had his St Crispin's day — the day on which he became one of a band of brothers, as did the army of Shakespeare's *Henry V*[6] on the day of the battle of Agincourt.

Henry proclaims:

> ... He that outlives this day, and comes safe home,
> will stand a tip-toe when this day is named ...
> He that shall live this day, and see old age, ...
> Then will he strip his sleeve and show his scars,
> And say, 'These wounds I had on Crispin's day.' ...
> ... he'll remember, with advantages,
> What feats he did that day ...
> This story shall the good man teach his son;
> And Crispin Crispian shall ne'er go by
> From this day to the ending of the world,
> But we in it shall be remembered —

We few, we happy few, we band of brothers;
 For he today that sheds his blood with me
 Shall be my brother ...
A middle-aged former Hagana fighter, living in Jerusalem, flaw-
lessly quotes this long passage to me whenever I give him the
opportunity.

War is so frequent and so close at hand that everybody, not
just the soldiers, lives through a St Crispin's day. The effect on
Israelis is profound. It makes a person appreciate his nation and
his life all the more and it motivates him. As children, many
Israelis lived through bombardments of their kibbutzim, and a
great many have seen mutilated bodies. When war comes virtually everybody has a war duty. For instance, schoolboys become
stretcher bearers and hospital workers to release the adult men
who have gone to the front. I know a 16-year-old boy, Itai, who
spent the Yom Kippur War of 1973 at Hadassah Hospital, Jerusalem; helping to lift stretchers from the helicopters as they
brought in wounded from the fighting on Golan Heights. At
such times everybody is desperately busy and youngsters are
given jobs they would not normally know exist. At one time,
when he was engaged on ward duty, Itai was beckoned by a
sister who nodded at something on a surgical table and ordered,
'Take that to the mortuary', 'That' was a stillborn baby, which
Itai dutifully picked up in his hand and carried to the mortuary.
'I grew up several years on the way', he told his parents.

Certainly the Israeli personality reveals pride in achievement,
but it is a muted and guarded pride — less obvious than it was
before the war of 1973. Pride shows itself in many ways. There is
a story much-quoted in Israel about a passing-out parade at an
aircrew school. After addressing the cadets the inspecting officer
invited questions, and this time, unusually, he got one — from a
religiously observant Jew, a fairly rare type among Israeli fighter
pilots. He said, 'You have taught us to become good pilots but
how do we become good *Israeli* pilots?'

'Before you leave here,' the senior officer replied, 'you will
make a solo flight in a jet. You will climb to 10 thousand feet
— and you will receive orders not to look down. Only at 30

thousand feet will you be allowed to look down. At that height you will see a clear dividing line on the earth beneath. On one side you will see sand, scrub and stagnation. On the other, green fields, good roads and many other marks of civilization. That is the point at which you become an Israeli pilot.' He was referring to the contrast between Israel and its neighbour, Jordan.

The term 'aggressive' is applied by both Israelis and foreigners, but each mean such different things that a dictionary entry might appear like this:

Aggressive 1: (*Israeli*): Self-reliant; disinclination to be 'pushed around'; confident; determined to the point of forcefulness. 2: (*Foreign*): Intransigent; abrasive; belligerent; inclined to ride roughshod over other people's feelings.

An examination of most adverse foreign criticisms shows that they come from people who have not travelled in Israel. Perhaps Israelis when abroad, by their confident bearing give an impression of aggressiveness which outsiders assume to be a national characteristic. Perhaps, too, exploits such as the Entebbe rescue — which had to be aggressive if it was to succeed — add to the notion that Israelis are belligerent by nature. They are not; they are merely direct in manner and speech. Anyone who talks with Israelis will find them painfully, even embarrassingly direct; they are not given to euphemisms and circumlocuitous speech, even among politicians. Abba Eban, as Foreign Minister, used circumlocution when among foreign statesmen because he knew it was expected of him, but within Israel he is as direct as anybody else.

Israelis who do not know Britain do not comprehend British understatement, that art which requires the listener to deduce or adduce information from an indirect or subtle statement. An Israeli politician, who is now a diplomat in Europe, once said to me, 'Why can't the British say yes or no? They're like Arabs the way they flirt with a decision. I never know where I stand with a British politican or diplomat.'

During Henry Kissinger's Middle East shuttle of 1974, when he was U.S. Secretary of State, he had a conversation with his masseur in Jerusalem. This exchange, which was to become famous, shows Israeli directness at its best, especially when an Israeli recounts the story,

Kissinger: Shall I break off negotiations? [Between Israelis and Arabs]

Masseur: Absolutely not. I would give up ten years of my life for peace.

Kissinger: How many kilometers would you give up?

Masseur: Not a kilometer.

Directness of another kind is shown by Israelis' refusal to accept old age; they fight it all the way. Most of them have to be forced to retire and then they will ferret out a part-time job or several part-time jobs. This reluctance to down tools is the result of living in a society where labour is a faith and the waste of time a crime against God. Also, Israelis are conscious of the enormous amount of work still to be done to make the state economically, commercially, militarily, socially and educationally secure. Few people in Israel question the value of work; it is an accepted value. A sizeable group would like more leisure time and favours a five-day week but there is no active demand for these social benefits. Most people are satisfied with their work and with the way they spend their leisure. The better educated are happier than the others at work and happier at play, and they also feel the shortage of time more keenly.

On first meeting an Israeli can also seem not just direct but abrupt or even rude. Appearances can be deceptive. The fact is, Israelis are among the least subservient people in the world and many are not aware of the forms of ritual politeness. Once the visitor makes allowance for this he finds that Israelis are informal, straightforward and willing to go out of their way to help the visitor. But willingness to help does not guarantee correctness when you ask advice or directions — for the Israeli is reluctant to say I don't know. I have been misdirected more in Israel than in any country except Australia — whose inhabitants are also notoriously reluctant to admit ignorance.

Sociologists and psychologists find little evidence of a generation gap. Israeli youth hold values and attitudes similar to those of their parents. Where youth and parents do differ both parties know exactly where the other stands, so the psychologists say.

CHARACTER AND PERSONALITY – WARTS AND ALL

David Reifen, Chief Judge and largely the creator of Israel's juvenile courts, has a different view. He says that children and youth in Israel have developed a feeling of superiority toward their parents, teachers and the older generation in general, because technological developments and the mass media have made them sophisticated. 'They look at the older generation with pity, disappointment and sometimes contempt, refusing to accept their values as worth imitating. Their elders are no longer those who have the know-how. Television has particularly changed the outlook of the young.'[7]

Mr Reifen should know but I must report that the 'pity, disappointment and contempt' levelled by children at their parents has escaped my observation and apparently that of many of Israel's academic researchers.

Contrary to a belief in some places abroad, the Israeli does not have a free-living, free-loving, free-wheeling personality. Israeli society has in fact been described as puritan and this may not be too wide of the mark — though the yardstick is not that of religion but of work.

Israelis do what they have to do, and they want to believe that what they do is right. Perhaps this is why, on the whole, they think well of themselves. This is no bad thing, for they also expect a lot of themselves. When they fail in something, they feel it badly. I have met several Israeli parents beset by guilt about having 'betrayed' their children before the Yom Kippur War. 'We could have prevented the war by putting out of power the men who caused it', one mother told me.

The Israelis hold human life and human relationships in very high regard, but it is possible that their lofty ideals have been tempered by the stark reality of prolonged war or near-war. It would be surprising if prolonged war had not made people less sensitive, thus decreasing their respect for their own lives and the lives of others.

Nearly all Israeli men and a good many women are afraid to be afraid; they feel that it is weak to show fear, unmanly, decidedly un-Israeli, and unfair to the team. Military psychologists have gone practically out of their own minds trying to get

203

shocked soldiers to let go their tight self-control, to unshackle their emotions and allow them to flood out — a technique calculated to bring them out of shock.

Emotion embarrasses the upper-class Israeli — except where Israel and its right to exist is concerned. Displays of deep emotion are an unpardonable indulgence, a weakness impossible to tolerate, an instability that will preclude the person concerned from any real responsibility; he is not the man you would want next to you in an emergency, for 'he is not being a man'.

Most of the world has seen Israelis in tears after a massacre or in fits of anger with the authorities for not having 'prevented it'. If Israelis were to see themselves being so emotional on film they would be mortified, and deeply self-reproachful for having given way to 'weakness'. The Sabra is specially concerned with self-control for he has rationalized that more is expected of him than of the immigrant, and as a thoroughbred Israeli he must set an example to the newcomers.

But he does not set a high example in dress. War, work, a long hot summer, the pioneering tradition and lack of money have together prevented Israelis from developing a taste for good clothes. Shabbiness is less obvious in summer when a shirt and a pair of trousers are adequate for a man and a simple cotton dress for a woman, but in winter, and especially on cold days, some ensembles have to be seen to be believed. Israelis do not lack a dress sense, but outer garments are a major investment to be put off as long as possible. Clothes are always clean, for Israelis are fastidious about personal cleanliness and physical appearance, which accounts for the large number of men's and women's hairdressers. Small children are the best dressed and best scrubbed. Israeli parents get much pleasure from seeing their children in good clothes and shoes.

The country makes much of its own clothing but the best quality items are sent abroad. And the quality is high. Gone are the days when men's trousers were the main clothing export; women's dresses have become more important. When an Israeli woman does dress to impress she has a grace that even Parisiennes cannot surpass. The women are attractive and have a natural elegance and vitality that seem more common in Israel than in many other countries. One place to see feminine beauty en masse is at the beach. Another is on the army parade ground.

Market research and psychological studies are Israeli commonplaces, but not until 1976 did anybody think to commission a report into the status of Israeli women. It was long past due. It must be understood that the pioneer Jewish women who help to found the Yishuv at the turn of the century saw themselves as worker-units rather than as wives and mothers to be protected. In a way, they played the parts of men because of their worker role; they asked for no favours or privileges and no task on the kibbutz was too heavy or unpleasant for them. As mates to their husbands under the arduous conditions imposed by heavy pioneering labour, hostile climate and raiding Arabs, they developed the type of backbone common among the early settlers in the American West, in Australia and New Zealand. Their men knew that these women could be counted on to the death. I have met some of them, now elderly, in kibbutzim such as Degania. They stand and sit straight and speak calmly and they have the deep quiet eyes of experience. You never hear them complain about anything.

Today's Israeli girls are no less dependable, no less courageous but they rate their femininity high — even higher than boys rate their masculinity. While able to bear the burdens of life as capably as her grandmother, the Israeli girl is more concerned with her appearance and she does not want to act in a mannish way. She joins the Army and dons a plain uniform only because the country has not enough men. Actually, she wants to be the 'real woman', and she believes she deserves a mate fit for her. The younger Israeli woman is liberated, but only to the extent that she will allow herself to be. She has, in fact, a form of split personality forced on her by the time in which she lives — as an Israeli she must have some masculine attributes, as herself she must be feminine. Perhaps the second is the consequence of the first. One of the most common sights in Israel is a young Israeli soldier on leave in uniform with his girlfriend; by order every soldier carries his Uzi sub-machine-gun everywhere and there is probably an order to say that he must not allow his girlfriend to carry it, but I have often seen the girl with the gun slung over her shoulder while the boy has his arm around her waist. It is a peculiarly Israeli sight, and it says much about the society in which the couple live.

Israeli men expect from their women pretty much what most Western men expect. She must, basically, be 'feminine', which, as the men see it, means not *too* independent minded, not *too* intelligent or articulate, not *too* obtrusive when men are talking. As a sexual partner the man expects his mate to be vigorous and voluptuous, but not to take the lead.

While in public life the Israeli woman is positive, even authoritative, in private life she is passive, even at times submissive. I have seen this in several married women I know well and I am struck by one marked contrast — at conferences during workaday life they make statements and initiate discussions; at home in the relaxing hours they ask questions and are reserved. And this can happen about the same topic in the one day. The reason for this change is not hard to find. At home the Israeli woman is happy to relinquish command or authority and to have her husband as head of the family.

Lesley Hazleton, a British-born Israeli who has studied the role of women in Israeli society, says[8] that sexism — or male chauvinism, as we would call it — is 'strangling Israeli women as surely as our foremothers were stifled into silence in the ghettos of the diaspora.' Ms Hazleton, who has lived in Israel since 1966, must have some justification for using these strong terms but I think they are extravagant. According to her, a triad of liberation, security and religion governs the lives of Israeli women. 'Until we confront the myth of our liberation, the power of religious tradition, and the effects of our national security/insecurity, we resign ourselves to the role assigned us by a male-oriented society.'

Israeli women have little option about conforming to a secondary sex role while Israeli society faces Arab hostility; the existence and acceptance of roles is a fundamental part of national defence. In times of great crisis — and Israel is perpetually in crisis — internal revolution against sex roles is a luxury and a diversion which the nation and its individual members cannot afford, and I think most women realize this. It is not a matter of resignation but one of practical possibilities.

After two years' study on the status of women, the government-appointed Namir Committee presented its report, *Status of Women in Israel,* in 1978. Headed by Mrs Ora Namir, a Knesset member, the committee comprised 92 men and two women, a disproportion some people might find disturbing, considering the nature of the report. Mrs Namir and her colleagues admit that Israel is a male-dominated society, a fact illustrated by example and statistic. For instance, of 700 types of job in the Israel Defence Forces only 200 are open to women.

The educationally disadvantaged woman is one of the report's main concerns. 'Our basic problem is not only the inequality between men and women but between women and women ... how to advance the weaker woman without holding back the progress of the stronger.' The less educated woman tends not to seek employment outside the home and remains uninvolved in her community; she is often poor and has many children. According to Mrs Namir and her colleagues, this woman is often virtually a prisoner in her home. Although her husband may be a functional illiterate he at least works outside, meets people and has opportunities to broaden his horizons. The only solution, the report recommends, is to break the vicious circle early in life. Education should be made free for toddlers and pre-schoolers, where it will do more good than at high-school level. Sex-roles, which the curriculum imposes on a child from as early as nursery school, should be uprooted. The report also demands a re-appraisal of vocational education programmes for girls and that traditionally male trades be opened to girls.

The lot of the career woman at the top of the socio-economic scale is not satisfactory, Mrs Namir's report states. Husband and wife may be equally well educated and both may work outside the home. 'Yet the husband comes home and expects to relax and find everything ready for him. It's a great sacrifice for him to take out the garbage or fetch something from the corner store. Such a division of roles in this epoch should be unthink-able. How can a woman be expected to do two days' work in one? How can she devote extra time to her job when she is con-stantly harried and preoccupied by what awaits her at home? Her male colleagues in the office are not similarly burdened.'

The report calls for the establishment of a public council of 30 men and women who would implement its recommendations while a smaller committee would formulate policy and draft bills for parliament. An ombudsman would be appointed to investi-gate cases of sex discrimination, with the power to appear in court as a prosecutor in cases involving women's rights. Because most things in Israel move fast the chances are that within a decade the life of women will change a good deal for the better.

At present a woman whose husband is declared insane may not divorce him until he has recovered, no matter how long it takes. If a woman remarries after her missing husband has been declared legally dead and he returns, she must divorce both men. Her second marriage is considered an adulterous union and any children from it are declared bastards. A woman also cannot marry a man she was involved with while legally married. Even more, if such a liaison is discovered she may not return to her husband. A childless widow is required to marry her dead husband's brother; she may not marry anybody else unless he legally releases her from this bond. And a woman can never be a judge in a religious court that decides on cases like this.

It is surprising that such laws were implemented in Israel, a new country founded on socialist principles, and in whose creation and defence women played such an important part. Fortunately, the legal status of women is changing, especially under the spirited leadership of women such as Shulamit Aloni, a member of the Knesset, and head of the Citizens Right Move-ment. Women in Israel often succeed in circumventing laws which discriminate against them and sooner or later the archaic Judaic prohibitions will crumble.

Despite certain equalities granted to women by law, they have not escaped from the traditional female jobs and obligations. Indeed, women seem to have surrendered some of the privileges which they won at such great cost and to have gone back to the kitchen sink. Even on the kibbutz more than two-thirds of female members are engaged in doing the work that woman have always done, in the kitchen, laundry, clothes stockroom, taking care of the babies, teaching school. It is almost as if, having shown that she could do anything a man could do, the woman has been content to return to her traditional role.

Some Israelis, especially the rabbis, want to reintroduce Jewish symbols in the home as the beginning of a return to tradition. Rabbi Adin Steinsalz, head of the Shefa Institute for Advanced Jewish Study, wants to stop Jewishness from further fading in Israel, and to do this he would like to see again mothers lighting sabbath candles and grandmothers making the gift of a prayerbook. Rabbis tend to place the responsibility for the reinculcation of tradition firmly on the shoulders of women, much to the annoyance of feminists. 'The Jewish home is created by the Jewish mother and if it breaks down it is her fault', Rabbi Steinsalz told me.

The traditional male terminology associated with the Divine Person also upsets Jewish feminists, who have proposed a glossary of substitutes for such words as 'Father', 'Master', and 'Lord'.

This is no more than another example of the dynamic nature of a lively society, notable for its many different facets. Yet a cultural mosaic exists in Israel rather than a cultural medley; the pieces fit together rather than clash and each piece shows up better because of the composition of the whole. The oriental Jews, who brought their own religious styles, tastes and customs provide a facet of special interest in the cultural mosaic. The influx of many immigrant groups with their different traditions and the difficulties of absorption constitute a crucial factor in the growing pluralism of the Israeli cultural scene. This emerging plurality is seen in the multiplicity of languages spoken, in patterns of dress, especially on holidays, in the different intonations of Hebrew, and in the patterns of cultural consumption. Yet, overall, there is a harmony that both intrigues and defies the observer.

209

It must be evident from several references in this book that the Israeli is a worried person, with causes for worry that do not enter many other peoples' lives. For instance, a 10-year-old boy who had been cycling down the coastal road between Haifa and Tel Aviv on the day of the terrorist massacre in March 1978 refused to go to school or leave the house for several days after. His worried mother contacted a psychologist friend, Professor Noah Milgram, for advice. Milgram told her that this was not a mental disorder requiring treatment by a psychologist or psychiatrist. It was an example of the everyday, normal stress which Israelis face.

He advised the mother to take her son back to the area where he had been cycling when he heard the shooting — which resulted in the deaths of 33 Israelis and the wounding of another 80. On the psychologist's instructions mother and son recreated the incident, emphasizing his bravery in turning around and cycling in the opposite direction instead of becoming paralysed with fear.

Milgram was one of the organizers of a conference on psychological stress in June, 1978 in Jerusalem. The hundreds of social scientists from all over the world could hardly have gathered in a more appropriate city.

Consider the stress suffered by Mrs Helen Morad of Hazor in northern Israel. In her mid-forties, her hair grew white in a single afternoon in 1974 as she watched helplessly while Israeli soldiers tried to free 85 children held in a school building by Palestinian terrorists. After the fight the soldiers found 22 children's bodies and nearly 50 wounded. Lilly, Mrs Morad's daughter was one of the dead. She was only 15. A notebook was in Lilly's hand. 'If I shall not be killed,' she wrote, 'I shall be kinder to mother. She did not like the idea of this excursion...'

Eight months earlier Mrs Morad had lost a son, killed in the Yom Kippur War of 1973. Her husband was killed in the Six-Day War of 1967. She has seven other children, though the two elder sorfs have emigrated to the U.S. and Canada. She worries that yet another child will be killed by terrorists.

Helen Morad is one of 250,000 Israelis living near the Lebanese border, where residents have been under strain since 1970, when Lebanon became a training ground and jumping-off place for terrorists in their attacks on Israeli civilians. When the Israeli Army drove the terrorists from the border area the tension lessened, though small children still panic at loud noises, such as a car back-firing or the slamming of a door. If stress in the frontier zones can turn a woman's hair white what must it be doing to her and to other people's characters and personalities? Toughening them, certainly. But perhaps having damaging results as well.

Another kind of stress is lack of money. Because of the recurrent financial crises which their state is required to face, Israelis have a fatalistic approach to the nation's problems and their own. As wave after wave of inflation hits them (the Bureau of Statistics reported a rate of 103 per cent in December 1978) they fall back on their we-shall-overcome attitude. They know that somehow or other they will manage.

The Jews of the diaspora and the Sabras of the Yishuv were always thrifty; they had to be because while they were poor they still had to save for the day of crisis, be it political, economic or family. The notion that all Jews were rich — a theme so constantly the subject of anti-Semitic propaganda — was always a fallacy. Some were very rich — but they were a handful. The Jews who came to Israel from Europe or from the Arab world were poor. They brought their frugality with them, and they saved in their new land. But their children do not acknowledge the virtues of saving; they have seen their parents' savings vanish under the impact of inflation, rises in taxation and the cost of living and now, with understandable cynicism, they prefer to spend their money on what they want *now,* rather than see the price of some desired article increase faster then their wages.

Jews, and especially the modern Israelis, do not *love* money; they respect it — and the respect is based on what money can do. In Israel it is not going to breed a fortune. No matter what business a man starts in Israel he knows that he has many competitors and a maximum home market of three million. That isn't much incentive for a large capital outlay. The real Achilles heel of Israeli economy is consumption; it was for many years rising consumption that ate up most of the increase in productivity.

Despite being struck by a large number of outrageous fortune's slings and arrows the Israelis have not allowed their minds to become numbed and their enterprise paralysed. The observer who travels around the country can find plenty of evidence of the spirit of experiment and initiative, in vastly different fields.

A recent example of agronomical inventiveness can be found at Ben-Gurion University of the Negev in Beersheba, where two specialists evolved a system of drawing geothermal water from underground reservoirs to control air temperature and warm the soil. Through this system high crop yeilds are achieved at a fraction of the cost of heating greenhouses by other energy sources. In the first season of applying the water-heated system, the specialists produced high yields of cucumbers and melons with a saving of up to 4,000 dollars an acre over that of heating the same land with oil. Greenhouse farming is increasingly popular in Israel as a method of conserving scarce water resources but the high cost of heating these structures during winter had greatly limited their economic feasibility. With the 'heated' plants maturing up to two months earlier, Israeli farmers can reach the lucrative European markets well ahead of their competitors.

Private enterprise is at work wherever you find a Bedouin with a camel, ready — for a price — to allow tourists to mount the animal and be photographed. If they want the Bedouin himself in the picture the cost is higher. One such entrepreneur in Beersheba, a handsome, dashing and exotically clad fellow, was much in demand among the visitors who descended on the town by the coachload. In fact, he was a Hungarian Jew, a musician down on his luck. It seemed that the original genuine Bedouin with camel had moved on with his tribe, and the Israeli, quick to see the opportunity, moved in. He did not even own the camel, but rented it.

Israel is a country not only of big problems, like war and monstrous income tax, but of little problems which would never occur to people in other lands. The Israelis are used to quick mental switches. For all that, there is a danger that Israel is producing fewer independent thinkers than in the days of the Yishuv or in the early days of the state. This is the result of a school system and a social pattern based on a security-above-all attitude. The emphasis is on conformity, for in Israel's precarious situation deviance is an un-Israeli activity. And yet deviance, original and lateral thinking, and independence of outlook, are essential to a country which must have its collective wits about it. The Army psychologists, fortunately for the nation, look for new officers among the boys who have withstood the school system to emerge as individuals. This individualism is what made the Entebbe operation successful.

A good many outsiders have wondered just how far the extroverted Moshe Dayan is typical of the Israeli. Dayan is cool, confident, self-assured, totally pragmatic, incisive and as far as Israel's survival is concerned he relies on the best technology rather than a faith that all will be well. He is a type of Israeli rather than the typical one since he has some less endearing traits that are not common to Israelis as a whole.

In the early days many Israelis, including Dayan as a young man, demonstrated 'chutzpah' — a cult of self-assertion sometimes bordering on impudence, of daring independent-mindedness and disregard for authority, all leavened with a sense of humour and plenty of common sense. Some foreigners still talk about chutzpah but it is an old-fashioned word in Israel; today it is used to describe downright rudeness.

Our portrait of the Israeli would not be complete without the warts, such as apparent rudeness. It cannot be pretended that Israelis, any more than Englishmen, Americans and Frenchmen, are without blemish, and they would be the last to claim such a thing — if only because their relentless surveys expose the flaws. The Israelis make public their own failings with a frankness which might surprise an observer.

213

THE ISRAELI MIND

Jack Yeriel of *The Jerusalem Post* is an honest observer of his fellow Israelis and in his newspaper[9] he related his experiences when he accompanied a party of 12-year-old pupils from his daughter's school on an excursion to Masada. Israeli fathers are sometimes called upon to act as armed guards on such excursions, in case of terrorist attack.

'By the day's end', Yeriel wrote, 'I was convinced that most of these youngsters will grow up to fit the well-known stereotype: the queue-jumper, the litterer, the polluter, the road hog — in short, the average Israeli who fights like a lion for his country and is capable of astounding acts of generosity and kindness in times of crisis, but who unfortunately turns into a self-centred, inconsiderate creature when engaged in normal activities, such as driving to work or waiting in a queue to buy a postage stamp.'

On analysis, it seems that the behaviour of the 120 Israeli school children are similar to that of those from many an English or French secondary school, but Mr Yeriel's profound distress is understandable. He would like to do away with the image of the 'ugly Israeli' and he knows that much of the responsibility for this rests on teachers. His article was much more a criticism of lax teachers than of bad-mannered children. And teachers are lax because parents are indulgent. And parents are indulgent because, hyperconscious of the fragility of life, they cannot force themselves to be strict with their children.

Israelis, too, go on strike. I doubt if I have ever visited Israel without finding a strike of some sort — among bus drivers, post office workers, El Al pilots, National Health doctors, seamen, miners, wharf labourers, high school teachers ... Some letters to the editors of various newspapers in Tel Aviv and Jerusalem complain that Israelis have a worse strike record that anywhere else in the democratic world. This is not so; Israelis strike no more than the British, French, Americans, Italians. Not that this can be much consolation for Israel; being a small country, it feels its strikes more acutely than other nations. Even the purveyors of mineral water struck against the Ministry·of Commerce and, wonder of wonders, merchants had a strike in opposition to iniquities imposed on them by Inland Revenue. Parents having a quarrel with a school headmaster will strike by keeping their children away from school. Everybody, not merely the 'working class', regards the strike as an acceptable weapon. Students at Mikvey Israel School went on strike over bad food and at Bar Ilan University they struck against poor teaching in the French Department.

I have only one personal complaint about Israelis — a generalization of course — they eat too fast. I like to talk over a meal and I want to eat slowly enough to enjoy the taste of my food, especially when I have paid a ransom for it. Many of my Israeli friends and acquaintances refuel rather than dine. Sometimes, barely started on a course, I look up to find my companions finished. I understand their haste; this is a society where work has to be done *now* and for a good many years there was not time for the luxury of a leisurely meal. When quick eating becomes a habit in the formative years it is difficult to switch to a slower style. The Israeli needs to be fed and ready. Also, unlike many Europeans, the Israeli prefers to talk after rather than during a meal. But he is tolerant about slow eaters and he betrays no impatience about wanting to leave the table.

Having written all this about the Israeli character and personality, I have come to the conclusion that it is not possible to paint or draw just one picture and label it 'The Israeli'. So much depends on a subtle and almost indefinable quality — mood. It has been said that in Israel there is mood rather than public opinion. A traveller certainly feels a tense mood when war seems imminent; a keyed-up all-pull-together mood after hostilities begin; a deeply sad mood when Israelis are mourning their dead, a bitter one when reacting to United Nations prejudice, and an angry mood after a terrorist attack. Perhaps the mood I have sensed most frequently is bewilderment — at why such a small and would-be inoffensive country should be so vilified. My daughter, who spent some time as a gentile worker on a kibbutz, would say that the mood she mostly saw was confidence. The point is, that Israel's mood can vary from pessimism to optimism, despair to euphoria. They have this in common with other peoples but in the case of the Israelis the change of mood can be profound, a reflection of the national vulnerability to external influences.

But even among these vital, volatile and dynamic people some qualities remain static and standard — such as a love of humanity, a fervent hope for peace and a great desire to be accepted on equal terms by the rest of mankind.

Most all, Israelis are sensitive to hurt. They do not like to hurt the feelings of others, perhaps because their own are so vulnerable. Over the last two thousand years Jews have learned to conceal hurt; to reveal it has all too often goaded their tormenters into further hurtful acts or words. As with the Jews so with the Israelis. They too, cover up, so that many foreigners get the impression that they are hard-boiled, that they can shrug off affronts and that they quickly allay any any pain by inflicting suffering on others. It is a false impression. They are worried about hurting others.

Among themselves, Israelis try to soften mental anguish, which they have all experienced any times. During the Yom Kippur War, Syrian troops captured Israeli soldiers in the Golan region, tied their hands behind their backs with wire, and shot them dead with machine-guns. When the bodies were found they were photographed in two different positions. One position, showing the dead man's face, was for identification and official record only; there is no way anybody can see these photographs. In the other position the dead soldier's face was hidden; the Army did not want to cause even greater grief to his family and friends. These anonymous photographs were released for publication but few editors used them. Nor were they used for propaganda. An Israeli propagandist told me, 'It is undignified and indecent to score political points over the bodies of our people killed in this way'. For the same reason, photographs of the bodies of children killed by terrorists have not been used in propaganda, and they are rarely published in the Israeli press. The hurt is bad enough without exhibiting the corpses. The press of other nations shows the mutilated bodies of Israeli victims; the Israelis will at most show covered corpses or their coffins.

I once reluctantly interviewed an Israeli mother soon after she had lost a child in a terrorist attack. She didn't cry; you don't let a stranger see you weep. 'You can tell the world that my son was only an Israeli', she said, 'but who cares when an Israeli dies?' She smiled very faintly to show she meant no personal offence, and shook her head and went inside her house.

17 'He went off to die a while'

In a concert hall near the Jerusalem railway station young Israeli singers and dancers sometimes perform for tourists. During each enchanting evening they sing with a verve and dance with a vitality that captivates the audience. Most of the dances and many of the songs come from the diaspora — leaping steps from Georgia, graceful glides from Rumania, pathos from Hungary and pride from Poland, all invested with Israeli panache.

Invited to join in the songs and dances, the audience never needs urging. People of all ages, sometimes to their own great surprise, find themselves on the stage where they quickly lose their shyness and inhibitions and dance with an enthusiasm they might not have known for years.

The performers are rarely professionals but amateur groups from the university or from a kibbutz or town district. They are there to enjoy themselves as well as to entertain. The dust rises from the stamping boots of the men, girls' skirts swing, bloused sleeves rise and fall in liquid, graceful gestures illustrating excitement or love or prayer, and sweat-beads glisten on faces never too intent to smile or laugh.

Here, in this crowded room, is young Israel. Here, on the elevated stage set almost in the centre of the hall, are young Israelis acknowledging their origins, proclaiming their independence and flaunting their disdain for prejudice, adversity and the climate. Around them are people from all over the world, holding hands, linking arms, weaving under arched arms, threading through intricate patterns — all in a pulsating rhythmic harmony and with a pure lust for life. The show lasts a few hours. The foreign visitors leave the hall sad that it is all over; some of the Israelis leave it with melancholia, all of them with regret. Some of them will tell you that they wish the union of performers with audience could be endless, if not on stage then elsewhere, if not in song and dance then in work and worship, trade and education.

But life for the Israeli is not like that. I'm not sure that living in Israel can be weighed rationally. One can assess the reasons which would take a Briton to reside in Mediterranean Spain or a Dutchman to the Canary Islands or an Irishman to Britain — but it is not so easy to analyse the reasons which might make a Jew want to live in Israel, or why, if he was born there, he would want to stay. After all, it is a place of tensions, the cost of living is high, the taxes are worrying and the climate takes a lot of getting used to. Israel is small and surrounded by countries which have declared themselves eternal enemies — now with the possible exception of Egypt — and closed their borders, so a leisure drive into another landscape and environment is impossible. Ships are few and the only practicable way out is by air, and that's expensive.

Some Israelis do not stay. About 200,000 — apart from diplomats, foreign service personnel and students — live outside Israel. Known as 'yored' (singular 'yordim') these people are not abandoning the ship and they are no less Israeli in feeling than those who choose to stay, but they are more restless. Some young people suffer from a territorial claustrophobia and want to see the big world outside, some become frustrated by their inability to buy an apartment or 'get rich quick'. Some say that the defence burden has driven them away or they dislike bureaucracy — though in this case they must surely be jumping out of one frying pan into another. Older people miss their friends and find it difficult to make new ones in a different environment.

Some new arrivals have been deeply disappointed to find that the reality does not match their expectations. They had expected still to find a pioneering country where a man could take an axe and a spade and carve himself a living. Instead, they find — generally speaking — the type of urban environment from which they had been fleeing. In fact, pioneering of a type is still possible in the 'development towns', which are usually sited in the less attractive parts of the country. But these romantics had a purer kind of pioneering in mind, the kind on which the history of Israel was built.

Yet other new Israelis leave because they expected too much of the nation in the first place. They arrive with the spiritual notion that Israelis are incorruptible, idealistic and efficient. They are shocked to encounter bureaucracy, crudeness, selfishness and corruption. Expecting saints, they found sinners, just as in other countries. Had they stayed longer, these leavers would have found that Israel has less crudeness, crime and corruption than other nations. But it can only produce people, not paragons.

Perhaps we should be asking why *more* Israelis haven't left Israel to live abroad. They could hardly be blamed for wishing to escape from the ever-present fear of war, if nothing else.

To the Israeli who stays the state is not just a legal and institutional framework or some kind of Judaistic entity. Nor it is a new idea, as some foreigners seem to think. For almost 2,000 years Jews had prayed, suffered and struggled if not towards their own statehood, then in reaction against the hardships inflicted on them by states where they were resident. The state of Israel is a secular transformation, giving new expression to the collective identity and independence of the Jews. Some writers say that the emergence of the state is the beginning of the end of the Jewish people, but this is unlikely. It is just that out of the collective yearning and striving of the Jews, the Israelis, a new Jewish people, has emerged. Some observers gloomily predict that the substitution of nationhood for ethnicity and religion will weaken ties to the Jews abroad who will increasingly assimilate with the local population.

One of them is Professor Simon Herman of the Institute of Contemporary Jewry at the University of Jerusalem who believes that Israel's young people are turning away from their Jewish roots. His Institute has conducted significant research[1] to find out if the Six-Day War and the Yom Kippur War had affected the Isrealis' thinking about religion. It was found that not only had their Jewish identity failed to deepen but it had actually weakened. I think that Professor Herman should also have set out to find if his subjects' *Israeli* identity had deepened. The impression of observers like myself is that this identity is more marked; that in turning *away* from their Jewish roots, Israeli youngsters are turning *towards* their Israeli birthright. An academic study on the point would be interesting.

It is certainly observable that the earlier Israelis lived with a strong sense of dependence on Jews abroad; this made them Jews first and Israelis second. In the second generation, with the sense of dependence in decline, the people became Israelis first, Jews second.

There are modern prophets who say that when peace comes at last to Israel — genuine, enduring peace — this solidarity of the Israelis will prove to be a myth, that it is a collection of ethnic, religious and ideological differences patched together for the sake of survival. These prophets questions Israel's cultural integrity and therefore its viability. My own prophecy, as a close foreign observer is that an irreversible integration of ethnicity, religion and ideology has already taken place and that it was too dearly bought ever to disintegrate. The primary binding factors are aloneness, the Holocaust, political will, devotion to children, the Army, the kibbutz, reaction to outside hostility. Judaism, while important, is only a secondary binding factor. Compared with these cohesive factors the differences of ethnicity, religion and ideology are weak.

It is also clear that Israelis face the perils of nationalism — and all responsible Israelis see the dangers. That chauvinism is at least latent is shown by the supreme pride in the state, the strikingly proud self-image of the people. Of course, antidotes to nationalism are ready at hand; the most powerful is the sense of mission to the world.

On 14 May, 1978, when Israel turned 30, *The Jerusalem Post* published a long editorial in which this was the key paragaph:

Risen from the pyre of the Holocaust, forcibly tested time and again in the crucible of battle, Israel today is at the peak of its prowess. No muscle flexing in military parades is needed

221

to demonstrate the obvious fact that [Israel] is now better equipped than ever before to cope with any attempt on its life or limb... Yet, inevitably, sheer survival remains the country's prime concern and first thought.

This significant passage has one error. Israel is not at the peak of its prowess, only at the peak of its military strength. It has yet to be given an opportunity to show its prowess in peace. That peace cannot be achieved (except apparently with Egypt) affects everybody, the young Israel's youth carries a burden which most young people elsewhere fortunately miss. They know that the future of Israel depends on them, that their parents and grand-parents depend on them — because most parents are too old to fight in modern war. A young person in Israel cannot think about ambitions and aspirations in the way that, say, his English, American and European counterparts do. The present is tense, the future perilous. Who can tell when an Arab threat of another bloody war might become reality? Careers may end, bodies may become shattered, life may end. The statistics are there to prove the hazards.

In the 1980s Israelis face the same problems that they faced on the eve of independence in 1948 — the need to establish an advanced society where the individual will find happiness and satisfaction, where an entire nation of people will not suffer as previous generations of Jews suffered.

The problems remain the same but the land has changed. Older Israelis have seen a dramatic transformation. Those who joined early kibbutzim found that farming was primitive and that a kibbutz might be set amid malarial swamps, as was Kfar Blum. Transport was also primitive and during the winter it was virtually impossible to get to the main road a few miles away. Telephones did not exist and the main method of communication in the evening was by code on flashlight; in this way the kibbutzniks could get some sort of message out.

Young Israelis have no first-hand knowledge of these particular hardships and take the existence of their state for granted; they were born into a going concern. It is not a dream as it was to their fathers and grandfathers but a fact. But to neither father nor son has Israel been a country of 'limitless possibilities', except in the human sense. It was and it remains a tiny, poor country and it is difficult to become rich in it. People make a decent living only because they work hard. The myth of the wealthy Jew is complete fiction here.

The real wealth of the Israeli is his energy and commitment. Abba Eban, the most eloquent of Israeli statesmen, expresses it this way:[2] 'The most distinctive attribute of Israel's character, the source of some weakness but of greater strength is the stubborn, tenacious refusal to recognize the distinction between imagination and reality'.

A superb example of this deliberate fusion of will and fact has been shown many times but on no occasion more vividly than in 1918 when Chaim Weizmann — who was to be President of Israel 30 years later — went to Mount Scopus, overlooking Jerusalem, to perform the ceremony of opening a new university. This resembled ceremonies in many parts of the world — the same oratory and proclamations, the same platitudes and pleasantries and ritual. But one circumstance made this opening day different from those in other countries. This was the fact that the university did not exist. It did not even have a foundation stone. The means for its erection also did not exist and there was no certainty that the people who most wanted to build a university would ever live in the country. But the establishment of a university was for the Israelis-to-be a matter of such passionate will that the lack of bricks on the site and money in the bank was of no consequence. They saw nothing amusing, quixotic, paradoxical or contradictory in the opening ceremonies. The university came into being within the next 10 years, the product of the same intensity of will. The Israeli imagination is rich with the fusion of imagination and reality and those who complain of intransigence should ponder on it.

The Israelis' refusal to admit that what the imagination inspires cannot be created in reality is the vital factor which has made the state viable. The same drive is constantly changing the face of the land. I once heard a frequent visitor to Israel say that he deplores the very thing he most admires — the pace of

223

change. I sometimes have the feeling that the Israelis are trying within this century to make up for the time lost during the previous two thousand years.

The one unchanging factor is the Israeli's feeling for Jerusalem, and that he shares with Jews everywhere. The inter-denominational and inter-religious Rainbow Group which exists to explain one religion to another, has said in one publications: 'Special attention should be paid to the peculiar bond uniting the Jewish people and the land of Israel to the capital city of Jerusalem. Jerusalem for the Jews is at once the heart of both the land and the people as well as the symbol of their total, physical and spiritual existence.'[3]

Its uniqueness as the centre of worship of the Lord dates from the period of David, who conquered the city some time after 1000 B.C. During the reign of Solomon (965 B.C.) the status of Jerusalem as 'the royal city' was established by the erection of the temple, which invested the monarchy, as well as the site, with an aura of holiness. The 'foundation stone' on Temple Mount, over which the Dome of the Rock is built, is regarded by both Jewish and Islamic tradition as the centre of the world. Temple Mount was referred to as Mount Zion and the name Zion also occasionally embraced the whole of Jerusalem. From this term the Zionists took their name.

The Babylonians destroyed Jerusalem and its temple in 587 B.C. and killed many of the population. After five desolate decades Cyrus, King of Persia, who had become overlord of Judah, issued a famous declaration, which allowed Jews to return to Zion and rebuild the temple on its historic site. It was completed in 515 B.C. only to be destroyed again in A.D. 70 by the Romans. It is the Western or Wailing Wall of this temple which today is the focus of Jewish worship. Dispersed by the Romans, the Jews hungered for the wall which they regained during the Six-Day War of 1967, when they captured East Jerusalem. Almost immediately after the capture an immense human stream surged towards the wall, to see it, to touch its stones, to weep and pray, to insert a prayer paper between stones, to rejoice.

There is something mystical about the wall of big rectangular stones, something transcending religion, logic and historical fact. All the longings for the Jewish people for Jerusalem are embodied in these ancient stones. The forever unyielding decision of the Israelis to hold all Jerusalem, regardless of any other concessions the state might make to the Arabs, is partly the result of Jordanian desecration. The large Jewish cemetery on the Mount of Olives was destroyed and many of the tombstones were used to build the walls of an Arab Legion barracks. Others were strewn in pieces all over the slopes of the Mount. The Arabs also destroyed the Jewish Quarter, including most of the synagogues, of the Old City. Many Christian holy places were also desecrated.

To the Israelis, recovery of the Western Wall was the most emotional event in the state's history; the heart of ancient Israel began to beat again in a new body. The notion that somehow Israel can be induced to return East Jerusalem, and therefore the wall, to Arab control is as naive as it is dangerous, since Arab nations could be encouraged to go to war to achieve this end. After his brief visit to Israel, President Sadat knew that the Israelis could not be moved from their Land and he said as much to those closest to him. Israel cannot be militarily defeated without the systematic wiping out of all Israelis or by somehow again dispersing them; while even a few are left alive they will fight. This is the nature of the people, as the Romans discovered.

President Sadat and the Egyptian journalists who accompanied him were deeply impressed with Jerusalem, especially those who had seen it more than 30 years ago. In spite of all the development and building in Jerusalem since 1967 the city's essential character has not changed. Its beauty is still there in the stone facing which gives a unifying texture to the various parts of the city. It remains in the picturesque alleys and courtyards of the older neighbourhoods, in the quiet and lushly planted streets of the middle-class neighbourhoods rich with the smell of jasmine, and in the sculpted hills surrounding the city.

Under Israeli rule eastern Jerusalem and its Arab population have achieved unprecedented prosperity. Before 1967 41 per cent of eastern Jerusalem homes has no running water and 60 per cent had no electricity; in 1977 less than 7 per cent remained without running water and every house has electricity. No park or playground existed in East Jerusalem in 1967 under Jordanian rule; now there are six. Where no kindergarten existed there are now 50. Where there was no lending library for adults there are now four plus a mobile library reaching outlying suburbs. Many thousands of East Jerusalem families get welfare and pension payments and National Insurance allowances. Beyond all this, the Israelis have done more to promote Arab culture in East Jerusalem than was ever done under Jordanian rule.

The period since 1967 has also seen in Jerusalem a religious revival of unprecedented proportions, not only for the Jews but for Christians and Moslems. The Jordanian defacements have been repaired and nothing remains which might cause offence to a member of any religion. Moslem worshippers are not always pleased that they have to pass a military guard on the way to pray in the great mosque on Temple Mount but the guard is necessary to protect it from vandals; a deranged Australian set fire to it some years ago, much to the Israelis' distress.

Israelis are always upset by disharmony in Jerusalem, which is one reason why the terrorists make it a prime target. In July 1976 a bomb hidden in a refrigerator and left in Zion Square caused 75 casualties when it exploded. Several bombs have been set off in supermarkets and produce markets; in June 1978 a Palestine Liberation Organization bomb killed two and wounded 42 in the central market. Outrages of this kind may occur in any part of Israel but the terrorists calculate that one in Jerusalem hurts the Israelis spiritually as well as physically. This is so, but it also hardens them and confirms their belief that any Palestinian state would be a dangerous neighbour — hence their implacable opposition to such a state.

Despite the occasional terrorist attack, Israel is a peaceful country, especially in its quieter corners.

I came across one of these corners in the summer of 1977, while driving along a narrow back road from Jerusalem to Tel Aviv. I stopped to take a photograph of a memorial to Israel's fighter pilots killed in action. This road is little used and I found myself alone at the site, except for an Army captain who was sitting hatless on a stone seat in the early morning sun, reading. He was waiting, he said, to be picked up by a friend with a car.

I sat with him and we looked across the hills and valleys towards Jerusalem. These brown-skinned Judean hills are covered with scrub and trees, many planted by visitors to Israel as a token of friendship. Around the fliers' memorial the ground is hard and stony but somehow the trees had taken root and were thriving enough to provide that most precious thing — shade. There are kibbutzim in these hills which look like oases because of their greater growth of foliage and in the valleys are irrigation crops. That morning water from a sprinkler was moistening the flower gardens around the memorial and where the stone surround was already hot from the sun water droplets hissed and disappeared as they landed.

The captain — he said his name was Zvi — was a tall man, aged about 30, with dark, fairly close cut hair and a lean physical hardness that one becomes accustomed to among Israeli soldiers. Not that his features looked 'military' — his lips had a firm line but his eyes were sensitive and his manner thoughtful.

I had recently visited the 'Good Fence' — the border between Lebanon and Israel in the north — so called by the Lebanese who have received Israeli kindness at the border. Deprived of most of the necessities of life by Palestinian terrorists, the Lebanese, mostly Christian, came to the Fence for good and water and medical help, and crossed into Israel to work in the town of Metullah. I told Zvi about the Good Fence and said that the Israelis were more Christian-like than foreign Christians themselves in the help they were giving to the hard-pressed Lebanese — admittedly as much for political considerations as for humanitarian ends.

'Christian-like?' he said, 'What's that?'

'We Christians like to think that we are charitable and compassionate,' I explained.

'You didn't act that way in the years before 1939.'

All I could say was, 'No, we didn't.'

A graduate in contemporary history and politics, Zvi knew all about the abortive Evian conference and the Christian world's other feeble attempts to help the Jews who had fallen under Hitler's boots. But as a professional historian and political scientist he was objective in his comments and his tone held no rancour.

After a while he said, 'We Israelis are offering the world the very first chance to see if a people can overcome a long and pitiless history. It's quite a spectacle, isn't it?'

I looked at the book which now lay closed in Zvi's hand and asked what he was reading.

'Poetry,' he said. 'I often carry a book of poetry. Do you know Yehuda Amichai's work?'

'I've seen some of his poems in English translation.'

'They're better in Hebrew. This is a piece I like, from a poem he calls "Psalm".' As he read he translated it for me, slowly; then he spoke the translation again, more confidently. I wrote it down. This is a fragment:

When I was a child I sang in the synagogue choir.
I sang until my voice broke.
I sang first voice and second voice. I'll sing until my heart breaks, first heart and second heart.
A psalm.

I had been at the memorial a long time. Friends were waiting for me at Kibbutz Nachshon and I had to press on. We shook hands and I said, 'Goodbye and good luck.'

'Luck?' Zvi said. 'The harder we Israelis work the luckier we get.' His tone was gently ironic. 'Have a good day.'

I left him on the stone in the hot sun and went back to my car. As I was driving away Zvi ran after me. 'If you ever get a chance,' he said, 'read Haim Gouri's poem, "Holiday's End".'

Months later I found an English translation of the Gouri poem. I think Captain Zvi wanted me to read it for the central two lines:

He went off to die a while
and then to rise from the dust, to come home from the desert.

18 Thoughts from Outside*

'Israel is a miniature world where men work to fulfil a pleasant social duty and have the satisfaction of watching growth. It is a world where each man strives for his own betterment through creative activity. Work is part of education.' *José Figueres, when President of Costa Rica.*

'Israel contributes to the enrichment of the free world by elevating and glorifying mankind.' *Vincent Auriol, when President of France.*

'Israel was not created in order to disappear — Israel will endure and flourish. It is the child of hope and the home of the brave.' *John F. Kennedy.*

'To see the country, to feel the throb of its extraordinary vitality, is to measure the immense debt of gratitude owed to Israel. The people of Israel, by their achievements, their great courage and pioneering spirit, offer the world new reasons for hope and optimism ... Israel stands out as a beacon of hope; if

*These quotations were all published in an anthology *The Mission of Israel,* edited by Jacob Baal-Teshura, Robert Speller & Sons, New York, 1963.

men are capable of such constructive work as is being done here, then we need not despair of humanity as a whole. *Pierre Mendès-France, when Prime Minister of France.*

'In this country of all countries it is easy to believe in miracles. The old Puritan motto, "Trust in God and keep your powder dry," might have been thought of for Israel; but Israelis could proudly add to it; "and to hell with time and space". ' *Professor Max Beloff.*

'A native-born Israeli is the toughest and most vital human being I have come across anywhere.' *Robert Graves.*

References

Chapter 2: Lust for Life
1. David Ben-Gurion, *Israel, A Personal History,* New English Library, 1972.
2. Abraham Shumsky, *The Clash of Cultures in Israel,* Greenwood Press, Westport, Conn., 1955.
3. Quoted in P. Lachower, *Bialik,* Tel Aviv, 1944.
4. Norman Bentwich, *The Hebrew University,* Weidenfeld and Nicolson, 1961.
5. Ephraim Kishon, *The Mark of Cain,* Shikmona Publishing Co., Jerusalem, 1976. Translated by Miriam Arad.
6. Maxime Rodinson, *Israel and the Arabs,* Penguin, 1968.
7. See *Israeli Statistical Abstract,* 1977, and A.L. Tibawi, *Arab Education in Mandatory Palestine,* Luzac, 1956.

Chapter 3: The Kibbutznik
1. Yosef Goell in *The Jerusalem Post,* 26 April, 1977.
2. Spoken by Shaul Daniel, of Kibbutz Ma'abarot, quoted by Yigal Pe'eri in *Hashavua,* April, 1977.

Chapter 4: Holocaust
1. From an undated report made to Hagana in 1945. Hagana had sent Gal to Poland.
2. Sources for the facts on the conference:
   a. High Commission for Refugees publications: Reports to the Assembly of the League of Nations, 1937-39; Proceedings of the Intergovernmental Committee, Evian, July 6-15 1938.
   b. The Co-ordinating Committee for Refugees, *Bulletin,* 1939.
   c. A paper by Eric Estorick, 'The Evian Conference and the Intergovernmental Committee' published in *Annals of the American Academy of Political and Social Science,* May, 1939.
   d. *The Last Escape,* by Peggy Mann, Pinnacle Books, 1961.
   e. *The Destruction of the European Jews,* Raoul Hilberg, Chicago, 1961.
3. Peggy Mann, *Golda: The Life of Israel's Prime Minister*, Washington Square Press, 1973.
4. Helmut Genschel, *Die Verdrängung der Juden aus der Wirtschaft im Dritten Reich*, Göttingen, 1966. (The relevant passage translated by B. Grey.)
5. Peggy Mann, article in *The Washington Post,* 1 May, 1978.

Chapter 5: Saving Jews for Israel
1. See Reitlinger, *The Final Solution*; André Biss, *A Million Jews to Save*, Hutchinson, 1973; and 'The British and the Slaughter of the Jews', *Wiener Library Bulletin*, XXI, Nos. 1 and 2.

Chapter 6: Arms for the Promised Land
1. Figures taken from the Hagana records in the Israeli government archives.
2. David Ben-Gurion, *Israel: Years of Challenge,* Holt, 1963.
3. From Ben-Gurion's speeches, as entered in his diary. Made available to the author privately.
4. The story of Fritzel is recorded in the private files of David Shaltiel, who commanded Hagana in Jerusalem.

Chapter 7: The Army
1. Quoted by a spokesman of the Office of Israeli Defence Forces.
2. Ben-Gurion, *Recollections*, Macdonald, 1970.

Chapter 8: People of the Family
1. Israel Government Statistics Office, *Israeli Statistical Abstract*.
2. Published on 28 June, 1977.

Chapter 9: Hunger for Learning
1. From the Knesset Records, quoted in David Ben-Gurion, *The Jews in their Land,* Aldus Books, 1966.
2. Ruth Bondy, *The Israelis*, Sabra Books, 1969.

Chapter 10: People of the Book
1. See also *Survey of Europe Today*, Readers Digest Association, 1970.
2. Leon Yudkin, *Escape into Siege*, Routledge and Kegan Paul, 1974.
3. In *P.E.N. Israel,* 1974.
4. Quoted in the Report on the conference, 1969.
5. Amos Oz, *The Hill of Evil Counsel*, published in English in 1978 by Chatto and Windus.
6. Yudkin, *op. cit.*
7. Abraham Megged, *P.E.N. Israel,* 1974.
8. Ehud Ben Ezer, *Nor the Battle to the Strong*, translated by Richard Flautz, Tel Aviv, 1974. 9. Yudkin, *op. cit.*
10. Y. Orpaz, 'Little Woman' in *P.E.N. Israel,* 1974.
11. From an article in *Ma'ariv* newspaper, 16 July, 1967.
12. Quoted in *Israeli Humour and Satire*, ed. Yishai Afek, Sadan Publishing House, Tel Aviv, 1974.

Chapter 11: The Serious Business of Spare Time
1. By Leah Isaac for the Communications Institute of the University of Jerusalem and the Israeli Institute of Applied Social Research.

Chapter 12: Settlement and Stress
1. Ian McIntyre, *The Proud Doers — Israel After Twenty Years,* B.B.C. Publications, 1968.
2. Chaim Bermant, *Israel*, Thames and Hudson, 1967.
3. Ian McIntyre, *op. cit.*
4. In *The Jerusalem Post*, 27 February, 1968.
5. From *Israeli Statistical Abstract*.

Chapter 13: Civil Religion v Orthodox Judaism
1. In *The Jerusalem Post,* 7 February, 1978.
2. In *The Jerusalem Post*, 21 June, 1977.

Chapter 14: Politics – Painful Pragmatism
1. *Administration in Palestine: A Handbook*, H.M.S.O., 1924 (and other editions).
2. Published in 1972 as *Why I Live in Israel* by the Anglo-Israel Association.
3. The document, entitled 'Significance of the State of Israel to the Jews', was made public by Cardinal Lawrence Shehan of Baltimore.
4. Amos Elon, *The Israelis*, Weidenfeld and Nicolson, 1971.
5. Speech in the Knesset, October, 1977.

Chapter 15: Scholarly Spies
1. Published in English by Israeli Students of Middle East Affairs, *Bulletin*, No. 3, October, 1969.

Chapter 16: Character and Personality
1. Ruth Bondy, *The Israelis*, Sabra Books, 1969.
2. *The Secularization of Leisure: Culture and Communication in Israel*, Elihu Katz and Michael Gurevitch, Faber and Faber, 1976.
3. Quoted by Katz and Gurevitch, *op.cit.*
4. Bondy, *op.cit.*
5. Quoted by Ian McIntyre in *The Proud Doers* (*op. cit.*). Quoted with permission.
6. *Henry V*, Act IV, scene iii, quoted by Ian McIntyre in *The Proud Doers*, B.B.C. Publications, 1968.
7. David Reifen, *The Juvenile Court in a Changing Society,* Weidenfeld and Nicolson, 1972.
8. In an article in *The Jerusalem Post*, 4 April, 1978.
9. *The Jerusalem Post*, 31 January, 1978.

Chapter 17: He Went Off to Die a While
1. See *Israelis and Jews*, Random House, 1970.
2. In a contribution to *The Mission of Israel*, edited by Jacob Baal-Teshuva, Speller & Son, New York, 1963.
3. *To Be or Not to Be*, Rainbow Group, University of Florida Press, 1975.

Bibliography and Acknowledgements

Many books have been written about various aspects of Israel and its people. I list here only those I found most useful.

For the serious reader the 15 paperback books in the Israel Pocket Library have the most authoritative reference. All are compiled from the material originally published in the *Encyclopaedia Judaica,* Jerusalem, 1971. They are:

Geography	*Anti-Semitism*
Jerusalem	*Archaeology*
Zionism	*Holocaust*
History (until 1880)	*Religious Life*
History (from 1880)	*Education and Science*
Immigration and Settlement	*Jewish Values*
Economy	*Democracy*
Society	

Avriel, Ehud, *Open the Gates*! Weidenfeld and Nicolson, 1975.

Baal-Teshuva, Jacob (ed.), *The Mission of Israel,* Speller & Sons, New York, 1963.

Ben-Gurion, David, *Recollections*, Macdonald, 1970.

Ben-Gurion, David, *Ben-Gurion Looks at the Bible,* W.H. Allen, 1972.

Bentwich, Joseph S., *Education in Israel*, Routledge and Kegan Paul, 1965.

Bermant, Chaim, *Israel*, Thames and Hudson, 1967.

Bondy, Ruth, *The Israelis*, Sabra Books, New York, 1969.

Bondy, Zmora, Bashan (eds), *Mission Survival*, W.H. Allen, 1968.

BIBLIOGRAPHY AND ACKNOWLEDGEMENTS

Collins, Larry and Lapierre, Dominique, *O Jerusalem*, Simon & Schuster, 1972.

Dekel, Ephraim, *B'riha — Flight to the Homeland*, Herzl Press, New York, 1952.

Dicks, Brian, *The Israelis, How They Live and Work*, David and Charles, 1975.

Eisenstadt, S.N., *Israeli Society*, Basic Books, New York, 1967.

Golden, Harry, *The Israelis*, Pyramid Books, New York, 1971.

Katz, Elihu and Gurevitch, Michael, *The Secularization of Leisure: Culture and Communication in Israel*, Faber and Faber, 1976

Kishon, Ephraim, *The Mark of Cain — a bitter smile from besieged Israel*, Shikmona Publishing Co., Jerusalem, 1976.

Larsen, Elaine, *Israel*, Batsford, 1976.

Leon, Dan, *The Kibbutz — a new way of life*, Pergamon Press, 1969.

Lucas, Noah, *The Modern History of Israel*, Weidenfeld and Nicolson, 1975.

McIntyre, Ian, *The Proud Doers — Israel After Twenty Years*, B.B.C. Publications, 1968.

Noy, Dov (ed), *Folktales of Israel*, University of Chicago Press, 1963.

Rapaport, Chanan and others, *Early Child Care in Israel*, Gordon and Breach, 1976.

Reifen, David, *The Juvenile Court in a Changing Society*, Weidenfeld and Nicolson, 1972.

Robinson, Donald, *Under Fire*, W.W. Norton, New York, 1968.

Shumsky, Abraham, *The Clash of Cultures in Israel*, Greenwood Press, Connecticut, 1955.

Sonntag, Jacob (ed), *New Writing From Israel*, Corgi, 1976.

Tiger, Lionel and Shepher, Joseph, *Women in the Kibbutz*, New York, Harcourt Brace Jovanovich, 1975.

Yudkin, Leon I, *Escape Into Siege, a survey of Israeli literature*, Routledge and Kegan Paul, 1974.

The series of more than 60 monographs published by the Anglo-Israel Association, 9 Bentinck Street, London, was useful to me, as they would be to anybody interested in the great experiment of Israel. They include: *Citizen as Soldier* (Dr. Louise Sweet-Combs); *The Kibbutz: Some Personal Reflections* (Lynne Reid Banks); *Urban Pioneering in Haifa* (Professor Bernard Crick); *The Welfare State Objectives in Israel* (Professor Richard Titmuss); *Israel, the United Nations and Aggression* (Arthur L. Goodhart); *Religion and Secularism in Israel* (S.C. Leslie).

Most of all I commend the English-Language *Jerusalem Post* daily newspaper to anybody interested in a full, frank and objective view of modern Israel. The *Post* publishes a weekly international edition on lightweight paper which reaches subscribers within a day or two of publication. The address is P.O.B. 81, Jerusalem. The *Post's* standard of journalism is high and, as a 'specialist' on Israel, I depend on its columns for much of my information. I am grateful to the editor for permission to make various quotations from the newspaper.

I owe a special debt to Mr John Levy of Friends of Israel, London, for practical assistance in recent research. Finally, I thank my wife for her unfailing good humour and keen observation in our many journeys in Israel — and other parts of the Middle East — for her work in the preparation of the manuscript, and for her support in this, her author-husband's eightieth published book.

John Laffin, 1978

Index